Béisbol on the Air

ALSO OF INTEREST
AND FROM MCFARLAND

Latinos in American Football: Pathbreakers on the Gridiron, 1927 to the Present (Mario Longoria and Jorge Iber, 2020)

Mike Torrez: A Baseball Biography (Jorge Iber, 2016)

Béisbol on the Air

Essays on Major League Spanish-Language Broadcasters

Edited by JORGE IBER *and* ANTHONY R. SALAZAR

Foreword *by* Curt Smith

McFarland & Company, Inc., Publishers
Jefferson, North Carolina

"Eduardo Ortega" by Jorge Iber originally appeared as "Béisbol as Part of 'Una Vida en Común en la Frontera': The Career and Significance of Eduardo Ortega, the Voz of the San Diego Padres" in *NINE: A Journal of Baseball History and Culture*, vol. 26, nos. 1–2, published by the University of Nebraska Press. Reprinted by permission.

LIBRARY OF CONGRESS CATALOGUING-IN-PUBLICATION DATA

Names: Iber, Jorge, 1961– editor. | Salazar, Anthony R., 1965– editor.
Title: Béisbol on the air : essays on Major League Spanish-language broadcasters / edited by Jorge Iber and Anthony R. Salazar ; foreword by Curt Smith.
Description: Jefferson, North Carolina : McFarland & Company, Inc., Publishers, 2024. | Includes index.
Identifiers: LCCN 2023042017 | ISBN 9781476687674 (paperback : acid free paper) ∞
ISBN 9781476649375 (ebook)
Subjects: LCSH: Baseball announcers—United States—Biography. | Hispanic Americans in radio broadcasting—History. | Hispanic Americans in television broadcasting—History. | Spanish radio broadcasting—United States—History. | Spanish television broadcasting—United States—History. | Radio broadcasting of sports—United States—History. | Television broadcasting of sports—United States—History. | Major League Baseball (Organization)—History. | BISAC: SPORTS & RECREATION / Baseball / Essays & Writings | SOCIAL SCIENCE / Ethnic Studies / American / Hispanic American Studies
Classification: LCC GV742.4 .B45 2023 | DDC 791.44/6579—dc23/eng/20231024
LC record available at https://lccn.loc.gov/2023042017

BRITISH LIBRARY CATALOGUING DATA ARE AVAILABLE

ISBN (print) 978-1-4766-8767-4
ISBN (ebook) 978-1-4766-4937-5

© 2024 Jorge Iber and Anthony R. Salazar. All rights reserved

No part of this book may be reproduced or transmitted in any form or by any means, electronic or mechanical, including photocopying or recording, or by any information storage and retrieval system, without permission in writing from the publisher.

Front cover: Orlando Sánchez-Diago and René Cárdenas at Colts Stadium (photograph courtesy of Orlando Sánchez-Diago)

Printed in the United States of America

McFarland & Company, Inc., Publishers
  Box 611, Jefferson, North Carolina 28640
    www.mcfarlandpub.com

This work is dedicated, as always, to my dear wife, Raquel, and our son, Matthew.

Additionally, I would like to dedicate this book to a dear friend and colleague who was a great help with this manuscript, Professor Jorge Zamora, of the Classical and Modern Languages and Literature Department at Texas Tech University.

Table of Contents

Foreword
    Curt Smith   1

Introduction
    Jorge Iber *and* Anthony R. Salazar   9

1. Legends

Buck Canel
    Luis Rodríguez-Mayoral   21

René Cárdenas
    Francisco Romero *and* Jorge Iber   25

Jaime Jarrín
    Richard A. Santillán *and* Frank C. Moreno   32

Felo Ramírez
    Lou Hernández   57

2. Veterans

Eduardo Ortega
    Jorge Iber   71

Orlando Sánchez-Diago
    Jorge Iber   81

Amaury Pi-González
    Jorge Iber   92

Uri Berenguer
    Bill Nowlin   102

Luis Rodríguez-Mayoral
    Lou Hernández   124

Héctor Molina
  JUAN JOSE RODRÍGUEZ   135
Tony Oliva
  CÉSAR BRIOSO   144
Jorge Jarrín
  SCOTT MELESKY   153
Pepe Yñiguez
  SCOTT MELESKY   164

3. Newer Voices

Francisco Romero
  JORGE IBER   175
Junior Pepén
  BILL NOWLIN   181
Jessica Mendoza
  ROBERTO AVANT-MIER *and* PATRICK J. MCCONNELL   186

Conclusion
  JORGE IBER   195
About the Contributors   199
Index   203

Foreword

CURT SMITH

In 1921, KDKA Pittsburgh aired baseball's first game on radio from Forbes Field. In 1939, the major leagues debuted on television at Brooklyn's Ebbets Field. For a long time, few Hispanics or other minorities vocalized the bigs. By contrast, many have now climbed baseball's broadcast stairway, the pastime carried on radio, TV, and the internet across this country and beyond.

At heart, baseball is individual, thus personal. The essence of Hispanic culture is communal, thus caring. Their union has forged a fun house of delight, enriching America's most fabled sport. This book relates many beloved Hispanic broadcast tales told by and about famed Spanish-speaking voices, all gleaned from memory's shelf. *Por ejemplo*: for example.

To *Sports Illustrated*'s Robert H. Boyle, Argentine Buck Canel lived a "double life" as a World War II correspondent and "the George Washington of Spanish-speaking baseball announcers." In 1959, ousting Fulgenico Batista in Cuba, Canel admirer Fidel Castro led his army into the city of Matanzas. Canel heard "the familiar voice shouting above the noise: 'Buck ... Buck ... Buck.'" Fidel left "the jeep to hug him," asking why Milwaukee Braves skipper Fred Haney had pitched Lew Burdette, not Warren Spahn, in 1958's World Series Game Seven.

Rafael (Felo) Ramírez became a synonym for Cuban baseball. The mother of longtime A's voice Amaury Pi-González told how "Amaury would go in the patio of our house, grab a broom, turn it upside down to look like a microphone, and imitate Felo's play-by-play!" No wonder. In 1951, Ramírez broadcast the first of 32 World Series. He liked to recount that during one of the games, a foul ball rolled up the netting to the press box, where he reached out for it just as someone in the adjoining box also made a grab. After a brief tussle, Ramírez came away with the ball—only to recognize the fellow he'd wrestled it away from as Humphrey Bogart. "I was just a rookie. I put the ball in my pocket. I didn't realize until later that I should have given him the ball—or at least have gotten his autograph."

Since 1987, Eduardo Ortega has announced for the kid within the fan, a spectator dropping a Budweiser on the San Diego Padres voice while trying to catch a foul near the booth. "An old beer ad went 'Tastes great or less filling?'" Ortega said. "This beer went O for 2." In Boston, Panama's Uri Berenguer, diagnosed at three with a rare form of cancer that almost cost a leg, never forgot a woman named Rosemary Lonborg—"my play lady"—volunteering at his cancer clinic. Later, he saw a 1967 video of Boston pitcher Jim Lonborg. "Look! There's Rosie's husband!" beamed Uri, ferrying the Red Sox since 2003.

Music is often deemed a "universal language." Historically, baseball has been too for a newcomer to America. To an immigrant child learning English a century ago, 90 feet between the bases and 60 feet, 6 inches from home plate to the mound seemed as vital as two times two equaled four. "Baseball was the essential and dominant feature of my Americanization," noted the *New York Times*' Leonard Koppett, leaving Russia for Depression-era New York at five. In the 1920s Big Apple, daily papers—you could choose among a dozen—"provided the main opportunity to learn the new language [English] and practice arithmetic."

At a certain age, most immigrant youth once ceased to use their native language. Today, bilingualism, including Spanish, is accepted, even cheered. Yet baseball as assimilator endures. "It's conversation," announcer Bob Costas dubs radio/TV broadcasting. "It's quirky. Tell us what you did today. Tell me about the guy sitting down at the end of the dugout. Is he a character? Did he always dream of being a big-leaguer?" Historically, Hispanics are a storytelling people, drawn to a storyteller's game.

The tempo of more frenetic sports leaves much less time for anecdote. By contrast, baseball's easy rhythm "lets our personality show," Ortega says of high-voltage Spanish voices "calling baseball in an arresting way." As example, he recalls how since 1994, the Padres have trained in Peoria, Arizona. For a time, the Milwaukee Brewers camped at nearby Chandler's Compadre Stadium, its two radio booths near "the last row of fans."

One weekday, Milwaukee didn't broadcast, Padres English and Hispanic voices filling each side of the press box. Attendees in the sparse crowd could hear Spanish speakers brandish what Eduardo terms "our festive Latin style." At first, patrons turned to stare, as if saying, "'Who the heck are you and what are you doing here?'" By game's end, most scattered. Ortega "not taking it personally" mused that the seventh-inning stretch is identical in any language: "It's baseball, all the same."

Picture the shortstop in the hole, nabbing a ground ball, the runner barely beating the throw to first base. In the 1860s, U.S. sailors, stationed in Cuba and Cubans once schooled in America, brought that vision to the isle. Esteban Bellán became the major leagues' first Hispanic player in 1871. By 1911, Cincinnati had to file affidavits to prove two Cuban players were European. In 1938, Miguel (Mike) Angel González managed the St. Louis Cardinals. Two years later, Washington Senators scout Joe Cambria told a young prospect to forget professional baseball. Castro did, pitching at the Universidad de la Habana.

"I can imagine a world without baseball," said Koppett, "but I can't imagine wanting to live in one." As recently as 2011, despite many Hispanic voices wishing to live in baseball's world, just 11 big-league teams boasted a Spanish-speaking network. Now 22 of 30 do, ferrying the pastime's pastiche of odd play, grand deed, glorious comeback, epochal collapse, and falling in love with a team.

Jorge Iber was born in Havana, Cuba, raised in Miami's Little Havana, and is a coeditor of this book and associate dean of the College of Arts and Sciences and professor of history at Texas Tech University. He notes a 2018 study in which Latinos comprised 32 percent and 47 percent of major- and minor-league players, respectively. Today, Hispanic play-by-play reaches an estimated major-league audience of 58 million people.

Depending on your age, you may recall a generation or more of mic men nearby or thousands of miles away. This book is partly statistical since baseball is. It is more about personality and narrative since humor, drama, syntax, and vocabulary stir a variety of phrase and mood. Most voices realize, to quote the Baltimore Orioles' late Chuck Thompson, how "on the field not a lot sometimes happens." The best accent what *does*, spurring what writer Doris Kearns Goodwin dubs the "most timeless of all sports."

Except for the equator, everything begins somewhere. Hispanic broadcasting began, as noted, with the man who was "for generations ... the voice of the World Series [a record 42] as heard by the collective ear of Latin America," wrote Jerry Izenberg in the *New York Post*. In and after World War II, Buck Canel's NBC Red Network *Gillette Cavalcade of Sport* (*Cabalgata Deportiva Gillette*) knit more than 200 U.S. and Latin American radio stations, then TV, once Cuba became wired.

Buck did New York Yankees games from 1942 to 1978, and 1970s Mets home games, often simulcast in Latin America on WHOM New York. A letter to the *Sporting News* said a listener "should hand [Canel] an orchid" as a bouquet even before the Brooklyn Dodgers aired 40 games in Spanish in 1957, their last year in Flatbush. Until his 1980 death at 74, Buck showed why the National Baseball Hall of Fame and Museum voted him the first Hispanic to receive the Ford C. Frick Award "for broadcast excellence" in 1985.

Throughout, Buck trumpeted what he styled his Spanish and English "two different personalities." If the Yankees' Héctor López homered, Boyle wrote, *Gillette* coverage led with the Panamanian's blast. If the Bronx Bombers' Mickey Mantle went deep, Canel led with No. 7. *Time* called Buck "the Graham McNamee of the Caribbean," referencing baseball's 1923–35 first network titan. Typically, Buck barbed that "Graham McNamee was the Buck Canel of the United States."

In the 1963 All-Star Game, the National League boasted third baseman Ron Santo of the Chicago Cubs and Cardinals at the other three infield positions. Canel's take was that the American League had no chance since the N.L. infield boasted three cardinals and a saint. The Cincinnati Reds, however, were special, being the first big-league club to use Cuban players. They thus became *el querido Cinci*—"the beloved Cinci." In 1961, they were trounced by the *Yanquis* in *La Serie Mundial*—"the World Series." McNamee could not have said it better.

In 1949, Canel invited Ramírez to help re-create his Red Network's *El Juego de Hoy* (*Today's Game*) on 24-hour Latin American radio. "If you have cardiac problems, back away from your radio now," Felo jibed. Few did. Ramírez had begun at a time where U.S. media Latinos were dubbed prop, joke, or foil. Unbowed, he aired Roberto Clemente's 3,000th hit, Hank Aaron's 715th homer, and Don Larsen's 1956 perfecto. Pi-González felt him "like a god to the people."

In 1993, Felo became Spanish voice of the expansion Florida Marlins. He aired them till his 2017 death, crying *Estan ganado, los Marlins!*—"the Marlins are winning!" The 2001 Hall of Fame Frick honoree nurtured America's fastest-growing minority, "tomorrow [lying] as much with them," wrote Peter Gammons, "as *Ozzie and Harriet* suburbs." The Spanish *Mi casa es su casa* means "My house is your house." As to Felo, Memorial Coliseum, then Dodger Stadium, became such a home.

In 1958 Los Angeles, the transplanted Brooks were the bigs' first club to serve the Spanish-speaking market, broadcast bilingually, and hire a Spanish-language voice: Nicaraguan-born René Cárdenas, grandson of Adán Cárdenas, who introduced baseball there in the late 19th century and became his nation's president. At 16, René began writing about the game, then airing it on Radio Mundial; 21, left for family in LA; 27, learning of the Dodgers' move in late 1957, pitched play-by-play to Spanish-speaking KWKW.

At the time, the Southland boasted "nearly a million Spanish speakers," René said. Dodgers boss Walter O'Malley needed no persuading. After four years in LA, Cárdenas joined the expansion Houston Colt .45s, later Astros, as director of Spanish broadcasting. In 1965, baseball's seminal Astrodome opened, René's signature embedded in the last beam used in construction. Next year, the now–U.S. citizen launched the first international radio baseball network, helping Houston recruit players throughout the hemisphere.

"When sorrows come," Shakespeare wrote, "they come not [as] single spies, but in battalions!" When the Astros ended 1970s Spanish-language wireless, Cárdenas returned to Nicaragua, where in 1979 the Sandinista National Liberty Front seized his home and other property and executed René's half-brother. Cárdenas and his wife, Jilma, fled to America, where he aired the 1981 Texas Rangers and, coming full circle, the 1982–98 Dodgers and 2007–08 'Stros, retiring after 38 years, said the *New York Times*, as "the first Spanish-language radio announcer at each stop."

In 2006, Vin Scully signed a reported $3 million per annum, holding his first-ever press conference. The Dodgers' Jaime Jarrín hailed "my mentor," Scully thanking *him* for "teaching me to say La Jolla and La Cienega"—streets in LA. In 1958, Cárdenas had mentored *Jarrín*: born, Cayambe, Ecuador, learning radio at a 750,000-watt station, and with "the bug to fly," leaving for California in 1955. "I unpack in time for the Dodgers-Yankees Series and can't believe the interest," Jaime marveled. "I'm like, 'What *is* this game?'"

Hired as a local sports/news director, radio Latinos rare, Jarrín immersed himself in "reading books on baseball" and watching the Pacific Coast League Angels and Stars in person. In 1959, like Cárdenas, he began to re-create, translating Scully and partner Jerry Doggett in studio with the Dodgers on the road. Jaime copied Vin's rhythm, envying his "choosing the right word in the right place." In turn, Scully liked the then–number two Hispanic voice's spontaneity. "I was in awe. Jaime would immediately interpret me."

Jarrin had intended to "do about six or seven years, then go back into news or boxing or soccer." Instead, as Columbia journalist Sandra Hernandez said, emigrating, "I listened to two things on the radio": Spanish soaps and "our evangelist" Jaime calling the Dodgers—*Esquivadores*—to suburb, city, and farm. By 1973, he baptized their 162-game live Spanish network. *La pelota viene como una mariposa* meant the ball moved like a butterfly. His *Se va, se va, se va* meant, in any language, "Going, going, gone!"

In 1980, Hispanics totaled 25 percent of the Dodgers gate. Next April, 20-year-old Mexican pitcher Fernando Valenzuela made the club. "Especially with more immigration, the interest was unbelievable," Jarrín referenced Fernandomania. Increasingly, "You saw Hispanic names on the field," he said. When would Hispanics thrive above it?

In 1997, Colombian Édgar Rentería's game seven hit won the Series for Florida. "A Hispanic hits it," said Jaime. "I call it. Our [Latina Broadcasting Company] audience of 35 million heard it," as many heard Vin on CBS Radio. That season, 35 Hispanics aired the bigs versus eight a decade earlier. Next year, Jarrín became the second Hispanic to get the Frick Award. Upon the Hall's phone call informing him, "my wife began to cry." He retired after the 2022 season, making the Golden State cry.

In 1999, Jaime began to mentor still-partner Pepe Yñiguez, who like other voices in this book, became an extended member of the family. Another, Orlando Sánchez-Diago, had joined the 'Stros in their first year in the Astrodome. Hearing him described as the Voice of Latin America and how he pined to work with Cárdenas, Houston owner H. Roy Hofheinz hired the refugee of the Cuban Revolution. Problem? "Orlando was stuck in Venezuela," said Hofheinz's son Fred, "so my dad called an old friend of his at the White House named Lyndon Johnson," then president, and wangled a special visa.

Sánchez-Diago's 21 straight years (1965–85) set a then-record for Astros Hispanic mic men, since topped by analyst Alex Treviño (1998–present, since 2008 teamed with play-by-play's Francisco Romero), each sustaining the club's following through the Americas. Among other voices, Colombian-born Joe Angel retired in 2019 after airing five clubs and ESPN Radio for 42 years in English and Spanish—19 with the Orioles, his *Hasta la viste pelota!* crossing a bilingual divide.

Referenced previously, Eduardo Ortega was first a disc jockey, reporter, and talk show host. Leaving Cuba in 1961, Amaury Pi-González, 17, has worked the bigs almost continuously since 1978, most notably the Oakland A's. In Minnesota, Tony Oliva merited that niche as a three-time AL batting titlist before a second career as a Twins analyst. As a boy, Luis Rodríguez-Mayoral moved from Puerto Rico to Panama, where his dad, a military officer, was stationed. Hearing Canel on the Series hooked him forever. Later, Luis aired the 1992–99 Rangers and earlier founded the Latin American Player's Day and Roberto Clemente Memorial Award, No. 21's memory hooking us, even now.

Juan Pedro Villamán was the youngest of nine children. His mother died giving birth to him. At 13, he called baseball in the Dominican Republic, raised by an aunt, who later watched two TVs simultaneously: soap operas and his game. In 1986, J.P., 27, immigrated to New York City, then Lawrence, Massachusetts, like thousands of other Dominicans. He beamed a Red Sox schedule, manned the Spanish Baseball Network, and led aide Uri Berenguer to muse, "He saw them [Sox] as the Almighty."

As the Olde Towne Team's Hispanic mouthpiece, J.P., his sobriquet Papa Oso (Papa Bear), "would hug, even kiss, players before interviewing them," said the *Boston Globe*. In 2004, Villamán's voice broke on the last out of the first Sox world title in 86 years, screaming, "*Boston gana!*" ("Boston wins!") seven times on air "with a simplicity of heart," as *The Great Gatsby* had read, "that was its own ticket of admission."

On May 30, 2005, Mother's Day in the Dominican, J.P. called his 88-year-old aunt. Driving home after a night game in New York, he lost control at the wheel, hit a truck and tree, and died at 46. That night, Uri,

23, broadcast from Fenway Park, crying about "a brother—every *hello* and *good-bye* a hug. It's Latino culture, and that's who he was." Villamán had nightly closed, "Keep the faith. God bless you. This game is yours." This evening, Berenguer said, "J.P., this broadcast is completely yours, *compañero*."

A continent away, Ortega exhibited a similar generosity of spirit. On December 11, 1980, his first day in radio, the then-17-year-old returning home heard his mother say, "Your brothers tell me there was a beautiful voice on the radio. I congratulate you for following your dreams and I love you very much. Remember, while you may not be before me, I will always listen with my heart."

For years, his *madre* clipped articles, photos, and game programs—mementos of a son's career—even though, being deaf, she never heard him. Yet she watched each game, thrilled to see the Padres, "but at the same time wonder[ing] how her son's voice must sound," Eduardo said. "My voice! A voice she hears not with her ears but heart." Like any voice of Hispanic radio/TV, Ortega knows what makes baseball sing—as do tens of millions of listeners and viewers.

CURT SMITH is the author of 18 books, including *The Voices in the Game* and *Memories from the Microphone*. Chicago Cubs announcer Pat Hughes dubbed him "simply one of the best baseball historians, ever." He also wrote more speeches than anyone for President George H.W. Bush. Since 1998, he has been senior lecturer of English at the University of Rochester.

Introduction

JORGE IBER *and* ANTHONY R. SALAZAR

As Major League Baseball (MLB) headed into the "unusual" Fall Classic of 2020 between the Los Angeles Dodgers and Tampa Bay Rays, Routine.com provided readers with a summary of the ethnic/racial breakdown of the sport. More than seven decades since Jackie Robinson reintegrated the game's highest level, there has never been more diversity among those donning MLB uniforms. As of October 2020, whites comprised just under 58 percent, Latinos encompassed a shade below 32 percent, the number of African Americans had dipped to slightly less than 8 percent, and players of Asian/Others backgrounds accounted for about 3 percent of all rosters.[1] Two of the most significant changes in the sport's ethnic/racial composition can be seen in the dramatic downturn in the number of African Americans and the drastic upsurge in the number of *jugadores* (players) of Spanish-speaking background in MLB.

An early piece dealing with this topic appeared in a 1965 issue of *Sports Illustrated* written by the late Robert H. Boyle.[2] In his essay, "The Latins Storm las Grandes Ligas," the author noted the dramatic increase in the number of players of this background between the late 1940s and mid–1960s. That figure, the article indicated, had increased from 1 (Mike Guerra of the Philadelphia Athletics) to 48 at the time of the article's publication. Boyle then detailed for his mostly white, middle-, and upper-middle-class readers that (in case they had not figured it out previously) "Latins" were great *fanáticos* of baseball. He then proceeded to shift into a series of broad-brush statements that can certainly come across as "problematic" to readers' sensibilities in the 2020s. Among some of the "traits" common to most of these athletes, he argued, were things such as "reckless individuality," being cliquish, overly sentimental, superstitious, fussy, and extremely sensitive to perceived slights. Although no doubt, some players might have exhibited some of these traits, what this author, and other writers of the time (and earlier), seldom went into details about was the racism, discrimination, and other issues such players confronted in the minors and the majors as well. Some of what white scribes perceived as cliquishness, for example, may have been simply a defensive mechanism caused by being unfamiliar with English (and being ridiculed for their use of that language in the press) as well as simply wanting to interact with others in similar circumstances.[3]

One crucial point Boyle included was a quick reference to the ties between MLB and Spanish-speaking fans on radio (both within and outside the United States) via the work of the legendary Buck Canel (who, of course, will be profiled in this work). In a 1963 essay, he presented Canel to his readers and provided extensive detail concerning the man's broadcasting career, both in sports and in news coverage. For example, in 1936, when NBC sought to start shortwave broadcasts in Spanish of the World Series, Canel started his employment in bringing *La Serie Mundial* to a vast *audiencia* (audience) in the Caribbean and Central and South America. Starting in 1939, he served as the voice of *La Cavalgata Deportiva Gillette* (The Gillette Cavalcade of Sports) sponsored by the razor company. By the late 1940s, he served as the *voz* (voice) of the Brooklyn Dodgers (*Los Esquivadores de Brooklyn*), and later, the Chicago White Sox (*Las Medias Blancas de Chicago*).[4]

Given the dramatic growth and broader geographic distribution of Latinos/as throughout the United States over the past 50 years, it is not surprising that MLB clubs have realized the need to reach out to these aficionados. An example of such efforts can be seen in MLB's recent *Ponle Acento* program from 2016, which introduced the placement of accents and tildes on players' jerseys, so that surnames would appear correctly in Spanish. How far we have come from the days (1957–1969) when Roberto Clemente's card listed his name as "Bob," even though Topps used "Roberto" in 1955 and 1956! To add further insult to the great man's legacy, his plaque in the Hall of Fame read "Roberto Walker Clemente" until 1999, when it was changed to the correct form (with his father's name listed first, as is customary in Spanish-speaking countries) to "Roberto Clemente Walker."[5] Indeed, demographics had changed so considerably that by the start of the 2021 campaign, 21 of the 30 MLB teams broadcast at least some of their games in Spanish.

Prior to the efforts of pioneers such as Canel, Felo Ramírez and the arrival of the Dodgers in Los Angeles (with the labors of René Cárdenas and Jaime Jarrín), the Spanish-speaking fans of the United States and Latin America had few, if any, alternatives for listening to games in their native language. Things transformed dramatically as MLB moved into markets with large, existing Latino constituencies (with a second team in Los Angeles in 1961, New York and Houston in 1962, and San Diego in 1969) and was already in locales that have witnessed substantial growth in their Spanish-speaking populace (with Chicago and the Cubs, for example).[6]

Whereas a large metropolitan area such as the Windy City might be expected to have MLB Spanish-language broadcasts, some clubs, such as the Twins, Cardinals, and Brewers, are not associated with locales that have "traditionally" been noted as containing substantial Spanish-speaking populations. The fact that franchises located in cities such as Minneapolis, St. Louis, and Milwaukee broadcast in Spanish is indicative of the expanding geographic footprint of the Latino/a populace in the United States, as well as the recognition of this fact by the sport's governing body. A narrative of the expansion of Spanish-language MLB broadcasts, through the stories of various announcers, will shed light on this history.

The writing on baseball's broadcasting past is extensive, with authors such as Curt Smith, Eldon L. Ham, Kirk McKnight, James R. Walker, and Tony Silvia, among others contributing to the narrative.[7] All of these efforts provide excellent coverage and discussion of various aspects of the history of baseball on the radio. Featured are overviews of the careers of legends such as Vin Scully, Red Barber, Mel Allen, Bob Prince, Harry Caray, and others. But within this extensive coverage, there is a major lacuna; over the hundreds and hundreds of pages of these works, there is but one brief mention of a broadcaster who covered MLB games in Spanish—that being the legendary Jaime Jarrín. Walker's work makes a passing reference to the "other" fabled voice of the Dodgers, acclaiming him to be among a list of what Walker calls the current "Hall of Fame announcers" such as Dave Van Horne, Bob Uecker, Tim McCarver, and others. One would think that such high praise for a broadcaster associated with one of the MLB's marquee franchises would merit a bit of discussion. There is certainly room for much more research on this topic, and this volume is, hopefully, a step in bringing this story to the attention of academic and popular audiences.[8]

To his credit, Smith's more recent endeavors purposefully included material on such voices, allowing these individuals to tell stories about their careers, upbringings, and the game's significance to their lives. Among those interviewed and discussed are Jarrín, Ramírez, Jose Ángel (born in Colombia, then broadcasting for the Orioles in English), Juan Ángel Ávila (born in Mexico and who broadcasted for the Padres until 2014), Uri Berenguer (born in Panama and broadcasted for the Red Sox through 2019), and Amaury Pi-González (born in Cuba and currently working for the Athletics). Although this is a good step toward inclusion, these narrators are not Smith's primary focus, as they will be in this project.[9]

The study of the relationship between sport and Spanish-language radio is not well documented. For example, the first major study on this topic appeared in 1979 by Felix F. Gutiérrez and Jorge Reina Schement. This endeavor examined the growth and development of Spanish-language radio in the southwestern United States. Although a worthwhile inquiry, nowhere does it mention "sport" or "baseball."[10] More recent works on this subject matter have provided broader coverage and focused on expanding the discussion of the history of Spanish-language broadcasting as well as a recognition of the growth and differentiation of the listening (and viewing) audience (Miami and Los Angeles, for example, are not peopled by the same types of Latinos!), but still, there is nary a word on sports (and, specifically, baseball). Some recent studies on television have, of course, mentioned ties to soccer/*fútbol*.[11]

A recent article focuses on a more "modern" method of MLB teams' communication efforts with such fans. A work by Kevin Hull et al. scrutinizes how clubs are utilizing social media (in this case, Instagram) seeking to "make Spanish-speaking fans feel more welcome." Part of how teams are accomplishing this goal is by emphasizing the activities of the Latino players. In this study, the researchers found that even though *jugadores* account for one-third of participants, they accounted for "nearly 50% of the players shown in the photos." Efforts along these lines "garnered more likes than posts that did not [feature Latinos]." The results of this project demonstrated that Latino fans are attached not only to certain clubs (in this case, the authors studied the Diamondbacks and the Yankees) but that it is important that when franchises reach out in *Español* they also highlight Spanish-surnamed competitors. "Although the followers may be fans of the Diamondbacks and Yankees, based on the number of likes, they appear to be greater fans of those teams' Hispanic players and Hispanic cultural events. This demonstrates that in the hierarchy of an individual's social identity, a Hispanic person's ethnicity appears to be of great importance." A logical assumption to draw from such research is that the role of the Spanish-language broadcaster is currently (and we would argue, has always been) an important aspect of the operation of MLB organizations.[12]

There are some works that have focused on the increasing presence and need to interact with (in a positive and respectful way), Latino/a fans of various sports. A prominent writer on this topic is Jorge E. Moraga of California State University–Bakersfield. In a stand-alone article and his dissertation (at Washington State University), Moraga has noted on the use of racially tinged commentary about the Spanish-surnamed/Spanish-speakers over the years on radio and other media (like what was happening with the phonetic writing used to discredit baseball players such as Roberto Clemente and others) and attempts to counteract such trends. Specifically, he concentrates on efforts by ESPN, the NBA, and other entities in the athletics business and how they confront the "new reality" of the "browning" of America and sports fans. In sum, Moraga argues that it is imperative for the industry to "pay heed to the growing Latino influence on U.S. media and society." This book seeks to present the role and history of how Spanish-language MLB broadcasters have been part of this significant trend.[13]

Although the coverage concerning the study of Spanish-language MLB *locutores* is limited, the cupboard is not completely bare. In addition to the increased attention provided by Curt Smith noted previously, there are three recent efforts, two of them in English, that build on the pioneering work done by Samuel O. Regalado on Jarrín and the Dodgers in the mid–1990s.[14] First, we turn to a self-published effort by Franklin Otto, *Locutores Hispanos: Perspectivas desde las Grandes Ligas*, in which the author interviewed 26 broadcasters concerning a myriad of issues, including how they began their careers, narrative styles, perceived differences between players of Latino and "Americano" backgrounds, and other themes. This is an excellent introduction but is limited by the small number of copies published (in a discussion with Mr. Otto, he noted that the run was only of around 60 books, with almost one-half being distributed to the participants). One goal here is to expand and contextualize much of what Otto discussed with his interviewees for a broader audience.[15]

The two recent works in English on this issue are by Patrick J. McConnell and Roberto Avant-Mier, and Jorge Iber. The first study is part of a collection edited by John Carvalho titled *Sports Media History: Culture, Technology, Identity*. The authors provided a very brief overview of the careers of Canel, Cárdenas, Ramírez, and Jarrín, as well as pointing to the "cultural cohesion" created by their efforts. The *locutores* helped the Spanish-speaking community rally around teams and helped humanize and introduce the broader public to the growing number of Latino players who populated the MLB. In sum, their efforts not only expanded a club's fan base but also shed light on the "complicated, complex, and sometimes contradictory" relationship between *peloteros* and *fanáticos* of the national pastime. Thus, they helped make this population of "others" (on the field, in the stands, and at home) a more prominent part of the game.[16]

Jorge Iber's recent contribution to *NINE: A Journal of Baseball History and Culture* provides similar coverage focusing on the life and career of long-standing San Diego Padres' broadcaster (39 years going into 2021) Eduardo Ortega. Significantly, because of the team's location, the Padres' Spanish-language broadcasts reach directly into Mexico and have helped forge ties between the Spanish-speaking community on both sides of the border.[17]

There are some early records that point to the potential and benefits of broadcasting games in Spanish: with four such examples present in the *Sporting News*. First, in 1940, an anonymous brief featured the headline, "Latins Like W.S. Broadcasts." This story noted that "more than 30,000 letters have been received ... expressing appreciations for the Spanish language broadcasts ... by René Cárdenas, sports announcer for CMQ-COCO, Havana." After the conclusion of the 1951 Fall Classic, another brief indicated that "broadcasts from Havana, Cuba, San Juan, Puerto Rico, and Mexico City sent Spanish language accounts to the CMQ network, Puerto Rican network, and Programas de Mexico, respectively." A "Voice of the Fan" letter sent during spring training in 1955 paid homage to Buck Canel as one aficionado from Oriente Province in Cuba stated that fans should "hand an orchid to ... the swell guy who broadcasts the major league games to us, the Spanish-speaking people." Finally, a 1957 article noted that "in an effort to develop more fans among the Spanish-speaking population of New York, the Dodgers will broadcast in that language over WHOM this season."[18]

Only a few academic exposés have dealt specifically with teams' early efforts to broadcast in Spanish and attract a following among that group. In addition to the essay by Regalado noted previously, there was an effort by Ron Briley concerning the Houston (then) Colt .45s which appeared in 2001. Briley's assessment of the new team's efforts was not as positive as those of the Dodgers. This author argued that the Colt .45s ignored the Mexican American and Mexican audiences that should have been a "natural" market for the expansion franchise, as well as not treating their first Latino star, Cuban Roman Mejías, properly. Briley claimed that not only did team ownership not assist Mejías with family reunification, but there was also constant stereotyping and noting of his "poor" English in the local press. Regarding broadcasting, this author argued, the club did not utilize Mejías to reach out to Spanish-speaking fans. Overall, Briley postulated that the Colt .45s made no attempt at "cultivating the local Latin market of Mexican Americans as well as that of neighboring Mexico."[19] Although certainly there were missteps, Briley's essay failed to mention that the Colt .45s/Astros hired two Spanish-language broadcasters from their inception in 1962; René Cárdenas, who came over from the Dodgers, and the Cuban-born Orlando Sánchez-Diago (who was with the club for 30 years). Indeed, in 1966, Cárdenas initiated Astro broadcasts into Mexico, the Caribbean, and the rest of the Americas. This work will feature an essay on Sanchez that runs counter to several of Briley's assertions about the early days of Spanish-language radio broadcasting by the franchise.

In 2003, Eric Ávila, a historian of urban life in Los Angeles, effectively summarized the value of the history of Dodger baseball and broadcasts by discussing what this has meant to the denizens of that Southern California metropolis:

Cultural officials in Los Angeles, Dodger owners, and radio management acknowledged the necessity of reaching out to the Mexican American community. Of course, as entrepreneurs, franchise owners were desperate to include Spanish audiences not only to reach out to a heretofore excluded group but also to maximize their own financial success.... The popularity of the Los Angeles Dodgers among southern California's Chicano community reflects a larger pattern of Mexican American participation in the institutions of American mass culture.[20]

While no other MLB franchise has broadcast in Spanish for as long as the Dodgers, it is fair to say that much of what Ávila notes about "los Doyers" can also be seen in the relationship between other clubs, such as the Red Sox, and their growing Latino fan base. This is a sport that Latinos/as embrace and having games broadcast in Spanish (as well as rooting for Latino athletes) certainly helps make these fans understand that they are valued and are part of the baseball community.

The goal of our project, then, is to present readers with a series of essays that examine the careers of some legendary, current but veteran, and younger Spanish-language broadcasters working in the major leagues. How did these individuals get involved in the business? How did they get jobs with their current team? How and why did the various teams make the decision to begin broadcasting in Spanish? Of course, for some franchises, such as the Miami Marlins and the San Diego Padres, the choice was obvious, given the demographic realities. But what about the Seattle Mariners, Minnesota Twins, and Milwaukee Brewers? What has been happening in those cities that prompted club ownership to broadcast in Spanish? It is questions such as these, in addition to detailing individual broadcasters' lives, that this work will address. It will be the first such effort undertaken in English to focus exclusively on this overlooked aspect of the Latino/a community's connection to MLB.

Whereas all of the broadcasters covered here do so in Spanish, we felt it was necessary to include the voice of Jessica Mendoza as well. As will become apparent, she is a pathbreaker who has broken down significant barriers in regard to the employment of Spanish-surnamed (and female) broadcasters. Her presence on ESPN's radio and television broadcasts, as well as being part of the NBC professionals who brought us the 2020 Tokyo Olympics, single her contributions as utterly unique. Perhaps she might inspire a young Latina to accept the challenge of calling games in Spanish. After all, if the Yankees can have Rachel Balkovec in charge of the Tampa Tarpons (Low-A level) and the Miami Marlins can install Kim Ng as their general manager, who is to say that a Latina calling MLB games in Spanish is not a possibility in the near future?

A final note worth mentioning concerning the essays included here is that not all of the contributors are academicians such as the two editors are. To wit, although most of the essays contain endnotes, some do not, as they are generated mostly from the personal recollections of the individual author, many of whom have had personal/professional interactions with the subjects of their piece.

In summary, in this work, of course, there are essays on *leyendas*, such as Canel, Jarrín, Cárdenas, and Ramírez. We also feature studies on *locutores* of long-standing: Amaury Pi-González, Eduardo Ortega, Héctor Molina, Luis Rodríguez-Mayoral, Uri Berenguer, Pepe Yñiguez, and Jorge Jarrín. We will also focus on younger broadcasters such as Junior Pepén and Francisco Romero. The essay on Jessica Mendoza will also be included in this section. Our goal has been to provide as broad a coverage as possible, but of course, not all individuals or teams are covered herein. Hopefully, this effort will stimulate further research by both academicians and writers for a popular audience. After all, the future of our national pastime is increasingly being written by *jugadores* of Latin backgrounds. As that population continues to grow in the United States, it is only logical that the teams that already broadcast in Spanish will expand their efforts. Further, it may not be too much longer before the nine franchises that do not offer their fans games in *Español* may find it rewarding to commence such endeavors.

Notes

1. "MLB Player Demographics," Routine.com, October 6, 2020. See https://www.routine.com/blog/post/mlb-player-demographics/. Accessed on June 10, 2021.

2. Robert H. Boyle, "Latins Storm *Las Grandes Ligas*," *Sports Illustrated*, August 9, 1965. See https://vault.si.com/vault/1965/08/09/the-latins-storm-las-grandes-ligas. Accessed on July 16, 2021.

3. There are many authors who have written about this topic, but for a concise summary of such issues, see Samuel O. Regalado, "Image Is Everything: Latin Baseball Players and the United States Press," *Studies in Latin American Popular Culture* 13, no. 3 (1994): 101–114.

4. Robert H. Boyle, "'El As' Is the Voice of America," *Sports Illustrated*, August 9, 1965, and October 14, 1963. See https://vault.si.com/vault/1963/10/14/el-as-is-the-voice-of-america. Accessed on June 16, 2021. For an example of local coverage on Canel, see Ben Gross, "Listening In," *New York Daily News*, June 12, 1943.

5. Jerry Grillo, "It's Roberto, Not Bob," March 14, 2020. See https://fourcrickets.wordpress.com/2020/03/14/its-roberto-not-bob/. Accessed on July 16, 2021.

6. "Cubs Broadcast History," July 26, 2007. See http://research.sabr.org/business/index2.php?option=com_content&task=view&id=119&pop=1&page=5. Accessed on July 16, 2021.

7. See the following: Curt Smith, *Voices of the Game: The Acclaimed Chronicle of Baseball Radio and Television Broadcasting—1921 to the Present* (South Bend, IN: Diamond Communication, 1987); Eldon L. Ham, *Broadcasting Baseball: A History of the National Pastime on the Radio and Television* (Jefferson, NC: McFarland, 2011); Kirk McKnight, *The Voices of Baseball: The Game's Greatest Broadcasters Reflect on America's Pastime*

(Lanham, MD: Rowman & Littlefield, 2015); James R. Walker, *Crack of the Bat: A History of Baseball on the Radio* (Lincoln: University of Nebraska Press, 2015); Tony Silvia, *Baseball over the Air: The National Pastime on the Radio and in the Imagination* (Jefferson, NC: McFarland, 2007).
    8. Walker, *Crack of the Bat*, ix.
    9. Curt Smith. *A Talk in the Park: Nine Decades of Baseball Tales from the Broadcast Booth* (Washington, DC: Potomac Books, 2011). Additionally, Smith is providing even more coverage of Spanish-language broadcasters in his just published *Memories from the Microphone: A Century of Baseball Broadcasting* (Cooperstown, NY: National Baseball Hall of Fame Books, 2021).
    10. Felix F. Gutierrez and Jorge Reina Schement, *Spanish Language Radio in the Southwestern United States* (Austin: Center for Mexican American Studies, University of Texas, Austin), 1979.
    11. See the following: America Rodriguez, "Creating an Audience and Remapping a Nation: A Brief History of U.S. Spanish-Language Broadcasting, 1930–1980," *Quarterly Review of Film & Video* 16, no. 3–4 (1999): 357–374; Maria Castaneda, "The Significance of U.S. Spanish-Language Radio," in *Latinos and American Popular Culture*, ed. Patricia M. Montilla (Santa Barbara, CA: ABC-Clio, 2013), 69–86; Alan B. Albarran and Brian Hutton, *A History of Spanish Language Radio in the United States* (Denton: Center for Spanish Language Media, University of North Texas, 2009). Two important works on Spanish-language television are Kevin T. Wilkinson, *Spanish-Language Television in the United States: Fifty Years of Development* (New York: Routledge, 2016); and Craig Allen, *Univision, Telemundo, and the Rise of Spanish-Language Television in the United States* (Gainesville: University of Florida Press, 2020).
    12. Kevin Hull, Joon Kyung Kim, and Matt Stillwell, "*Fotos de Beisbol*: An Examination of the Spanish-Language Instagram Accounts of Major League Baseball Teams," *Howard Journal of Communications* 30, no. 3 (2019): 249–264.
    13. See Jorge E. Moraga, "On ESPN Deportes: Latinos, Sport Media, and the Cultural Politics of Visibilities," *Journal of Sport and Social Issues* 42, no. 6 (2018): 470–497; Jorge E. Moraga, "Browning Sport: How Multicultural Markets, Halls of Fame, and Bilingual Media Construct Latinos/as in Late-Capitalist America" (PhD diss., Washington State University, 2017).
    14. Samuel O. Regalado. "'Dodgers Beisbol Is on the Air': The Development and Impact of The Dodgers' Spanish Language Broadcasts, 1958–1994," *California History* 74, no. 3 (1995): 280–289.
    15. Franklin Otto, *Locutores Hispanos: Perspectivos desde las Grandes Ligas*," (Slingerlands, NY: Earle Editors, 2016). See also Franklin Otto, "Bill Kulik: The *Gringo Malo* Speaks the Language of the Game," *NINE: A Journal of Baseball History and Culture* 21, no. 2 (Spring 2013): 135–139.
    16. Patrick J. McConnell and Roberto Avant-Mier, "Major League Baseball and the Development of Spanish-Language Radio Broadcasts," in *Sports Media History: Culture, Technology, Identity*, ed. John Carvalho (New York: Routledge, 2021), 107–120.
    17. Jorge Iber, "*Beisbol* as Part of '*Una Vida en Comun en la Frontera*': The Career and Significance of Eduardo Ortega, the *Voz* of the San Diego Padres," *NINE: A Journal of Baseball History and Culture* 26, nos. 1–2 (Fall–Spring 2017–2018): 125–141.
    18. See the following: "Latins Like W.S. Broadcasts," *Sporting News*, November 7, 1940, 6; "Record World's Series TV and Radio Coverage," *Sporting News*, October 10, 1951, 29; Mathias Rodriguez, "Cuban Orchid for Buck Canel," *Sporting News*, March 23, 1955, 20; "40 Brook Games in Spanish," *Sporting News*, March 20, 1957, 25.
    19. Ron Briley, "Roman Mejías: Houston's First Major League Latin Star and the Troubled Legacy of Race Relations in the Lone Star State," *NINE: A Journal of Baseball History and Culture* 10, no. 1 (Fall 2001): 73–88.
    20. Eric Avila, "Revisiting the Chavez Ravine: Baseball, Urban Renewal and the Gendered Civic Culture of Postwar Los Angeles," in *Velvet Barrios: Popular Culture and Chicana/o Sexualities*, ed. Alicia Gaspar de Alba (New York: Palgrave Macmillan, 2002): 125–140.

1. Legends

Buck Canel

Luis Rodríguez-Mayoral

Eloy "Buck" Canel had a unique deep rasp of a voice that as a kid I loved to hear while he was broadcasting baseball games in Puerto Rico's Professional Winter League. As I grew older, living in Panama during the l950s, I was always very attentive when he would broadcast the World Series every October. His knowledge of the game, his vocabulary, his anecdotes—all part of his artistry behind the mic—made him an exceedingly popular personality throughout Latin America and the Caribbean basin where baseball is followed.

Canel, in my appreciation, was an intellectual who loved to hold court while talking about diverse topics like politics, classical music, literature, arts, and boxing, to name a few. I dare say that among other pastimes he loved playing chess and expressing ideas as to how to fix the world. And I must not forget ... he enjoyed an occasional cocktail.

The "Buck" Canel I was fortunate to befriend was comparable to a poet behind the mic as he could keep the interest of listeners in the game while improvising stanzas about current events, food, and culture. He also was fantastic with wordplay and laughed at his own jokes!

He called the seventh inning—"El inning de la suerte.... The Lucky Seventh." However, the phrase that is truly unforgettable is—"No se vayan, que esto se pone bueno" "Don't go away because this is getting good." "Buck" also happened to be a magnificent boxing announcer.

"Buck" Canel was born in Rosario, Argentina, on March 4, 1906. His father was a career diplomat and his Argentine mother a journalist. As a man of the world, he grew up in his native country and in Staten Island, New York, while spending time as a young adult in Cuba, where he could trace some of his family roots.

I first met "Buck" days before the 1972 MLB All-Star Game in Atlanta. I saw him sitting alone a couple of hours before the evening game in the press box and did not hesitate to walk up to him and say, "Mr. Canel, I know who you are. Can I shake your hand?" The man, with an incredibly positive reaction, gave me a smile and instantly replied, "The honor is mine."

Our friendship was largely cemented that day. He even asked me about a relative of mine, Radames Mayoral, who for many years was the voice of the Leones de Ponce in the Puerto Rican Winter League.

When we met, he was 66 years old and had broadcast MLB games since about 1936, predominantly for the New York teams—Brooklyn Dodgers, Yankees, and Mets. However, his international fame, including Latin American Spanish-language markets in the United States, was by way of NBC's Gillette Cavalcade of Sports, which at its peak aired in more than 200 stations.

After our initial encounter, during the 1970s, he began growing a well-kept white beard and wearing beret-type hats. He reminded me of a writer I sincerely admired. One day in Yankee Stadium, with due respect, I addressed him as "Señor Hemingway," and he loved it! Like Hemingway, he started out as a journalist writing for the *Staten Island Advance*. He, perhaps better than Hemingway, was a master of English and Spanish.

In 1975, "Buck" told our late good mutual friend Tirso A. Valdez, for New York's *El Diario La Prensa*, "My first broadcast ever happened in 1933." I was the Associated Press correspondent in Havana, Cuba, when revolution led by Fulgencio Batista toppled dictator Gerardo Machado. "Days later, Batista asked me if in Miami his speech (minutes earlier) had been heard and then suggested that I translate it so that it could be understood there. He then escorted me to a mic and in front of media members present, I translated it from Spanish to English ... and I did not make an error!"

From the 1970s to the early 1980s, I was part of a broadcast team for WAPA Radio in Puerto Rico covering mostly MLB East Coast teams. Whenever in New York, he would happily join us in our booth. My invitations to him would renew his energies!

In a 1978 interview, "Buck" recapped his career during an interview which I used several times in Puerto Rico: He was the only Hispanic member of the media to cover the first MLB Hall of Fame induction ceremony on June 12, 1939, in Cooperstown, New York.

He served as a translator for President Franklin Delano Roosevelt and the United Nations. He was a writer for Associated Press, Agence France-Presse (the French news agency), and its predecessor, Agence Havas (the French wire service). He was the best man in the wedding of future Hall of Famer from Venezuela Luis Aparicio and Sonia Llorente (of Puerto Rican descent) in 1956.

Starting in 1937, he broadcast 42 World Series, a record that still stands. He did emphasize that it would have been 43, but in October 1964, he was assigned to Tokyo, Japan, to cover the Olympics. (This particular information proved to be of great interest to Hall of Fame officials.) He had many friendships with baseball players of which the most endearing were those of Luis Aparicio, Rod Carew, and Roberto Clemente.

During the last few years of his life we would talk on the phone frequently or when we visited Yankee Stadium. He would on many occasions suddenly become energetic and alive when dipping into his great vault of memories. "Buck" would recall experiences with Eva and Juan Perón in Argentina, Cuban dictators Batista and Fidel Castro, their Nicaraguan and Dominican Republic counterparts, Anastacio Somoza, and Rafael L. Trujillo, respectively. And then "out of the blue" came flashbacks of his experiences with the likes of former U.S. Secretary of State John Foster Dulles, Spanish bullfighter Manolete, or boxing heavyweight champions Joe Louis, Rocky Marciano, and Muhammad Ali. Like I have stated, "Buck" reminded me of Ernest Hemingway ... magnificent storytellers! They were so inexplicably similar.

One evening during the 1975 Caribbean Series in Puerto Rico, after attending a reception held by Governor Rafael Hernández Colón at La Fortaleza, his official residence, "Buck" suggested we walk around Old San Juan and visit his favorite restaurant, La Mallorquina, established in 1848. David Albarrán, a bartender there since the 1940s, immediately recognized "Buck" and minutes later showed us two remembrance logs dated March 30, 1948, and March 20, 1969. We found "Buck's" signatures along with those of Gloria Swanson, Nat King Cole, Eddie Fisher, and Luis Muñoz Marín, the first popularly elected governor of Puerto Rico. "Buck" was profoundly moved, and I saw it in his eyes.

In 1978, the National Baseball Hall of Fame and Museum established the Ford C. Frick Award presented annually to a broadcaster for major contributions to the game. The first two recipients were Mel Allen, the legendary voice of the New York Yankees, and Red Barber, the voice of the Brooklyn Dodgers before becoming Allen's partner on Yankees' broadcasts. During the course of that year, I undertook the mission of nominating "Buck" for the award without receiving any response whatsoever from anyone. In 1980, a good personal friend, Commissioner Bowie K. Kuhn, began promoting "Buck's" nomination through his own channels. His initiative coincided with "Buck's" passing at his home in Croton-on-Hudson, north of New York City, on April 9. He died from emphysema.

I will never forget that the next day I was on the air with Guillermo Portuondo Cala, the sports director for the USIA–Voice of America Radio Network, informing millions of fans in Latin America of his passing. At home in San Juan, I received a letter from Kuhn dated April 14: "I share your sentiments about 'Buck.' In addition to his professional abilities

Buck Canel being feted at Yankee Stadium, April 1979. The master of ceremonies is Luis Rodríguez-Mayoral (collection of Luis Rodríguez-Mayoral).

he was a great guy. I know I will miss him.... I will see that your further thoughts on the Ford Frick Award will be brought to the attention of the committee." Subject letter is well preserved in my archives 41 years later.

In March 1985, Bill Guilfoile, the Hall of Fame's director of public relations, pulled me aside prior to the annual banquet in honor of Major League Baseball held by the governor of Florida in St. Petersburg and said, "Your guy ['Buck' Canel] will be honored this year." I felt enormous joy! But the mission was not complete. We had to locate "Buck's" widow, Colleen, who had moved from their Croton-on-Hudson home in New York. Several weeks later, I located her living with her daughter, Alice, her husband, as well as their kids, at their Tri-Rivers farm in Moncure, North Carolina. On Sunday, July 28, 1985, Colleen, accompanied by her three grandkids (Chip, Nancy, and Steve), accepted the Ford C. Frick Award on behalf of her late husband ... the first Hispanic so honored!

As I had said the day after "Buck's" death in 1980, during a sad broadcast on the Voice of America, I say today, "As a writer, Ernest Hemingway conquered readers around the world. His fan and look-alike, 'Buck' Canel, conquered Hispanic baseball fans internationally with his voice and eloquence behind the mic."

René Cárdenas

Francisco Romero *and* Jorge Iber

The Los Angeles Dodgers went into the 2022 MLB season with high expectations of reclaiming the World Series title they earned in the pandemic-shortened season of 2020 (when they defeated the Tampa Bay Rays in six contests). A few months prior to the start of the campaign, however, the team got some not unanticipated but still poignant news, as their longtime (this season would be his 64th behind the microphone for the team) Spanish-language voice, Jaime Jarrín, announced that this would be his final year of work.[1] Although Jarrín's *voz* has become synonymous with the team, there is another person, René Cárdenas, who preceded Jaime and indeed served as the first broadcaster in *Español* not only for the newly arrived Dodgers but also for two other squads, the Houston Colt .45s/Astros and the Texas Rangers.

René Cárdenas was born in Managua, Nicaragua, on February 6, 1930, and unlike his partner with the Dodgers, the Ecuadorian-born Jarrín, was already quite familiar with baseball prior to his arrival in the United States in 1951. This was due to two reasons. The first was his family's connection to the sport; with his grandfather, Adán Cárdenas, who served as president of the nation between 1883 and 1887, introducing the sport to his countrymen.[2] One might say that *béisbol* was part of his life experiences from the very start, even though René did not play the game much. Second, by the time that he was in his mid-teens, Cárdenas was already authoring stories on boxing for the newspaper *La Estrella* in his hometown. He later moved on to another outlet, *La Prensa*, and covered basketball and baseball as well. His writing skills eventually helped him garner an opportunity to do a few spots on a local radio station. This in time led to a chance to do play-by-play for these sports with Radio Mundial. It was during this time that he earned the nickname *el chelito* ("the blond one"). By his early 20s, René sought to take his chance to work in the United States. He finished his schooling in California (where he had some family) and there learned English.[3]

Upon his arrival in Southern California, René continued working for *La Prensa* at the paper's local bureau. One of his tasks was to write about Pacific Coast League (PCL) teams, such as the Hollywood Stars and the Los Angeles Angels. One thing Cárdenas noticed while on this beat was that few Spanish speakers attended contests, in part, he believed, because "there weren't many Latin players in the PCL."[4] Still, René understood that given the dramatic rise in the number of Latinos in the region (in part, due to the opportunities made available for jobs during the era of World War II) that there was a potential market for baseball broadcasting in Spanish. When the Brooklynites announced their move west in late 1957, the young, hopeful broadcaster saw an opportunity. Shortly thereafter, Cárdenas, with a proposal in hand, visited with William Beaton, station manager of one of the only Spanish-language stations in Los Angeles, KWKW, with what would prove to be a brilliant idea. Why not have the Dodgers broadcast games in *Español*?

Beaton presented this proposition to the team, and this reminded the brass of a similar situation they had back east for "the Dodgers were able to establish a loyal fan base in a neighborhood with families of diverse ethnic backgrounds." Indeed, the Dodgers had broadcast some games (with Buck Canel) in Spanish prior to their departure from Flatbush.[5] Soon, Stan Evans, of the New York–based ad agency that worked with the team, auditioned up to 100 potential voices; René stood out from the rest. "We listened to hundreds of tapes and there was no question that René was absolutely outstanding." Thus, this planted the seed, although the Dodgers did not pay for this announcer to travel with the squad, with all games being Reagan-style recreations until 1961 when Cárdenas would follow the team to games in San Francisco. Not until 1964 did he travel to all away games. Starting with opening day of 1958, René was the team's voice in Spanish, to be joined by Jarrín in 1959.[6]

Although he would leave after 1961, René was on the air during some crucial early moments in the team's Los Angeles history. For example, the Dodgers won their first West Coast World Series title in 1959, certainly a great way to build positive connections to the new home base. That very same year, however, the team was embroiled in the controversy surrounding breaking ground in Chavez Ravine. The situation with 68-year-old Avrana Arechiga being dragged out of a house in the enclave did not make for good press for the club. Still, "the Dodgers and the city ... weathered the episode after local papers revealed that the Arechiga family owned at least nine homes. That the club employed Spanish-language coverage of its games was also of great help in restoring its reputation within the Mexican American quarter."[7] Shortly thereafter, René had the opportunity to pioneer MLB broadcasts in another market, this time in Houston, Texas.

In an interview with one of the authors of this essay in April 2020, Cárdenas noted that advertisers familiar with his work approached him to determine his interest in working for the new National League franchise. Eventually, the team's owner, Judge Roy Hofheinz, offered him the post. Although the market was smaller than Los Angeles, the job came with other opportunities that René found of interest. For example, he would work directly for the team, not a radio station. This was Judge Hofheinz's vision from the start. He simply "didn't want or need to give up control in exchange for a few extra dollars, so he did it his way."[8] Additionally, René also had the opportunity to select his broadcast partner, eventually deciding on Cuban-born Orlando Sánchez-Diago with whom he had worked previously.[9] The franchise was also interested in aggressively pursuing a Latino audience as ownership "saw a huge potential market in the Southern United States, Mexico, and in other parts of Latin America for Major League Baseball." One last aspect of René's early ties to the Houston franchise was the opportunity for him to help Hofheinz promote the construction of a new facility through a bond issue ($22 million for what would become the Astrodome).[10]

Last, given this focus, there was an opportunity to establish a radio network throughout various parts of the Spanish-speaking world. This started in 1966 with, eventually, a total of 82 stations in 13 different nations (in conjunction with the U.S. State Department, the Pan American Union, and the Office of the Commissioner of MLB). As part of this endeavor, team officials visited Nicaragua and other nations to check on the progress of talent in various winter leagues, as well as to help further develop an audience for the newly rechristened Astros. What an amazing moment this must have been for Cárdenas! Not only was he the lead announcer for another MLB team, but he was now being heard throughout Texas (the team had affiliates in locales such as Corpus Christi, Dallas, Amarillo, Brownsville, and San Antonio); his *voz* was now being heard in his homeland all the way from the United States. In addition to his baseball work, René also broadcasted championship boxing matches during the late 1960s and into the early 1970s. Among these were four title bouts featuring Muhammad Ali (in 1966, 1967, and two fights in 1971).[11] The broadcast duo worked for the Astros until 1975. At that time, due to changes in the organizational structure of the club (e.g., Judge Hofheinz had a stroke in 1970 and by 1975 his holdings were in a large amount of debt; ultimately, the team was sold to its two major creditors), both René and Orlando were terminated, as well as the south-of-the-border broadcasting efforts.[12]

This turn of events prompted René and his wife, Jilma (a second marriage for him; the couple married in 1957), to return to Nicaragua. There, they hoped to enjoy a peaceful and relaxing retirement, although he was still involved in sports radio broadcasting. Unfortunately, it was not to last long as by the spring of 1979, the Sandinistas came to take control of the country. The final days of the revolution saw fighting taking place directly in front of the entrance to the couple's hacienda. "They were fighting around my house every night. We had to go under the bed every single night for months. We were in a war without being soldiers." In addition to their personal peril, René endured the assassination of his half-brother Chester Escobar (though he would not know of this for years) due to his connection to the Somoza regime. As his Cuban partner had endured twenty years earlier, the Cárdenas lost most of their possessions. In addition to forfeiting his house for the benefit of "the people," there were irreplaceable mementos of the years with the Dodgers, Colt .45s, and Astros. "The bank account is nothing. But my furniture, my books. I lost all my clothing, my most intimate remembrances. Major league pictures and little trophies." Fortunately, the couple managed to arrive at the American embassy (René became a citizen in 1963) and eventually made their way out of the country.[13] Upon his return to the United States, Cárdenas managed to return to the MLB booth, first with the Texas Rangers (though only for the 1981 season) and then back to the Dodgers (starting in 1982).[14]

The main difference in this second go-round with Los Angeles was that René was now Jarrín's sidekick. This meant that the announcing duties worked a certain way: with Jaime calling seven frames, and René doing the fourth and fifth innings plus the pregame show. In a 1995 article for the *Los Angeles Times*, writer Kevin Baxter argued that the two giants of Spanish-language baseball broadcasting "share a microphone and a cramped radio booth for nearly eight months each year, but they no longer share a deep friendship." The article quoted an unnamed friend of both who said that "it's an ego thing. I have gotten out of them that there's a little war going on." Still, both men tried to downplay extant issues for the article. Jarrín for example, stated that "I don't know why there is an impression there is friction between us. I don't feel nothing against him at all. I think I'm a good friend of his." A bit later in the discussion, however, he argued that "in the last two, three years [René's] become a little colder. I don't know why. If you ask me to pick a reason, I would say it's because he doesn't want to admit that he's No. 2 in the booth. But that's not my fault." On the other side of the equation, Cárdenas counters that the ties were "excellent. And it's been that way for many, many, many years." Still, when asked about the division of innings noted above, René countered that "I don't know why it's the way it is."[15] Even though the two may have downplayed differences, they were obvious to Stuart Shea in his research on the team's broadcast history. In sum, Shea noted that "the booth eventually wasn't big enough" for the two legends.[16] René retired from the Dodgers in 1998 and returned to Houston but did have the chance to call another World Series for Los Angeles—their unexpected triumph over the Oakland Athletics in 1988.

After a 15-year hiatus, the Astros once again began to broadcast games in Spanish, with Sánchez-Diago returning to the air alongside fellow Cuban American Rolando Becerra on KXYZ in 1990. This pairing lasted until 1992, with both announcers leaving the Astros' booth. Francisco Ernesto Ruiz then took over until 2007. He had several partners over the years: Manny López in 1993, Danny González between 1994 and 1996, and Alex Treviño between 1997 and 2007. They were then followed by Alex Treviño and Francisco Romero.[17] René did make a return to the Astros' airwaves from time to time over the years and also returned for a television broadcast of 15 games in the 2008 season. He also continued to write for *La Prensa*.[18] One final highlight of this legend's time in Houston occurred in 2017, when the two teams he is most associated with, the Astros and the Dodgers, faced off in that year's Fall Classic. When asked to comment on the matchup, René tried to be diplomatic. "Where is my heart? With the Astros or the Dodgers? I have still not found a response. I do not know where my heart is. The only idea I can put forward is that is seems that I am in the middle and my heart is divided. I will celebrate with both teams" (authors' translation). Although he sounded noncommittal in this article, in another, with Alyson Footer for MLB.com, René did seem to tip his emotional hand a bit more directly. "'I remember starting with the Dodgers in 1958 and knowing I was starting something very special in my life,' Cardenas said. 'Those years with the Dodgers were the best years of my life. I thought I'd be with the Dodgers for several World Series.'"[19]

As René entered the latter stages of his octogenarian years, the significance of his place in the history of Spanish-language MLB broadcasting was increasingly ruminated. His fellow *leyendas*, Canel, Jarrín, and Ramírez, have all been enshrined in the Hall of Fame by earning the Ford C. Frick Award. Cárdenas was nominated in 2011, 2012, and 2015. Unfortunately, he was not selected.[20] More recently, in an interview with the *New York Times* author James Wagner, René discussed his continuing exclusion. The writer postulated that "out of sight does indeed mean out of mind." Jaime Jarrín also chimed in on this peculiar marginalization stipulating that Cárdenas's jumping from team to team might have "affected his case." Still, Jaime continues to push for his former colleague, even with the bad blood that had supposedly percolated over the years. "As the years pass by, new members are on the electing committee and they don't know Rení and the history, or study it. I always voted for him…. It'd be a great pleasure to have him in Cooperstown with me. Undisputedly, I'd love that. But it's out of my reach." In the meantime, he has been inducted into several other halls, among those being the Hispanic Heritage Baseball Museum Hall of Fame as well as the Nicaraguan National Hall of Fame. However, the most coveted prize continues to elude him. When commenting on his nominations, René noted that "it's an honor just to be nominated. There are a lot of people who would like to be in. It's a very exclusive club." While saying what is expected from all nominees who do not get in, he then went on to share his more honest sentiments: "I'd love to be elected while I'm alive, not after I'm dead. That's no fun."[21]

In the minds of many, there is no question that he belongs in baseball's holiest shrine. As one of the individuals who followed René in the Astro's booth, Francisco Romero, noted to James Wagner in 2018, "A lot of people don't know what he's done, who he was and that he was a pioneer. He was the first to be hired by a … team full time. He opened the door.… He's a maestro of the art of baseball narration. For his time alone, he merits it. How many of us have learned from him, including Jaime?"[22] If for no other reason, that last statement by Romero should resonate with those who care about the history of MLB Spanish-language broadcasting. If the man who helped launch Jaime Jarrín's 64-year-long career does not merit membership in the Hall of Fame, then who can claim to be worthy?

Notes

1. Chris Cwilk, "Dodger Broadcaster Jaime Jarrín to Retire in 2022 after 64 Years with Team," September 28, 2021. See https://sports.yahoo.com/dodger-broadcaster-jaime-Jarrín-to-retire-in-2022-after-64-years-with-team-203842680.html?fr=yhssrp_catchall. Accessed on June 24, 2022.

2. Kevin Baxter, "The Sunday Profile: Wins and Losses: René Cárdenas Brought Baseball to Millions with His Pioneering Broadcasts in Spanish. Now, Shaken by Tough Times, He Clings to His Claim to the Hall of Fame," June 18, 1995. See https://www.latimes.com/archives/la-xpm-1995-06-18-ls-14323-story.html. Accessed on June 24, 2022.

3. *Ibid.* See also James Wagner, "A Spanish Voice That Cries Out for the Hall of Fame," October 25, 2018. See https://www.nytimes.com/2018/10/25/sports/baseball/rene-Cárdenas-spanish-broadcaster.html#:~:text=Jarr%C3%ADn%2C%20his%20former%20radio%20partner%20who%20is%20the,heart%2C%20really.%20I%20hung%20up%20my%20gloves%20already.%E2%80%9D. Accessed on June 24, 2022; Samuel O. Regalado, "Dodgers Béisbol Is on the Air: The Development and Impact of the Dodgers' Spanish Language Broadcasts, 1958–1994," *California History* 74, no. 3 (Fall 1995): 280–289.

4. Regalado, "Dodgers Béisbol Is on the Air," 282–283.

5. See "40 Brook Games in Spanish," *Sporting News*, March 20, 1957, 25.

6. Regalado, "Dodgers Béisbol Is on the Air," 283–286. See also Kevin Nelson, "Los Angeles Dodgers vs. San Francisco Giants, April 1958," *California History* 82, no. 4 (2005): 44–61.

7. Regalado, "Dodgers Béisbol Is on the Air," 286.

8. Stuart Shea, "Raising the Roof on the Radio: Houston Colt 45s/Astros," in *Calling the Game: Baseball Broadcasting from 1920s to the Present* (Phoenix: Society for American Baseball Research, 2015), 251–259. Quote is from p. 253. The information on the bond issue is from Francisco Romero, email to Jorge Iber, June 29, 2022. Copy in Iber's possession.

9. Orlando Sánchez-Diago's career and significance will be discussed in a later essay in

this collection. The information on the boxing match is from Francisco Romero, email to Jorge Iber, June 29, 2022. Copy in Iber's possession.

10. *Ibid.*

11. Regalado, "Dodgers Béisbol Is on the Air," 288. See also "Astros Go Spanish, Si!" *The Bryan Eagle*, July 17, 1966; "Astro Latin Trip 'Better than Ever,'" *Marshall News Messenger*, January 29, 1967; "South of the Border Tour Pleases Astros Group," *Austin American-Statesman*, January 30, 1967; Edgar W. Ray, *The Grand Huckster: Houston's Judge Hofheinz, Genius of the Astrodome* (Memphis: Memphis State University Press, 1980), 279, 348, 387.

12. Jorge Iber interview with Fred Hofheinz, April 13, 2020. See also Jill S. Seeber, "Hofheinz, Roy Mark," in *Handbook of Texas Online*, https://www.tshaonline.org/handbook/entries/hofheinz-roy-mark. Accessed on August 12, 2020.

13. Wagner, "A Spanish Voice That Cries Out."

14. Stuart Shea, "Finally at Home on the Range: Washington Senators II/Texas Rangers," in *Calling the Game: Baseball Broadcasting from 1920s to the Present* (Phoenix, AZ: Society for American Baseball Research, 2015), 320–331. Information on Ruíz's partners provided by Francisco Romero, email to Jorge Iber, June 29, 2022. Copy in Iber's possession.

15. Baxter, "The Sunday Profile."

16. Stuart Shea, "A Tale of Three Redheads: Brooklyn/Los Angeles Dodgers Broadcasting History," in *Calling the Game: Baseball Broadcasting from 1920s to the Present* (Phoenix, AZ: Society for American Baseball Research, 2015), 115–139. Quote is from p. 136.

17. Francisco Romero's career and significance will be discussed in a later essay in this collection. See also Shea, "Raising the Roof on the Radio," 257.

18. David Barron, "Astros Bring Out Veteran for Spanish TV," May 7, 2008. See https://www.chron.com/sports/astros/article/Astros-bring-out-veteran-for-Spanish-TV-w-video-1781278.php. Accessed on June 24, 2022.

19. Enrique Rojas, "René Cárdenas tiene Corazón Dividido Entre Astros y Dodgers," ESPN Deportes, October 26, 2017. See https://espndeportes.espn.com/béisbol/playoffs17/nota/_/id/3658993/René-Cárdenas-tiene-corazon-dividido-entre-astros-y-dodgers. Accessed on June 24, 2022. See also Alyson Footer, "Former Broadcaster Cárdenas Has Ties to Astros, Dodgers," MLB.com, October 23, 2017. See https://www.mlb.com/news/former-broadcaster-has-ties-to-astros-dodgers-c259486254. Accessed on June 30, 2022.

20. Zachary Levine, "Former Astros Broadcaster Up for Frick Award," October 6, 2010. See https://www.chron.com/sports/astros/article/Former-Astros-broadcaster-up-for-Frick-Award-1714141.php. Accessed on June 24, 2022.

21. Wagner, "A Spanish Voice That Cries Out"; Kevin Baxter, "The Sunday Profile."

22. Wagner, "A Spanish Voice That Cries Out."

Jaime Jarrín

RICHARD A. SANTILLÁN *and* FRANK C. MORENO[1]

Introduction

"Se va, se va, se va, despídala con un beso."[2] For years, Spanish-speaking baseball fans around the world have heard this majestic signature call by 86-year-old Jaime Jarrín as he elegantly announces a home run. It astonishes the imagination that this 1998 Ford C. Frick Award recipient to the Baseball Hall of Fame, currently the longest major league–tenured baseball broadcaster in any language, and who has announced 30 World Series, 30 All-Star games, and 22 no-hitters (four of them perfect games), did not know essentially anything about American baseball when he arrived in Los Angeles, California, from Ecuador in June 1955.[3] Besides being one of the best-known baseball broadcasters around the globe, Jaime Jarrín has distinguished himself as an exceptional news reporter for most of his brilliant career. Books are required to accurately document and faithfully capture the immense achievements and profound legacy of this eminent icon and noble public servant who has, for nearly seven decades, effectively served as a bicultural ambassador between the Spanish- and English-speaking worlds.

As he continues to travel with the Dodgers after 63 seasons, Jaime is revered by his younger Spanish-speaking counterparts who call games for opposing teams. They respectfully pursue him with idolization for his insightful wisdom, valuable tutelage, and paternal advice.

This tight-knit network of colleagues accords him esprit de corps homage by addressing him as *El Maestro* (a wise, authentic, and distinguished figure), the highest title bestowed by the Spanish-speaking universe on an individual without equal in every occupation.[4] The rarest of the rare, the crème de la crème. This abbreviated narrative highlights his multifaceted and prototypal careers in the stadium and in the greater Latino community.[5]

Personal Background

Jaime Jarrín was born on December 10, 1933, in Cayambe, Ecuador. His father and mother, Leopoldo and Isabel Jarrín, had three sons and one daughter, Eduardo, Leopoldo (Polo), Jaime, and Concepción (Conchita). His father owned a ranch with cattle and agriculture. Sadly, his father died when Jaime was still young. Jaime's extended family was economically prominent in this regional valley, including five aunts who dominated its financial well-being for decades. Jaime attended several schools, including El Nueve de Julio, Academia Militar San Pedro Pasqual, El Instituto Nacional Mejía, El Colegio Nacional Montúfar, and La Universidad Central de Quito, where Jaime lettered in journalism. His favorite classes were history and geography, worthwhile subjects given his future careers.[6]

Around the age of ten, Jaime was mentored by his elder cousin Alfredo Jarrín, who was almost ten years his senior.[7] Alfredo was a successful and well-known radio announcer in Quito and credited his occupational achievements to his proficiency of the Spanish tongue as well as an impeccable gift of the gab. In an act of kindness that would change Jaime's professional trajectory forever, his cousin patiently rehearsed with him the precise phraseology of speaking his native language with grace, tone, speed, clarity, and style. Alfredo invested countless hours arranging for Jaime to read out loud classic books, influential newspapers, and recitation of traditional poems. These ingenious grammatical drills helped Jaime refine the artful techniques of projecting his baronial voice with an almost flawless linguistic system comprised of eloquence, pitch, tempo, fluency, and flair. By the time Jaime was a young adult, he had nearly mastered his innate linguistic flair. Alfredo hosted a program on Radio Quito, displaying musical talents, and often took his younger cousin to the station.

Jaime instantly fell in love with radio, the genesis of his prestigious career. He was told by the staff that he had a natural "microphonic voice." Alfredo underwrote the financial costs for Jaime to attend radio announcing school for six months. Alfredo himself went on to a brilliant career in advertising, joining the eminent firm of J. Walter Thompson. He became a prominent agent, serving in key positions in Mexico City, Miami, Los Angeles, and New York. He currently lives in the Big Apple at the age of 94; sadly, he is in failing health. When Jaime speaks of Alfredo, there is an indescribable sense of devotion, respect, honor, and adoration for his "segundo padre" (second father).[8]

Broadcasting Career in Quito, Ecuador

Jaime started his broadcasting career at the tender age of 15 in 1948, beating out 49 other aspiring applicants. He started his memorable career by working with a Protestant radio station, HCJB, in Quito, broadcasting cultural and religious programming throughout the world. The station, popularly known as "The Voice of the Andes," was sponsored mainly by the Protestant Church in the United States, which found the height of the Andes, at 10,000 feet, a perfect spot for broadcasting. With its 750,000 watts of power and its location along the Andes, the airwaves reached millions of people around the world. The station was commercial-free, broadcasting music, news, and community events. Since its target audience was diverse, programming was aired in several languages, with 60–80 announcers working behind the microphones.

Two years later, at 17, Jarrín was the leading announcer with a morning show highlighting news, music, and editorials. Eventually, he was a deft newsman, assigned to broadcast the political proceedings of the Ecuadorian senate in the National Legislature. For three years, Jarrín was the chief political correspondent in charge of C-Span and other public programming for his homeland.

Around this same time, Jaime met his future wife, Blanca Mora. Blanca was part of a girls' choir invited by the station to perform songs. Jaime immediately fell in love with her. She was beautiful with long black hair, intelligent, and extremely gentle and nice. Jaime asked Blanca's mother, Magdalena, for permission to accompany her since her father, Jorge Mora, was away working in Venezuela. They courted and were chaperoned for nearly two years before the 18-year-old Jaime and Blanca married at the church Divino Redentor. Jaime and Blanca were married for 65 years before his enchanting sweetheart unexpectedly died in 2019 in Flagstaff, Arizona. Blanca and Jaime were traveling to Santa Fe, New Mexico, during a brief break as usual from spring training camp in Glendale, Arizona, when she passed.[9] Jaime has created a pictorial memory of his darling Blanca in their home, including a huge portrait taken during her younger days. His son Jorge and his wife, Maggie, have moved in with his dad occupying his old childhood bedroom. Jaime calls Jorge's return a blessing; they enjoy each other's company very much.[10]

As a result of Blanca's encouragement, Jarrín soon came to realize in Ecuador, his broadcasting experiences, along with his distinctive status inside Ecuadorian political circles, might afford him occupational advantages in the United States. In 1955, at the age of 22 and with the open-handed assistance from the United States Consul General, Jaime secured a visa in three days. An impressive portfolio expedited the formal paperwork. Jarrín pondered job options, including becoming an airline pilot. He applied for a commercial pilots' course at the school of aeronautics at Teterboro Airport in New Jersey and was accepted.[11]

Jarrín, however, realized the profession he loved and knew well was broadcasting. He decided to come to Los Angeles, California, a city with a large concentration of Mexicans, sensing his career could flourish alongside this substantial Spanish-speaking populace. He and Blanca agreed that he would come to Los Angeles first, find a job and an apartment, then Blanca and baby Jorge, would follow.[12] Jaime's exodus from his homeland revealed early in his life the essence of his character: fortitude, boldness, self-confidence, brashness, adventurousness, an enterprising quality, and courage; in other words, he had guts and chutzpah.

The Ecuadoran senate provided Jaime free transportation to the United States. Jaime headed out to the seaport of Esmeraldas to sail to Tampa, Florida, and then travel onto Los Angeles. His transportation for the first leg of his journey was a German steamship carrying tons of bananas. Jaime encouraged two of his friends, Marco Pérez, and Arturo Bautista, to accompany him and convinced the captain to allow them free passage. The ship left for Tampa, via the Panama Canal, through the Caribbean before arriving in Tampa after five days at sea.

The three then purchased tickets on a Greyhound bus and crisscrossed the country in five days, arriving in Los Angeles on June 24, 1955.[13] As fate would have it, on this exact day, Sandy Koufax made his major league debut for the Brooklyn Dodgers. Unbeknownst to Jaime, within four short years, he would be calling games pitched by Koufax at the Los Angeles Memorial Coliseum. Jaime later noticed people everywhere crowded around radios and televisions listening and watching the 1955 World Series between the Dodgers and the New York Yankees. Because of the huge radio following, Jaime started attending weekend games at Wrigley Field and Gilmore Field, watching the Angels and Hollywood Stars. He had an intense curiosity about this unfamiliar sport that attracted so many fanatical radio listeners.

Jaime stayed one night with Manuel Romero, a former colleague at HCJB, before finding an apartment. Blanca and baby Jorge arrived four months later by plane. In 1960, Jaime purchased his first home in Altadena near both his workplace at KWKW and to Dodger Stadium. He purchased a larger residence in San Marino near Pasadena in 1965. He still lives in this same exquisite two-story Mediterranean house. He drives himself to Dodger Stadium barely 14 minutes from his driveway to his reserved spot. Blanca did not like baseball but was personally close to several of the broadcasters' wives including Gilma Cárdenas, Sophia Hoyos, and Margarita Mota. When it came to sports, Blanca enjoyed following the

World Cup games, cheering, of course, for Ecuador, and she accompanied her husband to several championship boxing matches including events in Rome and Tokyo. Blanca became a U.S. citizen in 1963; two years later, Jaime did likewise.

Jaime and Blanca had three boys, Jorge, James (Jimmy), and Mauricio. All three attended public schools in San Marino: Stoneman Elementary, Huntington Middle, and San Marino High. Jimmy passed away at the early age of 29 from a brain aneurysm.[14] Mauricio lives in Elfin Forest, California, on a ranch. All three attended and graduated with individual college degrees in performing arts, psychology, and business. Collectively, they attended Pepperdine University, the University of California at Santa Barbara, the University of Southern California, San Diego State University, and the University of California at Los Angeles. Jorge has given his father and mother three grandsons, Jaime Andrés, Phillip James, and Stefan Javier.

Radio Career in Los Angeles

Jaime found employment with a chain-link factory near Alameda Street in downtown Los Angeles in 1955. He soon learned there were two Spanish-language radio stations in Los Angeles, KALI 900, a part-time station, and KWKW 1330, a full-time broadcaster. Jaime was hired as a news broadcaster at KWKW in December 1955.[15] There were three well-known broadcasters working for the station: Teddy Fregoso, Martín Becerra, and Ernesto Cervera, who was also the program director. Jarrín had been hired to replace broadcaster Antonio Calatayud, who had died in a car accident.[16]

Jaime's initial responsibilities included stories and covering community events. In 1957, his duties expanded to announcing boxing matches at the famous Olympic Auditorium in downtown Los Angeles on 8th and Grand, and the coveted city hall news beat. His political coverage focused on state, national, and international news. Jarrín covered stories from Mexico, becoming the first announcer to broadcast political stories and Las Fiestas Patrias events directly from Mexico to Los Angeles, especially the ever popular El Grito de Dolores on September 16. Jaime's heartwarming and heartbreaking reports endeared him to an entranced audience of Mexicans and Mexican Americans, absorbing his stories about incredible achievements and the appalling plight of Mexican people on both sides of the border. His radio followers plainly recognized that Jaime was giving voice to the voiceless.

Jaime says Ecuadorian and Mexican Spanish are basically similar;

there are obviously unique differences in inflections and rhythms, but Jaime notes he always tried speaking "neutral" Spanish. He made a concerted effort to gradually integrate Mexican linguistic nuances and cadences, adding subtle word meanings, expressions, and intonations for his Mexican listeners. Jaime noted that during the late 1950s and early 1960s, 95 percent of his listeners thought he was from Mexico, surprised to learn he was from Ecuador. It is important to note that prior to becoming a Dodger broadcaster in 1959, Jaime had already established a far-reaching and faithful following after four successful years at KWKW before calling baseball games. Jaime has a one-of-a-kind distinct voice, weaving concurrently the echoes of romantic ballads, poetry, and storytelling; these three cultural characteristics, combined in a single vocal sound, led to an impressive surge in his popularity.[17]

The Dodger's Move to Los Angeles

In 1958, the Dodgers changed coastal venues from Brooklyn to Los Angeles, California. The Los Angeles Memorial Coliseum, built to host the 1932 Olympics and named in honor of World War I veterans, hosted the first major league game between the Dodgers and Giants, who had moved west to San Francisco.[18] Calling the game in English were Vin Scully and Jerry Doggett on KMPC 710, and in a nearby booth calling the game in Spanish were René Cárdenas and Milt Nava on KWKW 1330.[19] The Dodgers before 78,672 fans on April 18, 1958, beat the San Francisco Giants, 6–5.[20]

The now LA-based squad, the team that racially reintegrated baseball in 1947 with Jackie Robinson, became the first major league team to broadcast all its games in Spanish for the 1958 season. Team owner Walter O'Malley was a shrewd businessman who intuitively grasped the financial rewards of sewing together the ethnic and racial makeup of his teams to ideally mirror the same identical composition of ethnic fans in the stands. Brooklyn teams, with its Italian Americans and African American players, reflected two specific demographic groups residing around the borough of Flatbush. O'Malley also thought his signing of Sandy Koufax in 1954 might sell more tickets with Jewish fans in New York City.[21] Not as well-known were the outreach efforts by the Dodgers to Cubans and Puerto Ricans living in and around New York City. The Dodgers signed Sandy Amorós, a Black Cuban in 1950, and Roberto Clemente, a Black Puerto Rican, in 1954 as a marketing strategy wishing to attract Spanish-speaking fans to the ballpark.[22] Clemente had been sought after by several teams but wanted to play in New York where he had friends and family living in the booming Puerto Rican community. The legendary Buck Canel, who had previously broadcast baseball games for years from New York to South and Central America via Caribbean Radio Network, was hired by Brooklyn to call the play-by-play for a slate of selected games between 1955 and 1957.[23]

The 1958 initiation of Spanish-language broadcasts for all games by the Los Angeles Dodgers, though a significant milestone in American baseball, unfortunately has overshadowed the pioneering efforts by the Brooklyn Dodgers' outreach to Puerto Rican and Cuban communities and has likewise detracted from the profound history of Spanish-language Mexican American baseball in Los Angeles decades before the 1958 opening day game.[24] Baseball and Spanish-language media must be viewed as always going hand and hand, or in Spanish, *siempre como arroz con frijoles* (always like rice and beans). For most of its long history of Mexican American baseball in the United States dating back to the 19th century, Spanish has always been and continues to be the primary baseball language to generations of aficionados.[25]

Jaime Jarrín Joins the Dodgers

In 1957, the Dodgers announced that after failing to secure a new stadium in Brooklyn, the team moved to Los Angeles.[26] KWKW Radio acquired the rights to broadcast games in Spanish and hired René Cárdenas, a Nicaraguan broadcaster. In the 1940s, Cárdenas was a sportswriter for *La Prensa*, announcing Nicaraguan baseball, boxing, and basketball. In 1950, he came to Los Angeles and immediately enrolled in an English course. He worked at the Los Angeles bureau of *La Prensa*, covering local sports, especially the Pacific Coast League (PCL) Los Angeles Angels. Cárdenas quickly noticed that there were few Spanish-speaking baseball fans attending professional baseball games. Moreover, Cárdenas was impressed with the writings of Rodolfo "Rudy" García, a sportswriter for the Los Angeles Spanish-language newspaper *La Opinion*. García authored interesting stories about the handful of professional Mexican and Mexican American baseball players.[27]

Immediately upon hearing that KWKW had secured the rights to broadcast the games in Spanish, Cárdenas wrote a proposal and presented it to the directors of the radio station. At the same time, Walter O'Malley called the station requesting the hiring of Spanish-speaking broadcasters for his team. William Beaton, station manager, saw the real possibility of expanding the growth of listeners with Dodger games in Spanish. KWKW received over 100 applications and hundreds of tape auditions, eventually tapping Cárdenas as the first ever Spanish-speaking baseball broadcaster to call all games for one team. In 1958, there were about 600,000 residents of Mexican heritage residing in the city, a hidden treasure for KWKW since many of them played and supported community baseball.[28] At the time, Jaime was the director of news and information at KWKW in 1958. Station manager Beaton personally selected Jaime as Cárdenas's understudy because Jarrín had such a massive following on radio. Jarrín, however, felt like a *novato* (rookie) not knowing the basic intricacies and jargon of the game. Always striving for perfection, Jarrín's overpowering work ethic did not allow him to short-change his audience until he was 100 percent ready to call games. Instead, KWKW decided to team Milt Nava with Cárdenas. Nava, a Mexican American, was a KWKW broadcaster, serving as a short-term substitute until Jarrín joined the booth the following season.

The station management had so much faith in Jaime's impending baseball abilities (and the all-important bottom line) that they entrusted him with an extra year acquiring the finer points of the game. He visited Wrigley Field, home of the Los Angeles Angels, and dropped by Gilmore Field, home of the Hollywood Stars, jotting down baseball terminology and seeking out fans, ushers, players, coaches, sportswriters, announcers, and others learning the twists and turns of the sport. He paid close attention to René Cárdenas, Vin Scully, and Jerry Doggett on radio and read newspaper stories and box scores. Jaime, in reality, was ascertaining four new languages at the same time: first, learning the game in English; second, decrypting the rare tongue of baseball lingo, a vocabulary of silly code words and phrases that can sound like pure nonsense to a freshman baseball announcer; third, translating Caribbean baseball Spanish into Mexican baseball Spanish; and fourth, discovering the marvelous art of conjuring up to his listeners the mental images of a colorful and thrilling lifelike game through the pure magic of his vivid words.[29]

By 1959, Jaime, who had now learned a sizable part of the nomenclature and nuances of baseball, was ready for the big show (Major League Baseball). He was the second voice behind René Cárdenas.[30] Also in the booth was Miguel Alonzo, a Mexican, who worked at KWKW and stayed until 1961. Alonso would go on to make a bigger name for himself broadcasting wrestling matches at the Olympic Auditorium.[31] Jaime, during this time, believed he would call baseball games for maybe six seasons before returning to hard news. Jaime saw broadcasting games as a side job until he became an anchorman. But the Spanish-speaking gods of baseball had preordained plans for him. Cárdenas and Jaime called the games at the Los Angeles Memorial Coliseum in a makeshift booth in the stands

Jaime at the Los Angeles Coliseum (courtesy Los Angeles Dodgers).

behind home plate. It was a laborious task calling the games for René and Jaime with all the public distractions and physical obstructions of people standing in their way, especially when Hollywood celebrities like Frank Sinatra and Nat "King" Cole sat in front of them causing a commotion.[32]

Even more demanding for René and Jaime was reenacting road games from the KWKW studio in Pasadena. They were not allowed to hit the road with the team. They re-created road games for seven years, although after three seasons, they were finally permitted to travel with the team to San Francisco and later to San Diego. Re-creating games bilingually simultaneously within a two-second time delay is virtually impossible to do. Scully and Doggett called the games in their natural language, but Jaime and René had to first hear them and instantaneously switch from English into Spanish. This is not natural linguistically; it requires a verbal skill set that few humans can execute, especially when René and Jaime learned English as adults. Jaime and René always conveyed nonchalantly to their ardent listeners that they were re-creating the games from a studio in Pasadena.

Fortunately, Jarrín's inaugural season as a Dodger broadcaster in 1959 was an eventful season with the Dodgers winning a playoff series against the Milwaukee Braves and beating the Chicago White Sox in the World Series in six games. It was pure luck that Jarrín didn't start in 1958 when the Dodgers finished in seventh place out of eight teams in the National

League, a dreadful way to introduce the team to the Mexican community, who generally don't support losers. By the 1961 season, Cárdenas and Jarrín announced the games exclusively. In 1962, Cárdenas left KWKW to broadcast the games for the Colt .45s (later the Houston Astros). Cárdenas recommended José "Fats" García to take his place. García was the number one broadcaster with Jarrín sitting in the second chair. Jarrín has repeatedly said he learned the most about baseball from García, who stayed in the booth until his fatal heart attack in 1972.[33] In 1973, Jaime would take over the number one position.

Jarrín and his broadcasting chum García often patronized Tonita's Restaurant near Dodger Stadium that opened its doors in 1956, a favorite watering hole where Spanish-speaking players ate and mingled with Latin entertainers, elected officials, and media reporters.[34] Players, coaches, and scouts who frequented Tonita's included César Géronimo, César Cedeno, Pedro Borbón, Orlando Cepeda, Juan Marichal, Matty and Felipe Alou, José Pagan, Zoilo Versalles, Pedro Ramos, Vic Davalillo, Mike Brito, Roberto Clemente, Tony Pérez, Manny Mota, Vic Power, and Minnie Miñoso. There are a handful of vintage group photos of Jarrín and García with a cavalcade of players, movie and television stars, and musical entertainers, including Celia Cruz, José Ferrer, Tony Martínez, Anthony Quinn, Tito Puente, and Rosemary Clooney.[35] Tonita's closed its doors in 1986.

In 1973, Rodolfo Hoyos, Jr., joined Jarrín in the broadcasting cubicle replacing García. Hoyos was a Hollywood figure who appeared in several movies and numerous television programs. His father, Rodolfo Hoyos, Sr., had been an early pioneer in Spanish-language radio in the United States between 1932 and 1967. Jarrín and Hoyos worked together from 1973 until 1981 when Hoyos retired due to poor health. In 1983, he died at the age of 67.[36] In 1982, René Cárdenas rejoined Jaime in the broadcast booth replacing Hoyos, calling games until 1998.

Los Hermanos *(the Brothers): Jaime Jarrín and Vin Scully*

Jaime Jarrín enthusiastically credits Vin Scully for mentoring him and allowing him to absorb an assortment of broadcasting lessons over six decades of friendship and partnership. Jorge says that by mimicking the gifted style of Scully during the early years of reenacting road games, his dad became the perfect Spanish-speaking twin of Vin. Jaime publicly shares a handful of key tutorials that Scully instilled in him, such as sometimes it's best to say nothing, allowing the sounds of the crowd tell the story during thrilling parts of a game, preparing for each game as if it was your first game broadcasting, understanding that each game has its own idiosyncratic pulse, and never getting personally close to players because it might prejudice your objectivity.[37] For Jaime, however, there have been a handful of exceptions of being close to certain players.[38] Both Scully and Jarrín have never been considered cheerleaders for the Dodgers. They are not big devotees of stats and metrics, and both describe the games with their eyes and not their hearts, no sugarcoating. Both are men of unquestionable integrity, high degree of intelligence, unpretentious, willing to do the beneficent work, master storytellers, larger-than-life personalities, peerless play-by-play baseball announcers of their respective language, even-handed, believable, quick-witted, and recipients of countless awards, honors, tributes, and other public accolades.

The Dodgers are the only major league team to have two contemporaries with Ford C. Frick Awards in the Baseball Hall of Fame. When Jarrín was inducted into the Baseball Hall of Fame in 1998, he was standing next to Willie Mays and Stan Musial at a reception for Hall of Famers. He finds it hard to believe his amazing luck, coming to the United States, not knowing English, and having never seen a baseball game.[39] His son Jorge gives much credit to broadcaster Jack Buck who pushed the Hall of Fame committee to induct his father.

Fernandomania

The sudden and unexpected forces of Fernandomania were and still are the cultural, linguistic, and immigrant flashpoints that, without warning, instigated the gradual and large-scale reconfiguration of American baseball starting in 1981. There are dramatic milestones in this sport, with a key one being Jackie Robinson breaking the color barrier in 1947 and reintegrating African Americans onto major league rosters. And in 1981, Fernandomania directly challenged baseball's dubious status quo regarding the near invisibility of Latinos at all levels of professional baseball.

If Fernando was the heart and soul of Fernandomania, Jaime Jarrín was its earsplitting voice with his cultivated repertoire of matchless skills. Jarrín says that Fernando Valenzuela played a major part in making him a national celebrity. Moreover, it was Fernandomania that decided, finally, that Jaime would dedicate his life as a baseball broadcaster instead of a future news anchor.[40] Jaime modestly understates his magnificent status as a baseball broadcaster before Fernando. In truth, Jaime had already established a stellar reputation as one of the best, if not the best, sophisticated, Spanish-language broadcaster in the history of the sport.[41]

Jaime spoke about Fernando in much larger communal terms when he broadcasted games and translated for the rookie pitcher. For Jaime, Fernando was the timeless symbol representing generations of Spanish-speaking peoples coming to the United States, searching for a better life for their families, despite adversity. Jaime linked Fernando's immigrant struggles such as not speaking English to the collective experience of most working-class Mexicans, Mexican Americans, and other Latinos. Fernando and Jaime came to this country without speaking English, with no money, but seeking the American dream. Yes, Jaime was describing a baseball game when Fernando pitched, but more accurately, he was forcefully presenting and effectively relating Fernando's games as a weekly *novela* (soap opera) being played out in countless Spanish-speaking homes and workplaces.

By reporting Fernando's dynamic immigrant story, Jaime strenuously validated the day-to-day experiences of his spellbound listeners. Mexican culture, finally, had taken a small but hard-hitting spot within our nation's consciousness, harmoniously articulated by the empathic voices of Jaime and Fernando. It's true that Fernandomania amplified the Latino struggle against the reactionary and xenophobic traditions of baseball as an exclusively American, English-speaking, and lily-white sport. But it was significantly much more than that. Fernandomania became a cultural uprising, a national rally cry, adopted by grassroots advocates demanding social and economic change for the Spanish-speaking people in the United States, including police and immigration reform, better educational opportunities, fair housing, political empowerment, economic prosperity, affordable health care, and first-class recreational facilities in their neighborhoods.

Fernandomania was largely successful because Jaime weaved together his baseball knowledge with his news skills.[42] Jaime knew exactly the information baseball beat writers were seeking, and he knew, as a hard-nosed news reporter, what the non-baseball reporters were hunting for about Fernando, such as his family background. Because of his effortless aptitude in reenacting games in both languages, Jaime played both his roles seamlessly as a Spanish translator for Fernando and an English translator for the news media. Jaime was inundated with interview requests from media outlets about himself, generating greater national and international attention his way.[43] Moreover, he accompanied Fernando to the White House for a state dinner with President Ronald Reagan and the president of Mexico, José López Portillo y Pacheco.[44] The White House dinner clearly intermingled sports, immigration, and politics. Jaime was the only public figure who genuinely encapsulated the kinetic personality surrounding Fernando during this mind-boggling stretch of time.

In turn, Fernando introduced Jaime to two sets of new baseball fans, non–Latino English-speaking baseball fans and millions of Mexican American fans wanting to learn baseball in Spanish. He and Fernando were treated like rock stars wherever they went. Jaime proudly declares that he and Fernando became *como hermanos* (like brothers) during this glorious time, so much so that Fernando has served as color commentor with Jaime on radio since 2003.[45] Since 2015, Fernando switched to the color commentator job on the Spanish-language feed of SportsNet LA.

In 2021, Jarrín proudly asserted that Fernando became and still is one of the best ambassadors in baseball history, helping attract more Latino players, coaches, broadcasters, sportswriters, umpires, scouts, and stadium employees than ever before to the game. Jaime claims that baseball owes a great deal to Fernando. He is dismayed that Fernando's absence from the Hall of Fame is a combination of unwarranted and biased factors, especially ignorance about how Fernando profoundly revolutionized the cultural and linguistic demographics of the game. From Jarrín's vantage point, Fernando unquestionably belongs in the Hall of Fame, in large part because he also opened the stadium turnstiles to more immigrants, people of color, the working-class, and older Spanish-speaking fans. The proliferation of Latino players and coaches and other baseball personnel on the diamond, and the dramatic shift of skin color, economic class, foreign-born, ethnicity, and languages of fans in the stands can be traced, in large part, to Fernando Valenzuela.[46] Fernandomania is the ongoing catalyst that is fundamentally transforming the forever-increasing mixture of Latinos both on the field and in the stands. For Spanish-speaking fans, there was baseball before Jaime and Fernando and baseball after.

Today, over 30 percent of major league players are Latinos, and this percentage is gradually increasing every season; most of these players grew up hearing Jaime Jarrín and watching Fernando play. Jarrín cherishes a special photo of himself with Fernando Valenzuela, Edgar Martínez, Pedro Martínez, Alex Rodríguez, and two sons of the late Roberto Clemente. Like African American players, Latino players bring a special flair—a unique style of playing the game with high-octane energy, and so do Latino fans who bring an international *fútbol* (soccer) emotionality and intensity to the game of baseball around the country.

The Dodgers Spanish-speaking radio channel ratings more than doubled, with thousands of extra fans buying tickets when Fernando pitched at home and on the road. It is estimated that when the Dodgers came to Los Angeles in the late 1950s, the percentage of Mexican-heritage fans was less than 10 percent; today, for some games, 60 percent or more of those in the stands are Latinos.[47] Some of these societal changes can be directly linked to Fernando and Jaime; their fingerprints are nearly everywhere from a variety of Latino food to accent marks on uniform surnames, Mexican music being played by stadium organists, Hispanic/Latino Nights, and to nearly all games now broadcast in Spanish. Jaime and Fernando are equally responsible for changing further the culture, language, and immigrant status of baseball, enticing millions of Spanish-speaking fans into American baseball. Jaime says that almost 42 percent of the fans at Dodger Stadium are Latinos.[48]

The uncomfortable truth is that generations of Spanish-speaking fans do not know or have ever listened to Vin Scully call a baseball game. Since 1959, Jaime has been heard by more baseball fans than Vin because his Spanish-language broadcasts are aired throughout Mexico, Latin America, the Caribbean, and the United States, and he speaks English at countless baseball events. Countless fans still hear Jaime today. A few years ago, the Dodgers team sold for $2 billion. This investment and profit can only be sustained with an increasing Latino fan base, and Jaime has been the most influential connection for 63 wonderful seasons to this loyal community.[49] During Fernandomania, KTNQ carried 31 Spanish-language affiliates, which quickly expanded to 48 with games aired throughout the Americas. Scully had only 24 affiliates.

Untold numbers of people tuned in at home, work, parks, restaurants, and in their cars and trucks to listen to Jaime every time Fernando pitched.[50] He became the most popular Spanish-speaking baseball announcer since his idol, Buck Canel.

The sum impact of Fernandomania on baseball is incalculable. By 1994, 14 of the 26 major league teams were doing Spanish-language broadcasts. In turn, Spanish-language radio stations carrying Dodger games received considerable corporate support to reach the Latino market.[51] Jaime's direct influence as a linguistic trailblazer can be clearly seen and heard especially in Los Angeles as the Lakers, Clippers, Rams, Chargers, Kings, and Ducks broadcast some or all games now in Spanish. The three most important legacies of Fernando and Jaime are (1) they radically transformed baseball from its marginalization of Spanish-speaking people to its ever-evolving hybridization of Latino culture on the diamond and in the stands, (2) they both helped internationalized the game to nearly every corner of the globe, and (3) they provided immigrants a sense of cultural citizenship and *unidad* (unity) with baseball, legitimizing their civic status as first-class fans like everyone else who loves the game.[52]

The Struggle for Equal Access and Recognition

René, Jaime, and the other Spanish-speaking baseball broadcasters have struggled against being stigmatized as second-class employees by Dodgers top management since 1958. Walter O'Malley is outwardly given accolades for owning the first team to broadcast its entire season in Spanish and for aggressively seeking Mexican and Mexican American ballplayers for his teams, both, of course, driven by profit. Inwardly, the mindset among the top brass was to do virtually nothing in promoting its Spanish-speaking broadcaster team or supporting Mexican-owned businesses to advertise in their publications. From 1958 through 1968, it appears that no Dodgers yearbook ever mentioned in print the names of René, Jaime, KWKW, or any other Spanish-language broadcaster, highlighting only Vin, Jerry, KMPC, and KFI. This subordinated outlook toward Spanish-language broadcasters and crew, regardless of intentions, was sanctioned at the highest levels of the team.

This deplorable trend of invisibility lasted until 1969, when yearbook photos of Jaime and José "Fats" García were finally published, referring to them as the "Latin American radio counterparts" to Vin Scully and Jerry Doggett.[53] Yet, this ethnic and linguistic disparity continued but in a more degrading format in Dodgers publications. From 1969 through 1978, for example, almost all of the photos of Vin and Jerry are larger, often assorted photos, and nearly always carefully positioned higher than the photographs of Jarrín, García, and Rodolfo Hoyos, Jr. This wide-open disfigurement between photos speaks volumes regarding the observable linguistic hierarchies perpetuated by the Dodgers about the racial forms of worthiness in the broadcasting booths.[54] It was not until 1979 (22 years after the Dodgers started broadcasting their games in Spanish, and the season before Fernando Valenzuela's arrival in 1980) that Jaime, Rodolfo, Vin, and Jerry's photos were finally printed equally in the yearbook. This pattern of cultural negligence rings true with other Dodgers publications—for instance, game programs and media guides—although there are brief references in a few 1959 and 1960 game programs mentioning Jaime, René, and KWKW. A 1960 game program, for example, highlights a special night when Vin and Jerry were honored before a game for their broadcasting contributions and mentions kind words expressed by René and Jaime for their English-language colleagues, yet no photo of Jaime and René or their comments appeared. Dodger Stadium opened in 1962. From 1962 through 1969, it appears no Dodger game program mentioned Jaime, René, KWKW, or any other Dodgers Spanish-speaking announcer.[55] From time to time, Jaime has reluctantly shared stories of his disappointment of unequal treatment when Spanish-language broadcasters were not always assigned inside the mainstream broadcasting booths but rather dispersed to substandard whereabouts around the ballpark.[56] Jaime is a low-key individual but has strategically asserted himself when running up against circumstances regarding inequality toward him and his colleagues. Jaime has purposely commingled sports and hard news as humanitarian instruments for ameliorating the social consciousness of his listeners.

Walter O'Malley always asked Jaime Jarrín where he could find a Mexican "Sandy Koufax." O'Malley's business intuitions told him that a great Mexican pitcher would most likely attract thousands of new fans through the turnstiles.[57] Yet, Fernando had to hold out and insist on a fair contract in 1982 after his phenomenal 1981 season and then unceremoniously terminated in 1991 at the end of spring training.[58] The distressing timing and ill-treatment regarding his release were appalling since other teams had already finalized their pitching staffs. For years, Fernando rebuffed partaking in the annual Old-Timers' games and snubbed other team events. Eventually, with the advantageous benefit of Jarrín functioning as an arbitrator, Fernando returned to the Dodgers as a color commentator working alongside his "brother" Jaime.

To this day, Fernando's number 34, revered by the entire Spanish-speaking baseball world, has not been properly retired by the Dodgers, even though no player has worn this number since Fernando was brusquely released 30 years ago.[59] Not surprisingly, the Dodgers have mishandled a series of preventable blunders regarding the retirement of his jersey. The ball club continues to misjudge the public outcry, especially misreading the deep-seated sentiments percolating inside the Spanish-speaking fan base about seeing Fernando's number finally draped in the stadium. No Latino Dodgers player has had his number retired so far. If not Fernando, who? It is still taking too many years for the Dodgers to acknowledge and recognize Jaime Jarrín for his extraordinary broadcasting career also fully. On June 11, 2012, the Dodgers, finally, honored Jarrín for his 54 years of service. He was given a trophy, threw out the ceremonial first pitch, and proudly viewed a video tribute in his honor. Everyone in attendance received a promotional blue-colored T-shirt printed with his popular Spanish home run call. A belated Jarrín bobblehead came the following season after much public and media criticism. Both the Dodgers and Major League Baseball have dropped the ball, struck out, and committed a major error by not taking full advantage of Jarrín's immense popularity as a goodwill ambassador to Spanish- and English-speaking fans. The Dodgers continue to one-sidedly promote Vin Scully and Tommy Lasorda as the representational faces of the organization, while failing again to equally elevate Jaime Jarrín and Fernando

Valenzuela, hardening the ongoing disillusionment among many Latino fans.

Current Dodgers Spanish-Speaking Broadcasters

Besides Fernando Valenzuela as color commentator, Jaime has been extremely fortunate to work side by side with two extraordinary radio partners. One of these broadcasting associates is his son Jorge Jarrín. In 2004, Jorge joined the Dodgers as a temporary director of sales for Spanish-language radio. Spanish-language radio by far reaches more people than television and newspapers. Eventually, the position became full time, and Jorge worked diligently expanding the number of radio affiliates carrying the Dodger games in Spanish to 15. The combination of these stations covered Dodgers baseball from roughly Fresno to Calexico. In 2012, the Dodgers asked Jorge to call 30 games in Spanish along with Manny Mota for Fox Deportes, while keeping his job in the sales department. Jorge also cohosted the post-game show *Dodger Talk* on KLAC with Kevin Kennedy and David Vassegh.

In 2015, management changes teamed Fernando and Jose "Pepe" Yñiguez on Spectrum cable while Jaime and Jorge were paired on radio.[60] Jaime and Jorge became the first father and son in major league history to broadcast a game together.[61] There are a handful of broadcasting families like the Carays, the Bucks, and the Brennamans, but none have had father and son call a game in unison. Jorge's son, Stefan, played youth ball, high school, and college and was drafted by the Dodgers in 2011, but an injury with the Philadelphia Phillies cut short his promising career. For a while, Stefan collaborated with his grandfather and father in the broadcast booth, as a statistician and researcher—most likely the first time in major league baseball history that three generations of one family worked in the broadcasting booth side by side.

In 2020, Jorge stepped down from his broadcasting duties with the Dodgers to enjoy his retirement.[62] Jorge left at the apex of his profession and at the perfect time, having called the 2020 World Series with his dad, won by the Dodgers in six games against the Tampa Bay Rays. Both received World Series rings, and Jorge was proudly there at Dodger Stadium, along with the extended family, when Jaime was inducted into the Dodgers elite "Ring of Honor." Since 1884, the Dodgers have inducted only 12 remarkable individuals who have been honored in this fashion.[63] In fact, Jaime says his entrée into the "Ring of Honor," a hallowed place at Dodger Stadium, is the crowning achievement of his brilliant career, this from an extraordinary individual who has been inducted into the Baseball Hall of Fame, the recipient of the highest award given by Ecuador to a private citizen, and meetings with a pope, Mexican and U.S. presidents.

Currently working with Jaime and Fernando is Jose "Pepe" Yñiguez. He joined the Dodgers broadcast team in 1999. He grew up in Celaya, Mexico, playing baseball in Tijuana, Chihuahua, and Sonora. He came to the United States at the sprightly age of 16 and met with Jaime Jarrín about collaborating with him at KWKW. Jaime, with regret, informed Pepe that he was simply too young to work at the station and that it was imperative for him to go to school. Pepe took Jaime's advice and enrolled at the prestigious Columbia School of Broadcasting. After several years, Pepe's dream finally came true when he started broadcasting Dodger games in Spanish with Jaime. In the off-seasons, Pepe hosted a weekly sports talk show on KWKW called *Central Deportiva*. Pepe has broadcast numerous events for Fox Sports International, including the World Series from 1997 through 2005. He announced the 1997 Major League All-Star game, and the Caribbean World Series. From 1993 to 1995, Pepe served as the Spanish radio broadcaster for the Los Angeles Raiders. Beginning with the 2015 season, he called Dodger games on the Spanish-language feed of SportsNet LA alongside Fernando Valenzuela.[64] Pepe also played community baseball in East Los Angeles, including announcing games.

Final Thoughts

In reflecting back on his extraordinary baseball career, Jaime says there are two special experiences that pleases him the most. First, all the people who appreciatively flock around him sharing nostalgic stories about how generations of family members and friends grew up hearing Jaime calling Dodger games. They tell him too about his magical voice booming in their homes, workplaces, parks, beaches, restaurants, bars, and inside their cars. He loves being surrounded by multiple generations of adoring fans sharing how he blissfully brought everyday joy to them. The second experience that brings a big smile to his face is the significant percentage of Latinos playing on the field, watching from the stands, and as stadium employees. Jaime says a long time ago, he took his breaks during the third and sixth innings, going outside the press box for a few minutes hearing only English among the fans. Today, when he takes his recesses, he now hears a considerable amount of Spanish.

On September 28, 2021, Jaime Jarrín announced his retirement at Dodger Stadium, publicly saying that the 2022 season will be his final season calling the Dodger games in Spanish. Since 1959, he has uniquely witnessed firsthand a massive transformation of baseball from a basically a white sport into a fast-becoming-Latino sport. He understood the inherent conflict of this change because of baseball's unwillingness to change even though the country was changing from white to people of color and immigrants. For over six decades, Jaime has had a front-row seat, he was the right person, at the right time, and at the right place to chronicle this historic change. But Jaime just didn't announce baseball; he helped bring about this revolutionary transformation with his enormous energy and passion. His multi-special talents and public persona consolidated and codified the Latino culture and Spanish language in baseball. He helped shape baseball forever.

Jaime Jarrín is the patriarch of Major League Baseball's expanding universe of Spanish-language broadcasters. Over the decades, he has mentored a profound lineage of broadcasting announcers, a baseball family tree that has *locutores* (broadcasters) branches in nearly every ballpark. It is impossible to imagine baseball today without Jaime Jarrín. Entering the ninth inning of his brilliant baseball career (hopefully, extra innings), baseball fans, regardless of language, should now, more than ever, revere his broadcasts before he takes off his headphones for the last time. He will depart wistfully but with the satisfaction and jubilation that he gave his all for the love of the game, always striving to reach the level of perfection. His depth and knowledge of baseball is second to none; he has captured the full scope of the transformation of baseball from a white American game to an international game of people of color as players and fans but not yet in management or ownership. He is the gold standard of baseball, earning the distinction to join the Mount Rushmore of baseball orators. There will never be another like El Maestro. *Un brindis* (a toast).

Just as this essay was going to print, the Dodgers finally did announce that they are retiring Fernando's number 34. It is wonderful to see that on August 11, 2023, the team finally did what so many fans had clamored for.

Notes

1. Dr. Santillán dedicates this essay to his wife Teresa M. Santillán, and to his father, Carlos Veloz Santillán. For over 40 years, Teresa has been his guiding light on documenting the long and rich history of Mexican American/Latino baseball and softball. His dad, Carlos, introduced Richard to baseball by taking him to the old Wrigley Field in Los Angeles watching the Pacific Coast League Los Angeles Angels play in 1956 and 1957, and to Dodger games at the Los Angeles Memorial Coliseum from 1958 through 1961 before the Dodgers moved into their new home in 1962. Frank Moreno dedicates this article to two people. First, his father, Crispin Moreno, who worked restlessly to make a good life

for Frank being the first in the family to attend college. Crispin had several fascinating jobs with the Hostess Cake Company and Dodge Trophy Company. He sang with Vicente Fernández in Los Angeles in 1976. Second, to Frank's uncle Martín González, a former radio announcer in Guadalajara and Nogales, Mexico. He was the first one to take Frank to a Dodger game to see his nephew's hero, Don Drysdale, pitch against Juan Marichal of the Giants. Frank's father and uncle were young immigrants with a dream.

2. Roughly translated: "It's going, it's going, it's going, kiss it good-bye." Jaime has another beautiful signature call. Around the eighth inning, he will announce, "Estoy viendo mi casita del mi pueblo." This more or less translates to "I am seeing my little house of my village," meaning that he can see the game ending and he will be home soon.

3. Emily Bonilla, "Se va, Se va, Se va! Jaime Jarrín Set to Retire after the Los Angeles Dodgers 2022 Season," USC Annenberg Media, September 28, 2021.

4. This fraternity includes Polo Ascencio, Benji Molina, Eduardo Ortega, Carlos Hernández, José Mota, Amaury Pi-González, and Manolo Hernández-Doven, to name a few. Jaime is adored and embraced by the English-speaking corps of announcers as well including Bob Uecker, Joe and Jack Buck, Marty and Tom Brennaman, Rick Sutcliff, and Ron Fairly. Jon Miller has even adopted a home run call in homage to Jaime Jarrín: *"Adios Pelota"* (Good-bye, baseball). Jaime is also referred to as "Don" Jaime, a Spanish word reserved for royalty or a nobleman. It is an honorific title throughout Latin American culture.

5. The coauthors thank several special individuals who made this essay possible, including Jaime Jarrín, Jorge Jarrín, Fernando Valenzuela, José "Pepe" Yñiguez, and Ray Lara. Jorge Jarrín, the son of Jaime, went several extra innings sharing abundant information about his father's illustrious careers. Jorge sat side by side with his father calling Dodger games for seven seasons—Major League Baseball's first father and son baseball broadcasting team. We also appreciate the great support from Dr. César Caballero, dean of the library at California State University at San Bernadino and director of the Latino Baseball History Project, and Dr. Joe Price, former faculty member and current director of the Baseball Institute at Whittier College, Whittier, California. Finally, we thank Mark Langill of the Los Angeles Dodgers and renowned team historian for the use of the photos for this essay.

6. Interview with Jaime Jarrín, August 17, 2021, San Marino, California.

7. Interview with Jorge Jarrín, July 27, 2021, San Marino, California.

8. Interview with Jorge and Jaime Jarrín, August 17, 2021, San Marino, California.

9. Michael Green, "With the Passing of His Wife, Jaime Jarrín, the Sixty-One Year Hispanic Voice of the Dodgers Is Calling the Entire Schedule," *Sports Broadcast Journal*, August 15, 2019; Bill Plaschke, "Jaime Jarrín's Return to Dodgers Broadcasts Eases Pain of Wife's Passing," *Los Angeles Times*, May 11, 2019; "Blanca Jarrín, Wife of Hall of Fame Broadcaster, Dies at 85," *USA Today*, February 28, 2019.

10. Rowan Kavner, "Dodgers' Jaime Jarrín among 2020 Radio Hall of Fame Nominees," *Dodgers Insider*, July 2020.

11. Jaime's interest in aviation came about when he worked at HCJB. He befriended three Protestant missionaries who flew light aircraft evangelizing the Indigenous population in the Amazon jungles. One day, all three were killed while preaching the faith. Jaime was so shocked at this senseless slaying that he seriously thought about continuing their steadfast dedication by learning to fly. Interview with Jaime Jarrín, August 17, 2021, San Marino, California.

12. Interview with Jorge Jarrín, July 27, 2021, San Marino, California.

13. Interview with Jaime Jarrín, August 17, 2021, San Marino, California.

14. Larry Stewart, "Trip to LA Was the Road to Immortality for Jarrín," *Los Angeles Times*, July 28, 1998.

15. Interview with Jaime Jarrín, August 17, 2021.

16. Telephone interview with Frank Moreno, August 18, 2021.

17. As a young man, Jaime grew up fancying Spanish romantic songs, reading books of poetry, and enjoying telling stories from the novels he read. It seems that he meritoriously incorporated these three passions into a distinct and sophisticated style of broadcasting baseball games.

18. Other potential sites for the Dodgers to play their home games until Dodger Stadium was built included the Pasadena Rose Bowl and Wrigley Field, the home of the Pacific Coast League Angels.

19. Samuel O. Regalado, "Dodgers Béisbol Is on the Air: The Development and Impact of the Dodgers' Spanish-Language Broadcasts, 1958–1995," *California History* 74, no. 3 (Fall 1995).

20. Lincoln Mitchell, *The Dodgers, the Giants, and Baseball Goes West: The Shaping of the Major Leagues* (Kent, OH: Kent State University Press, 2018); Andy McCue, *Mover and Shaker: Walter O'Malley, the Dodgers, and Baseball's Westward Expansion* (Lincoln: University of Nebraska Press, 2014). McCue's book won the prestigious Book of the Year from the Society of American Baseball Research. See Mario Solis's Spanish-language interview with René Cárdenas, hRps://youtu.be/F2J_3vJVTK.

21. Amorós played for the Dodgers until 1958, their first season in Los Angeles. The Pittsburgh Pirates were able to "steal" Clemente from the Dodgers when he was left unprotected from other teams. David Finoli and Bill Ranier, *The Pittsburgh Pirates Encyclopedia: Second Edition* (New York: Simon & Schuster, 2015).

22. Stuart Shea, *Calling the Game: Baseball Broadcasting from 1920 to the Present* (Phoenix: Society for American Baseball Research, 2015), 124.

23. In the 1930s through the 1970s, many baseball fields had primitive wooden broadcast booths where announcers, utilizing old-fashioned public announcement equipment, called games in Spanish for those attending the games. José "Pepe" Yñiguez, a current Dodger Spanish-language broadcaster, played baseball in East Los Angeles and announced local games. Baseball and the Spanish language have for nearly 150 years been linked inside the hearts, souls, and minds of the Mexican people in Los Angeles.

24. The Mexican American Baseball History Project was established at California State University at Los Angeles in 2004. In 2009, the project, now the Latino Baseball History Project, moved to California State University at San Bernardino. The project's archives are housed at the John M. Pfau Library in Special Collections. Its holdings are the largest collection of Mexican American photos, memorabilia, and other vintage materials.

25. Neil J. Sullivan, *The Dodgers Move West* (New York: Oxford University Press, 1987).

26. Sullivan, *Dodgers Move West*; Regalado, "Dodgers Béisbol Is on the Air."

27. Richard A. Santillán et al., *Mexican American Baseball in Los Angeles* (Charleston, SC: Arcadia Publishing, 2011); Richard A. Santillán et al., *Mexican American Baseball in East Los Angeles* (Charleston, SC: Arcadia Publishing, 2016).

28. Interview with José "Pepe" Yñiguez, September 13, 2021, Los Angeles, California. Yñiguez has been calling Dodger games in Spanish since the 1990s. He currently shares the booth with Jaime Jarrín and Fernando Valenzuela. J.P. Hoornstra, "Jaime Jarrín's Spanish Broadcasts Are a Passport to Gardeners and Singing Ump," *Daily News*, August 28, 2019.

29. Interview with Jaime Jarrín, August 17, 2021.

30. Mike Lano, "Mat Matters: Remembering Beloved L.A. Miguel Alonso," slamwrestling.com., ca. 2012. Fascinating story on the history of Spanish-speaking wrestling broadcasters at the Olympic Auditorium. Alonso credits the legendary Dick Lane with helping him hone his craft.

31. The Dodgers were the first real showtime, attracting a glamorous who's who of Hollywood and sports royalty, including Dean Martin, Phyllis Diller, Mickey Rooney, Doris Day, Edward G. Robinson, Bobby Darrin, Cary Grant, Milton Berle, Don Rickles, Pat Boone, Soupy Sales, Bob Newhart, Johnny Mathis, Phil Silvers, Archie Moore, Rafer Johnson, Joe Louis, Buddy Hackett, Dale Robinson, David Jansen, Steve Allen, and Billy Barty. Jaime became a special friend to some of them, including Chuck Conners, Danny Kaye, Mario "Cantinflas" Moreno, and James Garner. Interview with Jaime Jarrín, August 17, 2021, San Marino, California. See also the Dr. Richard A. and Teresa M. Santillán Los Angeles Dodger Collection, the Baseball Institute, Whittier College, Whittier, California.

32. Jarrín recounts that José "Fats" García never received the immense credit he deserved as a significant broadcasting pioneer of baseball translation into Spanish, despite his extensive knowledge of the game and his uncanny ability to perfectly translate the analytical details of the game into the vocabulary for the common fan. Jarrín wonders quietly

that perhaps the unseen reasons that García did not receive widespread accolades he rightfully earned were because he returned to his native Nicaragua in the off season, and García was not successfully marketed locally in Los Angeles. For Jarrín, this is a shame since Jaime credits much of his career success to the baseball and friendly relationships both men enjoyed. Interview with Jaime Jarrín, August 17, 2021, San Marino, California.

33. Telephone interview with Héctor Menenes, September 7, 2021. Héctor's family owned Tonita's Restaurant, first in New York and later in Los Angeles.

34. Richard A. Santillán et al., "Mexican American Baseball in the Santa Maria Valley," Latino Baseball History Project, California State University at San Bernardino, 2019, pp. 184–188. There are nearly a dozen photos and captions of players listed in the text.

35. Telephone interview with Dr. Félix Gutierrez on August 20, 2021. Dr. Gutierrez is one of the foremost experts on the history of Spanish-language radio in the United States. Gutierrez interviewed Rodolfo Hoyos, Sr., around 1973. See also *A History of Spanish Language Radio in the United States* (Denton: Center for Spanish Language Media, University of North Texas, 2009).

36. Les Carpenter, "Jaime Jarrín: The Remarkable Story of the Latino Vin Scully," *The Guardian*, September 15, 2016. Also, interview with Jaime Jarrín, August 17, 2021, San Marino, California.

37. Jarrín was personally and professionally close to Sandy Koufax and Don Drysdale, two Dodger legends and Hall of Famers. Both Koufax and Drysdale worked on the broadcasting side of baseball and, like Jarrín, understood how hard the job was. Jaime was close to several of the early Spanish-speaking players in baseball, helping them navigate a new country, its customs, and a new language. He continues to this day to be a steadfast advocate for Latino players, coaches, broadcasters, sportswriters, stadium employees, and many more Spanish-speaking people. Jaime acknowledges others who have helped him during his exemplary career including Willie Davis (who played baseball and football at Roosevelt High School in Boyle Heights) and Orel Hershiser. Hershiser was especially supportive in 1988 when Jaime lost his son Jimmy.

38. Jaime Jarrín 1998 Ford C. Frick Hall of Fame speech. The speech is emotional and heartfelt, most of it in English but a significant part in Spanish. For the first time in Hall of Fame induction history, Jaime's speech was broadcast to the Spanish-speaking nations in the Western Hemisphere. https://youtu.be/mgN7mYqvXsu. See also Vin Scully interviews with Fernando Valenzuela, Jaime Jarrín, and René Cárdenas (ca. 1981), https://youtu.be/2nzo82VM034.

39. Prior to the arrival of Fernando, Jarrín was still envisioning a thriving career in hard news over baseball, even becoming an anchorman. He had covered Pope John Paul II's visit to Dodger Stadium in 1979, the funeral of President John F. Kennedy in 1963, the Chamizal Declaration with the president of Mexico Gustavo Díaz Ordaz and President Lyndon Johnson, his interview scoop with President Gustavo Díaz Ordaz and President Richard M. Nixon at the western White House in San Clemente, and his coverage of the Chicano movement, including the Chicano moratorium on August 29, 1970, protesting the war in Vietnam. Jaime's close friend Ruben Salazar, a *Los Angeles Times* reporter and news director of Spanish-language television station KMEX Channel 34, was killed by the Los Angeles County Sheriff's Department that day. Two other community residents lost their lives as well.

40. Jaime, himself, was nearly killed when his own car was struck by a bullet, missing his head by inches. Even with this near-death experience, he found his way to Dodger Stadium that night calling the game that saw the Saint Louis Cardinals defeat the Dodgers 3–2, one of nearly 4,000 games he announced between 1962 and 1984, 22 years without missing one game with little glitz and ceremony from the Dodgers organization, Major League Baseball, or the Los Angeles sports media establishment. Interview with Jaime Jarrín, August 17, 2021, San Marino, California.

41. In 1998, Jaime was honored by the National Association of Hispanic Journalists with its highest award and received his star on the Hollywood Walk of Fame. In 2002, Jarrín was inducted into the California Broadcasters' Association Hall of Fame and the Southern California Sports Broadcasters' Hall of Fame, and in 2003, into the Hispanic

Heritage Baseball Museum. In 2011, Jarrín was honored in Los Angeles, California, with the AFTRA Foundation's AFTRA Media and Entertainment Excellence Award in Broadcasting. In 1992, Jaime received La Gran Cruz al Merito en El Grado de Comendador (the highest civilian medal) from his native Ecuador for his immense contributions to the world. In 2019, Jaime received the Latino Spirit Award from the California Latino Caucus of the California State Legislature.

42. Fernando was thrust into the limelight (and into immortality) on opening day in 1981 at Dodger Stadium in front of a sell-out crowd of nearly 56,000. Jarrín said a star was born that day. Fernando shut out the Astros in a complete game and would go on to win seven more games, most of them shutouts. "Fernandomania" was born in front of the eyes and ears of millions of Spanish-speaking people, and all this hysteria was captured by Jaime Jarrín. He unpretentiously savored the national spotlight as the idolized translator for Fernando. Both conducted themselves at the highest standard of professionalism for the whole world to see. Fred Claire, the Dodgers public relations director, asked Jaime if he could serve as the official translator for Fernando. Other players, like Manny Mota, and staff had previously assisted Fernando, but it was important to have one person. Jaime said yes and the rest is history. See also the career-changing impact of Robert "Babo" Castillo on teaching Fernando the screwball: https:// youtube/2ODQ_-yC1xI.

43. Jo Ann Stevens, "Mr. Valenzuela Comes to Washington," June 10, 1981. The *Los Angeles Times* has produced a series of 12 short episodes highlighting the 40th anniversary of Fernando. One of these episodes draws attention to the White House visit: "Meeting President Reagan," https://www.youtube.com/watch?v=nfHkikIi9eQ.

44. *Ibid*. Michael Green.

45. Jarrín firmly believes one of Fernando's many impacts on baseball was drawing more fans from the Mexican and Central and South American communities to ballparks around the country than ever before. And it wasn't just the young who were becoming more attracted to baseball but also their parents, grandparents, and even great-grandparents. For the larger Latino community, Fernando was their own Jackie Robinson and Roberto Clemente combined, breaking down the color, language, and immigrant barriers that had haunted generations of previous Latino players, coaches, sportswriters, scouts, and umpires. Jarrín remembers a quiet young man with little, if any, knowledge of the English language in 1980 but saw a special gleam in the young pitcher's eyes that conveyed an unmistakable message that bigger accomplishments were awaiting Fernando in the major leagues and beyond. "A Changed Fanbase," https://youtu.be/YOKkbYU14HO.

46. *Ibid*. Les Carpenter.

47. Jorge Martín, "25 Years after *Fernandomania*," *Dodger Magazine*, August 18, 2006. See also the Walter O'Malley website highlighting Jaime Jarrín's Dodger career, March 9, 2006, http://walteromalley.com/hist_hof_Jarrín.php. Two California State University of Los Angeles students, Elizabeth Vasquez and April Provincio, interviewed Jaime Jarrín at Dodger Stadium on December 5, 2005. The interview was an oral history project for History 450 and Chicano Studies taught by Dr. Francisco Balderrama. The videographer was Ruben Martín and crew member Christine Campos. The interview is housed at the John F. Kennedy Library, Special Collections. See also Josh Peter, "Fernando Valenzuela's Impact Can Be Seen in Ballparks and beyond 40 Years after Fernandomania," *USA Today*, September 29, 2021.

48. *Ibid*. Les Carpenter.

49. Interview with Jorge Jarrín, August 17, 2021, San Marino, California.

50. Vic Wilson, "*Fernandomania*," in *The National Pastime, Endless Seasons: Baseball in Southern California* (Phoenix: Society of American Baseball Research, 2011); Jesse Sánchez, Natalie Alonso, and David Venn, "*Fernandomania* Still Resonates Decades Later," MLB.com, April 16, 2021. Outstanding comprehensive article chronicling the immense impact of Fernandomania on major league baseball and beyond.

51. Ben Chappell, *Mexican American Fastpitch: Identity at Play in Vernacular Sport* (Stanford, CA: Stanford University Press, 2021). Chappell has authored an outstanding book on Mexican American softball tournaments, mainly in Kansas and Texas. He views these community events through the lens of race, class, gender, immigration, language,

empowerment, and religion. We liberally borrowed for this essay his notions of racial hierarchies, hybridization, cultural citizenship, and racial worthiness.

52. The Dr. Richard A. and Teresa M. Santillán Los Angeles Dodgers Collection, the Institute of Baseball at Whittier College, Whittier, California.

53. Ibid. Ben Chappell.

54. A 1964 program mentions that the Dodgers opened a spring training exhibition game in Mexico City, including a photo of four Dodgers, one of them, Don Drysdale, is wearing an oversized sombrero. There is no mention of Jaime or García.

55. Jaime talks about the early years with the Dodgers when they were forced to call games in the worst parts of the stadiums. Vin Scully attempted to intervene but was not successful in having Jaime and the others join him in the press box. He told Jaime that one day, the Spanish-language broadcast teams would be allowed in the press box. About 10 years ago in Minnesota, Jaime was forced to call the game almost 20 feet behind the right field fence. When Jaime tells the story, it's clear that he was furious by the way he was treated. At the time, he was a Hall of Famer. He asked other Spanish-language broadcasters where they were placed and found out in the same terrible location. See his interview with LVBLive, "Legendary LA Dodger Broadcaster," April 24, 2019. His son Jorge expressed exasperation that he and his dad were stationed in an awful spot during the 2017 World Series in Houston. They raised a ruckus resulting in being repositioned to a better spot.

56. "Mexican Sandy Koufax," https://youtu.be/xW5NZUwaD5U.

57. "Fernando Valenzuela's Legacy Lives On," episode 12 of the *Los Angeles Times* Fernandomania video series, highlights the release of Fernando at the start of the 1991 season: https://youtu.be/x0l2o_64P5Q.

58. Major League Baseball in Mexico has already retired Fernando's number.

59. Jorge fondly remembers being only five years old when he visited his father in a makeshift radio booth at the Los Angeles Memorial Coliseum behind home plate and later seeing Wally Moon doing a postgame interview with Jerry Doggett. Jorge and his brothers often heard their father on radio since their mother had the radio on at home for each game. When Jorge was in high school, Jaime took him and his buddies to the games, leaving them in the hands of the ushers until it was time to go home. Jorge still remembers being in the booth with his dad, Jaime, during the 1974 World Series against the Oakland A's. This was the memorable game in Dodger lore when right-fielder Joe Ferguson threw out Sal Bando at home plate. The ballpark went absolutely nuts! Jorge says it was that magnificent play that converted him into a true baseball fan, when he finally realized how much entertainment and pleasure his father was giving fans each and every game. Jorge attended Pepperdine University and majored in broadcast sales, which, of course, came in handy when he worked in sales for the Dodgers starting in 2004. He proudly brags that like his father, he has a gift of the gab. In 1985, Jorge started working for KABC Radio doing traffic updates from a helicopter in the early mornings and late afternoons. He soon earned the moniker "Captain Jorge." Besides traffic, Jorge has covered natural disasters, the infamous O.J. Simpson car chase, and the Rodney King protests.

60. Eric Stephen, "Jaime Jarrín & Jorge Jarrín New Dodgers Spanish Radio Team," Truebluela.com, January 30, 2015. See also the interview with both Jaime and Jorge Jarrín, "Las Voces Latinas de Los Angeles Dodgers," https://youtu.be/vetrX61-jtE.

61. Eric Stephen, "Jorge Jarrín Retires after 17 Years with the Dodgers," Trueblue.com, February 5, 2021; "Dodgers Spanish Language Broadcaster Retires," *Los Angeles Times*, February 4, 2021, Associated Press story. See "Jorge Jarrín, Play by Play Announcer," Spectrum Sportsnet, n.d. The article highlights his impressive lists of awards and his great charitable work. He also manages the Jaime and Blanca Foundation, which supports educational and athletic programs, including the Jaime and Blanca Foundation Golf Tournament.

62. Scott G. Daves, "San Marino's Jaime Jarrín Inducted into the LA Dodgers 'Ring of Honor,'" *San Marino Tribune*, September 28, 2018. See also "Jarrín Inducted to Dodgers Ring of Honor," https://youtu.be/rDXnJNfoGnw.

63. Interview with José "Pepe" Yñiguez, September 13, 2021, Los Angeles, California. See also an amazing in-depth interview with Yñiguez: "LA Dodgers Spanish-Language

Baseball Broadcaster Pepe Yñiguez," https://youtu.be/ MaWOWScAyag; Cary Osborne, "Pepe and His Partner: Spanish-Language Broadcaster Yñiguez Keeps His Wife's Memory with Him Every Day," *Dodger Insider*, September 6, 2016, 56–60.

64. Interview with Ray Lara, August 20, 2021, Alhambra, California.

Felo Ramírez

Lou Hernández

He lived a lifetime behind the microphone, "with a voice as strong as café cubano and as sweet as tres leches cake."[1] Rafael "Felo" Ramírez spent 72 years as a sports broadcaster. Although he was also ringside announcer for many high-profile boxing matches, including pugilistic cards involving Muhammad Ali, the majority of those seven-plus decades were spent faithfully dedicated to his lifelong passion of baseball.

Rafael Ramírez Árias came into the world June 22, 1923, in Bayamo, Oriente, Cuba. He was the eldest of five children and only boy born to Rafael Ramírez Ricardo and Rosa Árias Bárzaga. His sisters, Carmen Luisa, Ángela, Rosa de la Concepción, and Urania, would complete the family over the next seven years.

"He redefined the category of sports narrator with a very simple recipe: inimitable style, deep voice, charisma, improvisation and a very friendly and pleasant manner," wrote Omar Claro, author of *Felo Ramírez el oráculo de la narración*.[2]

"I would describe my style as very peculiar," Ramírez would say well into his career, "very much my own, very spontaneous. I've had some famous lines, but they just came out of my mouth."[3] A particularly tense contest Felo would label as "*un choque no apto para cardíacos*," or as "a clash not for those with heart conditions." Or in a variation, "*Si tiene problemas cardíacos, aléjese de la radio*" (If you have heart problems, back away from the radio).

According to biographer Claro, Ramírez first began projecting his voice as a 16-year-old in his hometown. From moving automobiles he would announce, through a borrowed megaphone, the motion pictures showing at the local theater as well as advertising specials from the town's merchants. He was compensated with dress pants and *guayaberas* from one of the clothing stores.

Shortly thereafter, the teenager obtained his first baseball broadcast gig. On weekends, he described the action to fans in the stands at the local baseball field as play occurred. From 1939 to 1945, Ramírez estimates that he called nearly 500 contests and logged about 1,000 hours toward his burgeoning vocation.[4]

One of Felo's interim "day jobs" was as spokesperson for Bayamo's aspiring mayoral candidate. The postulant won the election in 1944 and encouraged Felo to broaden his horizons. A year later, Felo Ramírez took his first steps on the path to broadcasting immortality when he decided to venture (with three other friends) to the Cuban capital, almost 500 miles away.

Upon his Havana arrival, he applied for a job at a radio station which happened to be in desperate need for a broadcast voice for the upcoming Cuban Amateur League. The 22-year-old Ramírez impressed the station managers not so much with his voice but with his knowledge of the players and teams. Ramírez won the job at Radio Salas in Havana, broadcasting amateur baseball, an immensely popular sport on the island in the 1940s. "My career started in 1945 at Estadio Tropical de la Habana," Felo stated, "in the 18-team amateur summer league."[5]

He stayed on to broadcast the 1945–46 Cuban Winter League (CWL). He was teamed with established announcer Manolo de la Reguera. The pair became the most listened to sports duo in the country and kicked off a professional and personal relationship lasting more than four decades. The rookie announcer was named Broadcaster of the Year by the Association of Broadcast Journalists.[6]

The following season, Ramírez paired with veteran Carlos "Cuco" Conde to call games for the CWL and the 1947 Havana Cubans, the Class C Florida International League franchise.

On October 26, 1946, Felo described the action at the inaugural game of the 1946–47 Liga de Beisbol Profesional Cubana. What made the occasion extra special was the coinciding grand opening of the first million-dollar sports complex in Latin America.[7] The Cienfuegos Elephants and the Almendares Scorpions christened the season at Gran Stadium del Cerro de la Habana. The modern stadium had been built in a little over a year by Cuban businessmen Roberto "Bobby" Maduro and Miguelito Suárez and replaced Tropical Park as the main venue for the CWL. The Scorpions defeated the Elephants 9–1.

Not only did the young announcer have a chance to describe what is considered the most celebrated winter league season in Cuba's baseball history, with the "eternal rivals," Habana Lions and Almendares, clashing to decide the championship on the next-to-last day of the season, but the 23-year-old Ramírez also received the opportunity to broadcast the action between major league clubs for the first time. And what clubs they were!

A few weeks after the winter campaign ended, in late March, the Brooklyn Dodgers and New York Yankees (bound for a World Series meeting that October) came to Havana (during separate periods) for a partial training camp. The distinguished North American teams engaged in exhibition matches with the Havana Cubans and Cuban All-Star clubs.[8]

Two winter seasons later, 1948–49, Ramírez made history on the Cuban airwaves recounting the historical events of the inaugural Caribbean Series, held at Gran Stadium. A double round robin-formatted series that pitted the champions of four countries' winter leagues (Cuba, Puerto Rico, Panama, Venezuela), the first champion crowned was the home country's Almendares Scorpions with a perfect 6–0 record. Felo must have been inwardly pleased with the series' outcome, but like most of his contemporaries of the era, he maintained his impartiality. "You narrated those games with emotion in your voice," Ramírez recalled. "But always with objectivity in mind."[9]

A personally gratifying residual of that six-day baseball spectacle in Havana occurred for the now-established broadcaster. Ramírez met his broadcast idol, Eloy "Buck" Canel. Anyone who listened to sports in Latin America during the first half of the 20th century knew the name Buck Canel. Felo Ramírez was no different. He not only met Canel but also invited the Argentine-born radio personality to be a guest narrator for one inning during one of the games. Canel heartedly accepted.

Later that same year (1949), Felo engaged in a different kind of partnering, one that would be a mutually meaningful and enriching experience for both parties involved for a long time. Ramírez made the ultimate commitment to the woman who would become his steadfast companion throughout his lifelong journey achieving broadcasting excellence. While visiting cousins, he had met a woman named Luisa Rafaela Montano Fraga, whom he would affectionately call "Fela." Luisa was a native of Cienfuegos, a colonial city on the south-central coast of the island. She was attending the University of Havana at the time. Luisa and her mother were residing in the same apartment building as Felo's relatives. The couple married on September 25 at the Iglesia San Juan de Letrán in the Vedado municipality of Havana. Ramírez also added his second Broadcaster of the Year Award to his personal résumé that year.

In 1950, Felo jumped to Union Radio, the largest station in Cuba, after having left Radio Salas for COCO radio station a few years earlier. He found himself sharing the mic with René Molina, also youthful, and with a more complementary personality to Felo than his previous veteran voice associates. The move would lead to Cuban fans finally being able to put a face to the voice, as the station emerged as a dual television broadcaster, the first on the island, in the fall.[10]

During this period, Felo's growing profile did not escape sports biggest broadcast conglomerate. The *Gillette Cavalcade of Sports* (GCS) was heard, during its heyday, throughout 200 radio stations in the United States and branched out into the Spanish-speaking countries of the Caribbean and South America. Its primary sports headline attractions were baseball (All-Star Game, World Series, and then Game of the Week) and boxing, gaining a reputation for exceptional Friday night fights on television.[11]

The *Cabalgata Deportiva Gillette* approached Felo in 1951 to join their Spanish broadcast team. He jumped at the opportunity. The Cuban native's first broadcast was live from Madison Square Garden in New York, on Friday, May 25. The main card featured lightweight champion Ike Williams and challenger Jimmy Carter. If that was not a starry occasion in and of itself, Ramírez was partnered with his idol, Buck Canel. The same idol a young Felo would never grow tired of listening to on the radio in Cuba.

In the fall, thanks to his new employer, the "Pride of Bayamo," as he was nicknamed in Cuba, nestled behind the microphone for his first World Series extravaganza. Starting in 1951, Ramírez went on to call 31 of the next 32 World Series. During one of his initial Fall Classic games at Yankee Stadium, Felo liked to recall an incident that occurred with a foul ball skipping all the way back on the screen to the lip of the press box. He reached over for the ball and found himself in a tussle for it with an outstretched arm from the adjoining box. "I'm fighting, and finally I grab the ball and see that it's Humphrey Bogart," said Ramírez. "I was just a rookie. I put the ball in my pocket. I didn't realize until later that I should have given him the ball—or at least have gotten his autograph."[12]

The Canel-Ramírez GCS teaming was the beginning of a beautiful broadcast friendship. During the 1950s, the pair would go on to "paint the pictures" for their Hispanic audiences to boxing's and baseball's biggest showcases. In particular baseball, for which Cavalcade had purchased the World Series rights in 1939.[13] "He had a great voice and great personality," Ramírez said of Canel. "He developed a great appreciation for me. Canel would say I was the only one who did not try to imitate him."[14] One of the duo's most memorable World Series was in 1955, the storied Brooklyn Dodgers' only world championship, and the 1956 Classic, which included Don Larsen's perfect game.[15]

Felo's streak of Fall Classics was interrupted in 1961, when he was not permitted to leave Cuba, two years after the Cuban Revolution. Its guerrilla leader, Fidel Castro, and his Marxist sociopolitical turn had convulsed the island and altered baseball in the Caribbean for the remainder of the century. "[That was] the year of the great home run race between Mickey Mantle and Roger Maris," Ramírez recollected. "They [the government] told me I couldn't talk about it [on the radio]. I talked about it every day. I wanted them to fire me."[16]

Felo's career might have stagnated for who knows how long if not for a life-affecting whim imposed by one of the new usurpers of power in the country. "I got to leave [Cuba] because of my house," Ramírez said. "A captain in the army lived in my neighborhood, and his wife wanted my house. She told her husband to get my house for her. One day, a lieutenant from the army approached me and asked me if I was doing the winter-league games in Venezuela. I told him I had a contract, but I couldn't leave. He gave me a note and told me to go to an office. I went the next day, and everything was arranged for me to leave…. It was like a miracle for me. I was dying to leave Cuba."[17] The liberating experience was not without personal cost and sacrifice, however. Ramírez left Cuba on November 6, 1961. "It was difficult leaving my parents and sisters," Ramírez reminisced decades later. "I never saw my mother again. My father I did see once more but he was 92."[18]

Ramírez eventually continued the craft he loved on a permanent basis in Puerto Rico, delineating games for the winter circuit's San Juan Senators, beginning in 1962. "When Felo arrived in Puerto Rico, he was already internationally admired as a great broadcaster," attested Luis Rodríguez-Mayoral, who narrated over 2,000 major league games in Spanish. "He was always there to help and give me orientation in the world of baseball."[19]

It would not be a stretch to say a love affair between Ramírez and Puerto Rico and its people ensued, culminating with the dedication of a life-size statue of Ramírez at the National Sports Museum in Guaynabo in 2004. The love affair had its roots in the minds of many older island baseball fans in 1960. Those fans could excitedly recall Bill Mazeroski's World Series–winning home run, handing the Roberto Clemente–led Pittsburgh Pirates their upset victory over the New York Yankees—the game and series narrated by Felo and Buck Canel.

Even as Felo established his primary residence on the Island of Enchantment, he made more international inroads in the 1970s, reproducing games for three of the Venezuelan Winter League's teams, at one time or another. The Magallanes Navigators were one of the clubs. Over the airwaves, Felo recorded the last outs heard of the championship campaigns of 1976–77 and 1978–79 for *los Navegantes*. The Caribbean Series had restarted again by this time—after the dictator Castro's abolishment of professional sports in Cuba in 1961 had ended the games—and Felo had dutifully returned to his usual press box spot for these annual and popular tournament contests. His signature home run call of Mitchell Page's deciding blast for Magallanes, which clinched the 1979 Caribbean Series for the Andean team became as historic as the blast itself for Venezuelan fans: *"La bola se va elevaaaando.... Y la booooola seeeeee llevó la cerca!"* (The ball is riiiising.... And the baaaaaall caaaaaaries over the fence!). Ramírez wound up broadcasting an amazing 40 Caribbean Classics in his career.

Earlier in the decade, Felo was privileged to transmit Roberto Clemente's 3,000th base hit to his Spanish-speaking public. *"Lo logro! Lo logro!"* (He did it! He did it!) Ramírez punctuated, after describing Clemente's historic two-base hit on September 30, 1972, at Pittsburgh's Three Rivers Stadium. The entire call would later be placed in the National Hall of Fame's archive collection. The audio elevated Ramírez as the first Hispanic broadcaster to have his narration included within Cooperstown's hallowed halls. Less than two years later, the 50-year-old Ramírez relayed to his Iberian audience Henry Aaron's record-breaking 715th four-bagger.

For years, Larsen's perfect game, Clemente's 3,000th hit, and Aaron's home run stood as the loftiest of Ramírez's major league baseball archiving achievements. He gladly ended up expanding the career highlight list not long after H. Wayne Huizenga, video chain and waste management mogul, brought major league baseball to Miami in 1993. Who else but Felo Ramírez could be considered as the Spanish broadcast voice of the new Florida Marlins?

Ramírez broadcast the expansion team's inaugural game, April 5, 1993, against the Los Angeles Dodgers, with Manolo Alvarez handling the color commentary. Felo did the play-by-play for the Marlins' first no-hitters, Al Leiter in 1996 and Kevin Brown in 1997. The same latter year recorded the Marlins in a late-season spurt that gained the team a wild card position and spot in the playoffs for the first time. The Florida Marlins became the first wild card–World Series champion with a thrilling seven-game victory over the Cleveland Indians, and Felo Ramírez was the event's principal articulator for Hispanic posterity. "Being part of the World Series was tremendous," Ramírez said. "The playoff games, Liván Hernández's strikeout record. It was a very emotional experience."[20]

As Miami evolved increasingly into an international city at the turn of the new century, Felo Ramírez's international voice was fittingly recognized at the highest level by the sport he adored. In early 2001, Ramírez was informed of his selection as that year's Cooperstown's Ford C. Frick recipient, honoring outstanding baseball announcers. Ramírez was at his home in Puerto Rico. "When I found out I was voted in, I cried," he said, "just as I cried when Roberto Clemente got his 3,000th hit and when the Marlins won the World Series."[21]

On August 5, 2001, Felo Ramírez became the 24th broadcaster and third Hispanic honored under the Hall of Fame's (HOF's) "Scribes and

Mikemen" library exhibit, which annually recognizes famed sportswriters and announcers of the past and present. The first HOF Hispanic elocutionist had been Felo's idol, Buck Canel (1985). The second was Jaime Jarrín, longtime Spanish voice of the Los Angeles Dodgers (1998). Excusing himself to his audience in a self-deprecating manner by saying his English was the halting equivalent of that of Tarzan, Ramírez asked Jarrín to translate his acceptance speech into English from the Cooperstown podium. "Felo has that special charisma," offered Jarrín. "He has opened the door for new fans in Latin America."[22]

The veteran orator shared the Cooperstown stage that afternoon with J.G. Taylor Spink honoree Joe Falls and baseball legends Dave Winfield and Kirby Puckett, along with Veterans Committee selections Bill Mazeroski and Negro Leaguer Hilton Smith. "I could talk about being here today and about how a dream has been finally realized," declared Felo. "But I never dreamed to be in Cooperstown."[23]

In his speech (which can be found on YouTube), Felo revealed, among other things, that "broadcasting baseball games was a childhood dream, and it is still, more than six decades later, the driving force behind my life." He redressed the sweeping breath of his baseball trajectory, calling amateur and professional games in the Caribbean Basin countries of Cuba, Nicaragua, Venezuela, Dominican Republic, and Puerto Rico and through both phases of the Caribbean Series tournaments, All-Star Games and World Series—a total of 56 years of uninterrupted service in baseball. Ramírez, of course, paid tribute to Buck Canel. He also mentioned he was filled with pride to be alongside other great Cuban baseball stars, Martín Dihigo and Tony Pérez, along with Latin American icons such as Clemente, Cepeda, Marichal, Aparico, and Carew. He was glad that his wife, Fela (in the audience), was able to partake in "the happiest day of my broadcast career." The 78-year-old Ramírez became most emotional when he lamented that he was unable to share his honor with his closest family members, including his sisters, in his "beloved country Cuba" and when he expressed his desire, in spite of the brief time he speculated he had left, to broadcast baseball in a free Cuba.[24]

In spite of having had four heart-bypass surgeries by the time of his 80th birthday in 2003, Felo Ramírez showed no signs of slowing down. One might say he experienced a rejuvenating season that year when he described the action to the Marlins' second improbable post-season run. Again the wild card winner, the South Florida team won two league championship rounds and upset the New York Yankees in the World Series to gain the franchise's second World Series trophy. Twenty-three-year-old Josh Beckett shut out the Yankees 2–0 at Yankee Stadium in the clinching sixth game, in a contest that must have seemed reminiscent to Felo from his Fall Classic broadcast of 1955, when 23-year-old Johnny Podres of Brooklyn blanked, by identical score, the Yankees in the same Bronx ballpark, albeit in game seven.

During the Marlins' championship defending campaign of 2004, Ramírez was forced to endure the loss of his wife and steadfast companion.

Felo Ramírez in New York City (collection of Lou Hernandez).

Six weeks shy of their 55th wedding anniversary, Fela passed away on August 13, "following a prolonged illness."[25] She was 79. Felo missed his first ever Marlins games during the subsequent period of mourning. He returned the same season, without thought of retirement. Felo would inevitably be asked about his loss in the years that followed. He would often say, "Being a sports announcer has been my life. My other great love was my wife of more than five decades. She lives in my heart."[26]

Ramírez began his seventieth year of broadcasting in 2014, and his third at the Miami Marlins' new state-of-the-art, retractable-roof ballpark. At 91, he continued to travel with the team. Three seasons later, the ageless Ramírez still displayed no indications of slacking off. But on April 26, 2017, while accompanying the club on a northeastern road trip, the veteran announcer slipped or tripped stepping off the team bus, fell, and hit his head. The Marlins were returning to the team hotel following a game with the Philadelphia Phillies. Bleeding from a head wound, Felo was taken to a Delaware hospital and remained there for two months. He was then released to return to Miami.[27] However, the broadcast legend never fully recuperated and, on August 21, succumbed to complications from his injury. He was 94. His obituary was carried in every major newspaper and internet outlet in the country. Baseball commissioner Robert D. Manfred and the Marlins released prepared condolences statements. He and his wife were childless. Felo Ramírez was laid to rest at Our Lady of Mercy Catholic Cemetery in Miami, next to his beloved Fela.

Shortly before his passing, Miami–Dade County passed a resolution naming a baseball field at one of its largest public parks after Felo. Field #3 at Tropical Park was officially named Rafael "Felo" Ramírez Field, complete with dedication ceremony, attended by Felo and mascot Billy the Marlin, among others. Prior to Marlins Park opening, one of the four streets surrounding the innovative ballpark had been renamed Felo Ramírez Drive (formerly NW 6th Street).

Following Ramírez's death, the Marlins honored his memory outside of Marlins Park. Felo's recognition became part of a dual homage, including deceased pitcher José Fernández, who was killed in a boating accident in September 2016. "The Marlins have been fortunate to have had some truly talented individuals within our organization through the years," Marlins chief executive officer Derek Jeter said. "Jose, on the field, and Felo, in the booth, each left a lasting legacy in Little Havana and throughout baseball. We wanted to commemorate them with plaques on the West Plaza for our fans and family members. Their memories will live on in our hearts and in our community."[28]

During the twilight of his career, I met and interviewed Felo in 2016. Never a tall man, age had permanently hunched his shoulders to burden him with an even shorter stature. He maintained an envious amount of hair well into his 90s, though with copious amounts of gray. His thick eyebrows sprouted erratically over his prescription glasses. His chin struck me as his most prominent feature; it was carved out with almost permanent laugh and age lines, helping to strengthen his sagging jowls and flappy neck folds. During our time together, he spoke in a surprisingly faint voice. Yet when he settled behind the mic, even in his final years, his voice resurged to its natural baritone level. I came to realize Ramírez instinctively knew he had to conserve his vocal cords for his treasured ball games.

Throughout his life, the most recognized baseball voice in Latin America remained faithful to his humble origins. Following his death, local Miami sports reporter Bobby Salamanca expressed that "Felo's head never swelled over his acquired fame and celebrity status that accompanied him everywhere."[29]

"When the Marlins won at Yankee Stadium," said Ramírez's last broadcast partner, Luis "Yiky" Quintana, "Felo described the emotional last out and in the midst of all that we saw each other, and we hugged and enjoyed the moment. That will always be my favorite moment with Felo."[30]

Tony Pérez, Hall of Famer and former Marlins community relations assistant, stated the following in memoriam: "He was that kind of person who loved people and wanted to be around people. He wanted people to listen to him. He didn't speak good English, but to people who speak Spanish, he's a hero."[31]

And always will be.

Notes

1. Mike Phillips. "Ramirez Has Become the Voice of the People," *Miami Herald*, August 5, 2001.
2. Omar Claro, *Felo Ramírez el oráculo de la narración* (Self-published, 2018), 16.
3. Linda Robertson, "F. Ramirez a Longtime Radio Legend," *Miami Herald*, March 1, 2001.
4. Claro, *Felo Ramírez*, 42.
5. Interview with Felo Ramírez, Big Five Club, Miami, Florida, September 16, 2016.
6. Award presented by the Asociación de la Crónica Radial Impresa (Spanish acronym ACRI).
7. The stadium was expropriated by dictator Fidel Castro and its name changed to Estadio La-tinoamericano. As a testament to those who built it, the stadium has endured as the principal venue for baseball in Cuba, more than seven-and-a-half decades later.
8. The Dodgers had Jackie Robinson, Don Newcombe, Roy Partlow, and Roy Campanella on their expanded roster. Whereas their Caucasian teammates stayed at the luxurious Hotel Nacional, these Black players were relegated to second-rate accommodations in another part of the city. The decision to intentionally segregate the players was made by Branch Rickey.

9. Marino Martínez Peraza, "Felo Ramírez: la Voz del Béisbol," *El Nuevo Herald*, December 12, 2010.
10. Union Radio Television, Channel 4, transmitted its first broadcast on October 24, 1950. Cuba, along with Mexico and Brazil, were the first Latin American countries to initiate the new broadcast medium.
11. According to Wikipedia.org, the *Cavalcade of Sports* program ran from 1942 to 1960. The Gillette sponsorship began in 1948, coinciding with the program's first television appearance. During the 1940s, boxing matches were shown twice weekly, Monday and Friday.
12. Robertson, "F. Ramirez a Longtime Radio Legend."
13. https://en.wikipedia.org/wiki/Gillette_Cavalcade_of_Sports. It should be noted a third in-ternational broadcaster, Francisco José Croquer, also was part of the celebrated team for a time. Better known by his Spanish nickname Pancho Pepe, Croquer was considered the most recognized sports voice in his native Venezuela. A true sports aficionado, Croquer competed professionally in race car driving events. Sadly, in December 1955, the auto he was driving in one of those races crashed and killed him at the early age of 35.
14. Emily Martínez, "Este Domingo Don Felo llega a Su Casa," August 1, 2001, https://espndeportes.espn.go.com/beisbol/columnas/beisbollatino-08-01-01.html.
15. It is probable Felo, as junior member, would have done the final four and a half innings of Larsen's masterpiece.
16. Phillips, "Ramirez Has Become."
17. *Ibid.*
18. Peraza, "Felo Ramírez."
19. Phone interview with Luis Rodríguez-Mayoral, May 8, 2020.
20. Christy Cabrera, "A Baseball Authority," *South Florida Sun Sentinel*, August 6, 2001.
21. Robertson, "F. Ramirez a Longtime Radio Legend." Part of the voting committee that elect-ed Felo included Ernie Harwell, Joe Garagiola, Bowie Kuhn, and Vin Scully.
22. Cabrera, "A Baseball Authority."
23. Mike Phillips, "Ramírez 3rd Hispanic Broadcaster in Hall," *Miami Herald*, August 6, 2001.
24. Youtube.com/watch?v=S7zgDgYF8Y. Besides Cooperstown, Felo Ramírez was recog-nized with pantheon honors in the Halls of Fame of Cuba [in exile], Miami (1997), Caribbean Baseball (2003, first broadcaster), Puerto Rican National Sports Museum, Guaynabo, PR (2004), Latin American International Sports Hall of Fame, Laredo, Texas (2004), Latino Baseball, La Romana, Dominican Republic (2010). The Magallanes baseball club set aside a day to recognize Ramírez's more than 60 years of broadcasting in Valencia, Venezuela, in 2012.
25. Juan C. Rodríguez, "Sports Notes," *South Florida Sun-Sentinel*, August 14, 2004.
26. Peraza, "Felo Ramírez."
27. During this period, after having described the first five no-hitters in franchise history, Ramírez missed calling the Marlins sixth no-hitter (Edinson Vólquez, June 3) due to his incapaci-tating injury.
28. Joe Frisario, "Fernandez and Ramirez Are Two of the Most Iconic Figures in Franchise History—Marlins to Honor Fernandez, Felo with Plaques," March 8, 2018, https//www.mlb.com/news/marlins-to-honor-jose-fernandez-felo-ramirez-c268171434.
29. "Fallece en el Exilio Felo Ramírez, Lyenda Cubana de la Narración Deportiva [television news report]," Radio Televisión Martí, August 22, 2017.
30. Manny Navarro, "Marlins' Spanish-Radio Voice Dies," *Miami Herald*, August 23, 2017.
31. Manny Navarro, "Felo Ramirez, Legendary Spanish-Radio Voice of Marlins, Dies at 94," *Miami Herald*, August 22, 2017.

2. Veterans

Eduardo Ortega

Jorge Iber

When the National League granted the city of San Diego a franchise to commence play in 1969, the club's brain trust, led by E.J. "Buzzie" Bavasi, began the process of securing ballplayers, establishing a managerial structure, and, importantly, issuing contracts for both radio and television affiliates. The team's location, hemmed in by Los Angeles (by then hosting two clubs) and the border, "caused some concern that the Padres would be hampered in their local negotiations." The agreements for both sets of rights were awarded eventually to KOGO. The initial broadcast team was comprised of Jerry Gross and Frank Sims.[1]

Like the Dodgers before them, the Padres recognized the need for broadcasting in Spanish, immediately considering that they could reach into Baja California as well as appealing to the substantial Mexican American population that existed in their home base. A recent work on the history of baseball broadcasting noted that "one area in which the Padres were very progressive was in Spanish-language radio. Starting in 1969, XEXX [based in Tijuana] aired the new club's games." One of the early and most enthusiastic listeners to these broadcasts was Eduardo Ortega-Díaz, particularly after Mario Thomas Zapiaín (known affectionately as "Don Thomas") began broadcasting games in 1970.[2]

The early years of the Padres were certainly lean, as the team did not notch its first winning season until 1978, when they went 84–78.[3] During an interview with this author (which is the source of much of what follows in the latter section of the chapter), Eduardo Ortega recalled those years as being "*los años de las vacas flacas*" (the years of skinny cows). Although the action on the field was more often than not abominable, the young Ortega was captivated by the images on his television (with the volume turned all the way down) and the dulcet tones and delivery coming through on XEXX. It would come to be the inspiration for his professional career as well as a community-building activity that tied together fans on both sides of the border.⁴

Eduardo was born on June 5, 1963, in the Colonia Juárez section of Tijuana. He was the youngest of four children of Maria Amparo Díaz-Valdez and Salvador Ortega-Becerra. There were two older brothers, Salvador and Rodolfo, and a sister, Amparo. His parents divorced when Eduardo turned three, and he recalled that event as "a very important part of my childhood."

Salvador senior was a laborer who toiled mostly in the construction industry, and his mother was a stay-at-home parent. After the couple's separation, María Amparo turned to some of the traditional employments of women suddenly left to manage alone with children to raise: she took in laundry, ironed, and made tortillas. The two older boys would peddle these wares throughout the neighborhood. Eventually, both also took part-time jobs after school selling newspapers and delivering groceries. Eduardo commenced his contributions to the family till around the age of eight, working as a bagger for tips at the same grocery store. Compounding the family's difficulties was the fact that María Amparo was deaf due to an illness she suffered at the age of 14.⁵ Although María Amparo did not have much formal education, all of the siblings were required to go to school. Ortega attended the Ángel Bustamante School for his *primaria* (elementary) and then moved on to Lazaro Cárdenas–La Poli for his *secundaria* (high school). Although this institution was tied to the Instituto Politecnico (the national equivalent of a "tech" university), it did not offer any studies focused on the field of broadcasting or communications. It was not the high school curriculum that attracted Ortega to his professional endeavor; rather, it was watching his brothers play as well as attending games at the amateur and professional levels in and around Tijuana (and the Padres' contests) that made him fall in love with baseball and radio.

Ortega's path to the booth began in the late 1960s and involved both the Padres' broadcasts as well as his lack of athletic capability on the diamond. From listening to Don Mario, he memorized all of his catchphrases and expressions. He had a lot of time to practice among his teammates as, like many other Mexican youths, he loved to play baseball, but "I was so bad. They sent me to right field, but I was always benched." Ortega would scamper up a tree and become the *cronista* (chronicler) of the action. He quickly earned a local reputation for his aptitude in describing athletic contests. Ortega's capabilities also came to the attention of another one of his heroes in the industry, Juan Manuel Martínez-Pérez (who has been broadcasting about sports in Tijuana for almost 60 years), who provided encouragement and even helped him get one of his first "gigs": serving as master of ceremonies at local graduations (Ortega was 17 at the time).⁶

The voice of Don Mario was not the only connection between Ortega and the Padres. One of the most important memories of his youth took place in the mid–1970s when Ortega got the opportunity to attend a home game courtesy of another San Diego legend. Ortega recalled the importance of the Dave Winfield Pavilion and how he appreciated all that the player did to assist disadvantaged youths on both sides of the border. When, in 1995, the broadcaster (then working the World Series for the CBS Americas Radio Network) had an opportunity to visit with the Hall of Famer, he reminded and thanked Winfield for using his wealth and the sport of baseball to reach out to the needy above and below the international divide: "I just wanted to tell you, on behalf of my family, thank you very much. You motivated me to pursue a life in baseball." A friendship developed between the two, and when Winfield was inducted into the Hall of Fame in 2001, he asked Ortega to attend the ceremony in Cooperstown.

After finishing high school, Ortega reached out to the Sindicato de Trabajadores de Radio y Televisión, or the STRT (Syndicate of Radio and Television Workers). Part of the requirements for his chosen profession was the need to go down to Mexico City and take a test for his *licencia de locutor* (broadcaster's license). He was awarded this designation by the National Secretary of Education. He then returned to his hometown, where his goal was to work at the station that employed Juan Manuel Martínez-Pérez.

Here, he learned all aspects of radio operations. This was *la mejor escuela* (the best education), Ortega recalled during our interviews. In turn, this led to a plethora of narrating opportunities: boxing matches, bullfights, beer commercials, and serving as a disc jockey. He even attained another pinnacle of Mexican broadcasting: working as an announcer for *lucha libre* contests alongside Juan Manuel Martínez-Pérez. Still, his dreams of broadcasting baseball was always at the forefront.

The process by which Ortega broke into baseball is tied directly to the efforts of Juan Manuel. He, along with his broadcast partner Gilberto Delgado-Lizárraga, were the radio announcers for the Tijuana Potros (Foals) of the Mexican Winter League. Through their suggestion and Ortega's growing local reputation, the young broadcaster got the job as the Potros' public address announcer. Satisfactory results in this area eventually led to stints on pre- and postgame radio for the club, and he began calling play-by-play for the early innings of Sunday games. In 1982, Delgado-Lizárraga moved on to direct the operations of a newspaper, and Ortega took his place alongside Juan Manuel through 1986.

Ironically, while his voice graced the airwaves throughout his teen years and early 20s for his hometown team, there was one person, his biggest fan and beloved mother, who could not hear any of it. Although she was not really a sports fan, María Amparo grew to love baseball because of her son's passion for the sport. In an interview with Curt Smith for *A Talk in the Park*, Ortega recalled how she reacted to his first appearance on the radio. "Your brothers tell me there was a beautiful voice on the radio.... Remember, while you may not be before me, I will always listen with my heart." Amparo passed away during the off-season of 2011. Ortega noted, "It gets me sentimental ... because I took inspiration from her.... I wanted to make her proud."[7]

The next path on the way to San Diego took Ortega to the state of Coahuila through his interactions with yet another Mexican baseball legend, Don Guillermo "Memo" Garibay. The great former catcher was then serving as general manager of the Torreón Algodóneros (Cotton Pickers). In the 1980s, Garibay would often attend winter league contests to scout for talent. He had listened to Ortega's efforts with the Potros and liked what he heard. This was a critical moment in the young broadcaster's career. In order to be able to accept the job in Torreón, he would have to resign from his current post in Tijuana, and the likelihood of returning should things not work out was zero. With great anticipation and hope, Ortega took the chance and worked the campaign with the Algodóneros. He then returned to Tijuana to spend time with family during the off-season. The timing of his arrival back in his hometown could not have been more fortuitous.

In the late summer and early fall of 1986, personnel changes were taking place at Radio Ranchito, the station that broadcasted Padres baseball into Baja California. At that time, Don Mario continued to work the games with Gustavo López-Moreno serving as both sidekick and station general manager. Due to López-Moreno's other duties, he was looking for another voice to work the Padres' road games. This was the opportunity Ortega had waited for his entire life. Starting in 1987, not only would he be broadcasting MLB contests for his hometown team; he would also be doing so alongside his childhood idol.

Ortega noted during our interview that working his first game with Don Mario was a very emotional experience, but he realized quickly that the seasoned veteran broke no lack of professionalism. In short order, the mentor reminded the youthful sidekick that his primary job was to "watch me work and if you have questions, ask me. I'll show you how it's done." Not only did Don Mario share with Ortega the intricacies of calling the sport at its highest levels; he also instructed him on how to deal with the players, managers, and other broadcasters. This guidance helped Ortega move forward with his career. Unlike his instructor, who never worked directly for the Padres, Ortega has been an employee of the franchise since 1991. There have been several changes in stations and color commentators over the years, but Ortega has been the constant. By the late 1990s, as Don Mario's career was winding down, he only did day home games and Ortega became the main announcer. Don Mario retired after the 1997 campaign and passed away in 2009.

Over his career on-air, Ortega has noted numerous changes that have taken place in the game and the acceptance of Spanish-language broadcasts and players.[8] He indicated that in more recent times, many English-speaking fans visit with him and mention how much they enjoy listening to the contests in Spanish because of his enthusiasm and flair. They particularly like that "we Latinos are very *escandalosos* [loud], with a very amicable culture!" It was not always this way. In his interview with Curt Smith, Ortega related that early in his career, the lively style of Spanish broadcasters did not appeal to some fans attending a spring training contest against the Brewers in Chandler, Arizona.

The number of fans at the contest was minuscule, and Ortega began to count up the balls and strikes in "our festive Latin style." Not surprisingly, not everyone appreciated his narrative technique. Several attendees seated in the stands in front of Ortega stared intently and asked, "'Who the heck are you and what are you doing here?' By game's end, no one was sitting directly in front of us, moving to different sections to get away. I haven't taken it personally."[9]

Another significant transformation has been that contrary to the way that Latino players' names were routinely butchered by non–Spanish-speaking announcers without a second thought, now broadcasters such as Ortega are seen as resources on how to properly pronounce names and certain words.[10]

Just as MLB decided to *poner acento* on the backs of jerseys, many English-language broadcasters and public address announcers now come up to Spanish-speaking colleagues and ask, "How do I pronounce this name, or how do I pronounce this hometown?" Ortega even noted that now many of his English-language colleagues keep pronunciation lists/guides handy in order to provide the correct (or as close to the correct as possible) iteration of the various ballplayers' names.[11]

Ortega has also made a name for himself at the national and international levels. Since 1993, he has broadcast games in Spanish covering playoff series, World Series, and the World Baseball Classic. Among the highlights in this aspect of his career was working the 1998 and 2001 World Series alongside the legendary voices of Jarrín and Ramírez. He has also broadcast All-Star Games and worked MLB contests for entities such as the Latin Broadcasting Company, CBS America, and Radio Caracol (out of Colombia). In addition, since 2005, Ortega has served as the radio voice of the Mexicali Aguilas (Eagles) of the Mexican Pacific League. This broadcaster has become the *voz* of the Padres for the local Latino community as well as fans in Mexico. In a recent interview, historian of San Diego baseball Bill Swank indicated that the presence of Latinos in the stands at Petco Park is, to a substantial extent, due to the relationship that Ortega has helped to forge between the team and the *comunidad*. An example of this can be seen in the fact that by the late 1990s, the Padres often shuttled busloads of *fanaticos* from Tijuana for home games dubbed *Domingos Padres Tecate* (Padres' Sundays with Tecate).[12]

In addition to his on-air duties, Ortega is active as a volunteer on both sides of the international divide: raising funds for scholarships, leading toy drives, visiting hospitals and homes for the aged, attending Little League events in Tijuana, being part of the Padres yearly caravan into Baja, and as a presence (mostly as a master of ceremonies) for charitable community activities. The caravan is not only a way to promote the club, but it also includes a charitable element, as Ortega makes sure that plenty of souvenirs are provided for children in the city's poorer neighborhoods. Additionally, when the Padres had a retail establishment in his native city, Ortega provided not just a visible presence in town; he also made sure to be available to visit with youths/children dealing with life-threatening illnesses who wanted to meet with the Spanish-language voice of "their" hometown team. A particular treat for these individuals was when Ortega would re-create important moments from a Padres game using the patient's name as the player making the fantastic catch or hitting the game-winning homer.

Furthermore, Ortega visits elementary schools north and south of the border and reads to children in both languages, many of whom are now doing what he did as a youngster, mimicking their favorite announcer's calls and catchphrases. Ortega considers his work with youth to be among his most important endeavors. One of the institutions he often visits is Willow Elementary, located in the border town of San Ysidro. The school is almost exclusively populated by children of Mexican families. He seeks to inspire children to read and to think about the possibilities available to them. He also wants them to know the immense pride he has in being Mexican and having succeeded in such a competitive industry. These youths are not only future paying customers for the Padres; they are the next generation that will live in the area and build, hopefully, a better and more well-assimilated community. For older students, he has repaid his ties to the STRT by doing professional presentations on baseball broadcasting for younger members of the organization. He has also performed similar duties for sportscasters in Venezuela as well as the National Association of Sports Writers in Nicaragua.

In all, Ortega is a wonderful ambassador for not only his employer but for all of MLB with the Spanish-speaking world.[13] His professionalism and

Eduardo Ortega (Iber) 77

Eduardo Ortega at his "office," Petco Park (courtesy Eduardo Ortega).

longevity led, in recent years, to his nomination for the most important recognition in baseball broadcasting: the Ford C. Frick Award. Although he did not receive this honor in 2013 (he was also nominated in 2011 and 2012), no less of a legend than the late Dick Enberg (himself a Frick winner in 2015) noted, "Oh, he's going to be in the Hall of Fame one day. He's that good."[14] During our discussion, Ortega's modesty did not permit him to classify himself as approaching the heights of a Canel, Jarrín, or Ramírez, but he referred to these men as *"modelos de excelencia"* (models of excellence) that he and today's Latino baseball broadcasters must strive to emulate.

Although he has still not achieved entry into the Baseball Hall of Fame by being honored with a Frick, Ortega wants to earn the designation not necessarily for his own sense of accomplishment but to bring recognition to his native land and family: "My mom was my inspiration and learning about Mexico's baseball history pushed me to make it to the majors." He noted that as of 2018, there were around 140 Mexican-born players in the minor leagues. Additionally, there have been more than 120 such competitors in the majors.[15] Although the Mexican nation is well represented on the field, there is not yet a single individual from the country enshrined at the sport's pinnacle. Ortega indicated that since the hall flies the flags of the various nations of enshrinees, "I see the flags of the United States,

Puerto Rico, Cuba, and other nations before the hall. It would be so wonderful for me to be able to see the tricolor raised in Cooperstown!"

For the present, Ortega is quite content to see the changes that have taken place in baseball and its relations to Latino fans and players. He recalls that when he started in the 1980s, only about five or six teams broadcast in Spanish, and even those would often leave the Spanish-language announcers behind during road trips. Now, it is a different situation. As the game has become more responsive to Spanish speakers, a new generation of broadcasters is presenting the action to this population. When asked to name some of the "younger" lights among today's Spanish-language baseball announcers, Ortega mentioned the following: Ángel Castillo (with the Phillies since 2012), Alberto "Beto" Ferreiro (with the Marlins since 2018), Oscar Soria (with the Diamondbacks since 1999), Francisco "Paco" Romero (with the Astros since 2008), Jorge Jarrín (with the Dodgers since 2004), and Néstor Rosario (with the Mets since 2011). "What these individuals are doing is to make known the talent of the Spanish-surnamed athletes to the aficionados of the sport," he said. These players, and Latinos' ties to the game, are an "essential part of our culture." As Ortega argued toward the end of our interview, "This is a way to bring our cultures/peoples together: through our mutual love for this wonderful game."[16]

New publications, in 2017 and 2018, by the highly respected and University of Central Florida–based TIDES (The Institute for Diversity and Ethics in Sports) have noted that MLB has done a fairly effective job of fielding players of color, with 42.5 percent of opening day rosters in 2018 being comprised of Latino, African American, or Asian participants (Latinos make up the majority of those athletes of color and approximately 34 percent of all MLB competitors). Given this makeup, the work that Ortega and his cohorts do is of prime importance to maintaining the relationship with current fans, as well as developing the next generation that will come through the turnstiles of MLB parks.[17]

A recent article by Jose de Jesús Ortíz for the online journal *La vida baseball* provides support for the arguments presented above regarding Ortega's (and indeed, about other Spanish-language baseball broadcasters') significance and contributions to the sport and the community. Ortíz's essay summarizes his baseball recollections of growing up in Southern California. What initially generated the ties to sport was that he and his Mexican-born father "became baseball fans by listening to Jarrín, a fellow immigrant who was born in Cayambe, Ecuador, and learned baseball only after arriving in Los Angeles in 1955 at age 19." Indeed, Ortíz goes on to say, his household, certainly one of many in the region, was a place where (like Ortega's domicile in Tijuana) the family "often lowered the volume on Scully's television broadcast ... so we could listen to Jarrín *en Español* on the radio." The sum total of this, he argues, can be seen in the stands at Dodger Stadium. "There's no telling where the Dodgers would be without Jarrín, but you cannot deny that this impact on the organization is felt daily. If you don't believe me, just look at our *gente* in the crowd."[18]

Likewise, a Mexican-born friend of Bill Swank informed him that in regard to the Padres, "'most people think that all Mexicans are soccer fans, but in Baja California and Sonora, they love *béisbol*.' He and his family can't wait for the season to start! [Then] he'll start reciting [a list of] his favorite Mexican players: Aurelio Rodríguez, Roberto Ávila, Fernando Valenzuela, Memo Luna."[19] Another example of the cross-border support for the Padres comes from a 2006 article in the *San Diego Tribune*. In an article titled "Spanish-Language Announcer Celebrates Milestone with Padres," Irasema Mayoral Liera quoted an individual who has been listening to the team on Spanish-language radio for 38 years. "Eduardo describes the game in a way that makes you feel like you're in the stands." This fan's son even did a college-level thesis based on his many years of listening to Ortega. A final, and poignant, example of the significance of these broadcasts is also cited in this article: "Last weekend against the Arizona Diamondbacks, Ortega said a fan had emailed to say he could no longer go to games because his visa renewal was late."[20]

Even more significant than his accomplishments with the Padres are Ortega's efforts to connect the Latino community with the broader society of the United States, and baseball is a perfect mechanism with which to accomplish this. He is a consummate professional and always argues that the presence of the Spanish-surnamed in our nation is a promising development.

Not only are there more Latinos than ever on the field, but also by introducing these players to a national audience, broadcasters such as Ortega help to unite our nation's diverse groups through our mutual love for the sport. Here, he follows in the grand tradition of his idols: Canel, Ramírez, Jarrín, and of course, Don Mario. Eduardo Ortega is a shining example of the power of baseball to unite individuals of various backgrounds through a passion for the "national pastime." Certainly, he, and his predecessors, are worthy subjects for study by historians of the game of baseball. It is time for scholars to notice this critical thread of the game.

Notes

1. John Bauer, "It's a Major League City or It Isn't: San Diego's Padres Step Up to the Big Leagues," in *Time for Expansion Baseball*, ed. Maxwell Kates and Bill Nowlin (Phoenix: SABR, 2018), 195–203. Quote is from p. 197.

2. Stuart Shea and Gary Gillette, *Calling the Game* (Phoenix: Society for American Baseball Research, 2015), 306.

3. See https://www.baseball-reference.com/teams/SDP/index.shtml. Eduardo Ortega interviews with author, April 26, 2018, and December 19, 2018.

4. Eduardo Ortega, interviews with author, April 26, 2018, and December 19, 2018.

5. Unless otherwise noted, biographical information is taken from the author's interviews with Eduardo Ortega.

6. In addition to the interviews noted above, see Bryce Miller, "Padres' Eduardo Ortega Is a Spanish-Language Star," March 27, 2018, https://www.sandiegouniontribune.com/sports/padres/sdut-eduardo-ortega-baseballs-boy-in-a-tree-2016mar27-story.html.

7. Curt Smith, *A Talk in the Park: Nine Decades of Baseball Tales from the Broadcast Booth* (Washington, DC: Potomac Books, 2011), 230..

8. See Jorge Encinas, "How Latino Players Are Helping Major League Baseball Learn Spanish," March 26, 2017, https://www.npr.org/sections/codeswitch/2017/03/26/519676864/how-major-league-baseball-came-to-officially-speak-spanish; Jerry Milani, "On the Airwaves and Online, Spanish Language Baseball Business Grows," March 27, 2018, https://www.portada-online.com/2018/03/27/on-the-airwaves-and-online-spanish-language-baseball-business-grows/.

9. Smith, *A Talk in the Park*, 230–231. Also Curt Smith, interview with author, March 16, 2018.

10. For more information on this, see Samuel O. Regalado, "Roberto Clemente: Images, Identity and Legacy," *International Journal for the History of Sport 25*, no. 6 (2008): 678–690.

11. James Wagner, "When Spanish Names (Don't) Flummox English-Speaking Baseball Announcers."

12. Bill Swank, email messages to author, February 13 and 14, 2019. See Bill Swank in conjunction with the San Diego Historical Society, *Baseball in San Diego: From the Plaza to the Padres* (Charleston, SC: Arcadia Publishing, 2005), 42, 45, 47, 58, 59, 61. Mr. Swank also provided further details in emails to this author on February 13 and 14, 2019.

13. Eduardo Ortega, email message to author, March 23, 2019.

14. Miller, "Padres' Eduardo Ortega Is a Spanish Language Star." See also Alexandra Mendoza, "Eduardo Ortega: 30 Anos Como Voz de los Padres," April 9, 2016, https://www.sandiegouniontribune.com/hoy-san-diego/sdhoy-eduardo-ortega-30-anos-como-voz-de-los-padres-2016apr09-story.html.

15. See http://www.baseball-almanac.com/players/birthplace.php?loc=Mexico.

16. See the following websites: https://www.mlb.com/phillies/team/broadcasters; https://www.linkedin.com/in/alberto-el-beto-ferreiro-94344834; http://arizona.diamondbacks.mlb.com/ari/team/exec_bios/soria_oscar.jsp; http://houston.astros.mlb.com/hou/team/exec_bios/romero_francisco.html; http://www.sportsnetla.com/on-air-team-sportsnet-la-talent/jorge-jarrin-play-by-play-announcer-sportsnet-la1; https://www.mlb.com/mets/team/broadcasters.

17. Richard Lapchick, Mark Mueller, Todd Currie, and Destini Orr, "The 2017 Racial and Gender Report Card: Major League Baseball," April 18, 2017, http://nebula.wsimg.com/d96daf1e011b077b2fd9ff4cfe4bf1bc?AccessKeyId=DAC3A56D8FB782449D2A&disposition=0&alloworigin=1. See also Richard Lapchick, Blair Neelands, Brett Estrella, Paris Rainey, and Zachary Gerhart, "The 2018 Racial and Gender Report Card: Major League Baseball," April 12, 2018, http://nebula.wsimg.com/2b20e1bb7ea3fad9f45263b846342d04?-AccessKeyId=DAC3A56D8FB782449D2A&disposition=0&alloworigin=1.

18. Jose de Jesus Ortiz, "Why I Fell in Love with Baseball," February 2019, https://www.lavidabaseball.com/jaime-jarrin-dodgers-voice/.

19. Bill Swank, email to author, February 11, 2019.

20. Irasema Mayoral Liera, "Spanish-Language Announcer Celebrates Milestone with Padres," August 27, 2006, http://legacy.sandiegouniontribune.com/uniontrib/20060827/news lz1j27ortega.html.

Orlando Sánchez-Diago

Jorge Iber

The infatuation of many Spanish speakers (in the United States, Caribbean, and Central and South America) with Major League Baseball (MLB) is long-standing, but the consistent broadcasting of MLB games in that language to fans both inside and outside of the United States is a more recent phenomenon. A perusal of the "bible of baseball," the *Sporting News*, documented World Series broadcasts being transmitted to Cuba, Puerto Rico, and Mexico as early as 1940.[1] Still, as historian Samuel O. Regalado noted in a 1995 essay, through the mid–1950s, "Spanish-speaking fans in the United States had no avenues for listening to any games in their native tongue."[2] The breakthrough for connecting the sport, and a specific team, with such a fan base occurred when the Dodgers left Brooklyn in 1958 and moved to Los Angeles, a community with approximately 600,000 Spanish-surnamed people (according to the 1960 census), many eager to hear games of the new hometown side.[3] Aficionados in Southern California thus bonded with the franchise through the voices of René Cárdenas, later to be joined by Jaime Jarrín.

The story of the Dodgers' offerings in *Español* are well known, but a similar effort, which has generated little academic attention, is that of the team in another city with a substantial Spanish-speaking population: Houston, Texas. When the National League awarded an expansion club to the Bayou City in 1960, which had a Latino populace of around 75,000,[4] the principal owner, Judge Roy Hofheinz, presciently recognized that such broadcasts would be valuable for promoting the team in the Southwest (and, eventually, into Mexico and other parts of Latin America). The newly christened Colt .45s, just as the Dodgers had earlier and the Padres would do later, sought to attract those fans from their on-field genesis in 1962.

A recent publication by the Society of American Baseball Research, titled *Calling the Game: Baseball Broadcasting from 1920 to the Present* by Stuart Shea, provides readers with a team-by-team history of how franchises have reached out via radio and television. The chapter on the Colt .45s/Astros, while noting the team's Spanish-language efforts, provides but superficial coverage. Importantly, Shea noted that Judge Hofheinz decided to retain control of the team's broadcasters. In this way, he countered a trend that saw sponsors exclusively determining announcer hires. This was done because he "didn't want or need to give up control in exchange for a few extra dollars, so he did it his way."[5] This decision played a key role in the career trajectory of Orlando Sánchez-Diago. Shea noted that the team immediately worked with KLVL, "the city's first exclusively Spanish-language station, as the flagship …[for] a large slate of live home games and road re-creations over a five-station network from 1962 to the mid–1970s."[6] Hofheinz made this decision because he "saw a huge potential market in the Southern United States, Mexico, and in other parts of Latin America for Major League Baseball."[7]

Although it is customary for expansion clubs to follow an ideology of going with "youth" when fielding a team, the Colt .45s took the opposite approach when deciding on the composition of its Spanish-language crew: going with two experienced and respected announcers. The first individual selected was already well known in the United States: the man who started Dodger broadcasts back in 1958, René Cárdenas. In an interview with this author, he indicated that advertisers familiar with his work bought the rights to Colt .45 games and asked if René would serve the new franchise. Eventually, Hofheinz offered him the post. The judge then asked Cárdenas to select his partner. Having worked previously with Orlando in Nicaragua and knowing that Sánchez-Diago was calling games in Venezuela after his exile from Cuba, he suggested the veteran broadcaster. The judge telegrammed and asked Orlando to visit Houston for an interview.[8] At the time he arrived in Texas, Sánchez-Diago was already a well-seasoned, well-traveled, and established *voz* in the world of sports.

Orlando was born on December 16, 1908, in Cienfuegos and eventually made his way to Havana. According to his son, Orlando Sánchez, his father began his career in the early 1930s. "He worked for CMQ, wrote articles, called horse races at the Hipódromo de Marianao (also known as Parque Oriental),[9] and even served as MC for events at the Tropicana. He was also reporting on the All-Star Game and the World Series back to Cuba by the late 1930s."[10] In the next decade, he was working for Cadena Oriental and was a cohost of a popular program called *Tribunal Deportivo* (Sports tribunal) discussing amateur baseball. This show featured another aspect of the sport beloved by Cubans: arguing about the quality of individual players and strategy.[11] Sánchez-Diago would also man the microphone for COCO, being part of a triumvirate of announcers at that network (the other two being Felo Ramírez and Pedro Galiana) eventually inducted into the Cuban Baseball Hall of Fame. Orlando also is remembered for calling the last Amateur World Series held in Cuba, in 1943. Indeed, he is mentioned on various occasions in the classic work by Roberto González-Echevarría, *The Pride of Havana*. By the late 1940s, that author argued, Orlando was recognized as the nation's "dean of announcers."[12]

After the installment of the Castro dictatorship, Sánchez-Diago left his homeland to work in the Venezuelan capital, calling games for Los Tiburones de La Guaira and the Leones del Caracas. Shortly thereafter, he sent for his family; his wife, Olga (they had met, appropriately enough, at the Gran Estadio de La Habana in 1955), son, Orlando (born in 1957), and daughter, Gemi (born in 1959). The family remained in Venezuela through the latter months of 1961. It was during this time that Orlando got the telegram from Judge Hofheinz with the invitation to visit about the job. There was one issue, however: how to get visas for him and the rest of the family quickly? René asked the judge if he "knew" anyone in Washington who might make it possible to expedite the requests. Hofheinz then called his friend, Vice President Lyndon Johnson. After the Colt .45s' owner connected with Blair House, arrangements took but a couple of days. Orlando and his family would be in Texas (and he, eventually, in Apache Junction, Arizona, for spring training) in time for the start of the team's inaugural campaign. Orlando and Olga were eternally grateful for this assistance and named their last child Lynda (born in 1965) in honor of now-president Johnson.[13]

The novelty of the team's broadcasts in this language was noted in various parts of Texas during the lead-up to the first regular season game on April 10, 1962. By that time, the Colt .45s had established a network of stations (23 in total), including five in Spanish. These were as follows: KCOR (San Antonio), XEO (Brownsville), KOPY (Alice), XEOR (McAllen), and KVOZ (Laredo). Given that Orlando was in Arizona with the team during spring training, it is interesting to note that articles in the lead-up to the start of the campaign did not mention him at all. Indeed, one story, from April 6, indicated that René was on board and "another ... announcer will be added to the Latin Network and announced later."[14]

Cárdenas and Sánchez-Diago would work at the stadium when Houston was in town and do re-creations based on the call by Gene Elston and Loel Passe for road games. Initially, Orlando did not know much English, and his partner translated for him. During our interview, René noted that the process worked well, except for when Passe would throw out one of his southern witticisms. "It was a nightmare trying to understand Loel

Orlando Sánchez-Diago (right) and René Cárdenas at the Colt 45s' first spring training in Arizona, 1962 (courtesy Sánchez-Diago family).

Passe because of his unusual phrases.... After all, how would you translate 'Hot ziggety dog and sassafras tea?'"[15] Orlando was quite fortunate in not speaking sufficient English during these first years to even attempt to decipher such a statement.

The game broadcasts were not the only endeavors by the club to attract Spanish-speaking fans. There was also a tour guide out of Corpus

Orlando Sánchez-Diago (center) and René Cárdenas (right) at Colts Stadium (courtesy Sánchez-Diago family).

Christi who would pick up folks from his city as well as Harlingen and other locales in the Rio Grande Valley to bring customers to the ballpark. Additionally, the broadcast pair served as guides for tours of Colt Stadium and, eventually, the Astrodome. Overall, the two men operated as "the franchise's ambassadors to Houston's Latino community."[16]

In addition to continuing to reach Spanish-speaking fans throughout Texas, Cárdenas and Sánchez-Diago broadcast on an even broader stage when, in 1966, the team, now with the Astros moniker, established a radio network targeting "82 radio stations in 13 countries throughout Mexico, Central America, South America and the Caribbean" in conjunction with the U.S. State Department, the Pan American Union, and the office of the Commissioner of Baseball. This endeavor sought to serve three major purposes. First, the team hoped to establish itself among the many millions of MLB fans in this part of the world. Second, there was a patriotic motive, as Judge Hofheinz noted that "it creates a great deal of goodwill for our country and presents a product that is common to the people of all languages and faiths." Last, this was an opportunity for the Astros to be in a better position to recruit talent in various Spanish-speaking countries.[17] The initial reactions were positive, as René noted that "we have had hundreds of letters saying how the people of their country now regard the Astros as 'our ball club.'... The commercials on our broadcasts sell four primary products—the United States, the City of Houston, the Astrodome, and the Astros.'"[18]

In 1967, team officials visited Nicaragua, Venezuela, Panama, and Costa Rica to review the progress of players in winter ball and also received the good wishes of many fans for their Spanish-language team.[19] Given that the United States was in direct competition with the communist world (spearheaded by Cuba in this region), having a Cuban exile behind the microphone of MLB broadcasts was likely an added benefit as far as the Department of State was concerned. Unfortunately, the network was never profitable, as indicated by Fred Hofheinz in an interview with this author, and eventually ceased operation toward the end of the family's ownership of the club.[20] Even though the international efforts may have struggled to pay their way, by the early 1970s, the local (in Texas) version of the broadcast was proving quite popular and, according to at least one report, profitable. At this time, the stations included XEAM (Brownsville), KRBZ (Freeport), KINE (Kingsville), and KBUY-FM (Fort Worth).

An article leading into the 1972 season provided readers with a bit more background on Orlando than had previously appeared in print. It noted that his career started in Cuba in 1930, "where he was the first sportscaster to recreate major league baseball. He later was the first man in South American history to broadcast live a professional baseball game." Unfortunately, the article did not indicate when this occurred, and the family did not have any materials providing greater specificity concerning these events. The piece also noted that Sánchez-Diago had been named "Outstanding Sportscaster" in South America on five separate occasions.[21]

In 1962, the team put up the Sánchez-Diago family upon their arrival in Texas at the Surrey House, which also served as the team's hotel. From there, given the generosity of the Hofheinz family, who paid him year-round, and Orlando's continued excellent work, the family prospered and became an integral part of the Houston community. During the years they worked together, René and Orlando and their families' households became a hub for Latino ballplayers visiting Houston. Among the many guests Orlando, Gemi, and Lynda recalled were Orlando Cepeda, Preston Gomez, César Cedeño, Felipe Alou, and many others. Gomez, a fellow Cuban, in particular, enjoyed visits to the domicile when San Diego was in town as some of Olga's good Cuban food surely helped ease the pain of the dismal early Padres campaigns. Other visitors included the legendary owners of teams from Venezuela, such as Pedro "Panza" Padrón (the owner the Tiburones). Overall, the family's house was a center for a Latino baseball milieu during those years.

In addition to the sport's predominance in his house, the young Orlando also visited the Astrodome for all home games, warming up legends such as Roberto Clemente by playing catch with outfielders during mid-innings. He also served as a press runner for the team until he graduated from the University of Houston at the age of 22. Further, the Sánchez-Diago residence was a center for many of their countrymen who settled in the area during the 1960s; dinners were often followed by games of domino as well as more discussions about baseball. Orlando enjoyed his time with the Astros and was able to connect directly with the mostly Mexican American populace in the region. Many in the community embraced his most famous catchphrase, "*Swing y se avànica*" (Swing and he fans). The fact that the Astros' broadcasters were of Nicaraguan and Cuban extraction was never an issue with local fans. Cárdenas and Sánchez-Diago did their job and helped to make the team a vital part of the Latino community.

The Spanish-language duo worked for the Houston franchise between 1962 and 1975. After that season, the team terminated both announcers and decided to stop broadcasting in Spanish. *The Handbook of Texas*'s article on Judge Hofheinz notes that he had suffered a stroke in 1970 and was subsequently confined to a wheelchair. By 1975, his myriad real estate holdings (which included Astroworld, Ringling Brothers, and a series of "Astrodomain" hotels) was "burdened by high interest rates" and around $38 million in debt. Eventually, ownership of the team passed to two of his major creditors, General Electric Credit and Ford Motor Credit. (The two organizations ran the club between 1975 and 1978, then Ford was on its own for the 1979 season—subsequently, John McMullen bought the club that year and operated it until 1992.[22]) René returned to his homeland and remained there until the 1979 Sandinista revolution forced him to leave (his half brother was shot for having worked for the Somoza regime).[23] Orlando Sánchez, however, would remain in Texas, and begin working for several local Spanish-language stations between 1976 and 1987. Olga also helped the family make ends meet by working at the local Coca-Cola bottling plant for more than 20 years as well as cleaning offices at night.[24] Although no longer directly employed by the team, the Astros continued to be the senior Orlando's passion. Subsequently, he worked at a couple of stations, including KLVL (1480 AM, also known as Radio Morales) out of Pasadena, Texas, and also with La Tremenda, where he would watch games and describe the action (KXYZ 1320 AM). He also authored articles on sports for a local Spanish-language newspaper called *La Informacion*.

It was at La Tremenda that Sánchez-Diago came into contact with another Cuban, Rolando Becerra, who had made the move to Texas from Miami in 1980. Becerra encouraged station management to pursue a deal with the Astros, now under the ownership of McMullen. This made perfect business sense from both the team's and station's standpoint, given the dramatic changes in the city's demographic mix. According to the 1980 census, the Hispanic (using the term utilized at that time) population of Houston had increased to more than 281,000 and would grow by another 60 percent by 1990.[25] Given the striking upsurge, it was not surprising that the team's new leadership moved to reestablish the Astros' connections to Spanish speakers. Radio broadcasts resumed in 1986, pairing Becerra with a man he affectionately referred to as "El Viejo" (Orlando was now 78). This line-up would continue through the end of the McMullen period in 1992.[26]

Rolando Becerra was born in Cuba in 1949 but left the country in early 1961. As he indicated during our interview, though born on the island, his "cultural life" (he spent his teen years in Pahokee, Florida) was pure "baseball, guitars, and rock and roll"; in other words, by the time he reached adulthood, Rolando was a "typical all-American kid." He hoped to start a musical career and wound up in Miami (with stops in Puerto Rico), eventually settling into a radio career in the Cuban American mecca. After marriage, he sought a more stable occupation, and that led to his move to Houston. When he met with Orlando, he "was totally unaware of how legendary" his new color commentator was. What most impressed Rolando was his sidekick's encyclopedic knowledge of the sport. "He had been to Ebbets Field, the Polo Grounds, and interviewed legends of the game. He even worked for a rich man who chartered a plane to get the signal for a World Series in order to rebroadcast the game to Cuba in the 1930s." The audience, not surprisingly, was comprised primarily of Mexican Americans. As previously with René, Orlando's excellent announcing and knowledge of the game continued to attract fans, regardless of ethnic background. Although continuing to re-create games from Houston while the team was on the road, Becerra and Sánchez-Diago did get to travel with the club to New York as the Astros played the Mets in the National League Champion Series in 1986, and were behind the microphone to call Houston's heartbreaking loss in game six of that series, a 7–6 Mets victory in 16 innings. Additionally, the two also broadcast spring training games in 1987 and 1988 from Kissimmee, Florida.[27]

As had occurred with René, Orlando and his family became close to the Becerras, and the two men continued to work well together until the club's sale to Drayton McLane in 1992. Rolando indicated that shortly after the completion of the transaction, the new owner stopped by the Spanish-language radio booth and stated that he would continue to emphasize this part of the club's operations. Shortly thereafter, however, Jaime Hildreth, the organization's director of broadcasting, contacted the announcers and indicated that team management had decided to go in another direction. The pair was then replaced by Francisco Ernesto Ruiz (who covered the team between 1993 and 2007) and Manny Lopez (1993).[28] Orlando took his firing extremely hard, and his children indicated during our interviews that his termination haunted him until his death in 1998.[29]

So, what to make of the career/life of Orlando Sánchez-Diago? On the surface, it is easy to point out some of his many accomplishments: he was the *voz* of the Colt .45s/Astros for over two decades; considered to be one of the greatest sports broadcasters in the history of prerevolutionary Cuba; and one of the first Spanish-language announcers of an MLB team to be heard internationally. The team has continued to broadcast in Spanish ever since the 1986 season, indicating that the market is a worthwhile one and that it forms a core element of the team's fan base. It is to the major credit of Judge Roy Hofheinz, René Cárdenas, and the subject of this essay that the Houston franchise, with some fits and stops along the way, was a pioneer in such endeavors for MLB. Whereas the Dodgers were the first to broadcast in Spanish (even prior to their arrival in Los Angeles, with Buck Canel broadcasting some Brooklyn games between 1954 and 1957[30]), the Colt .45s/Astros have the distinction of being the first club to broadcast in Spanish and English from their inception.

A recent article by American studies scholar Jorge E. Moraga focused on some key trends in sport and broadcasting in *Español*. At the current moment in time, Moraga argued, Spanish-language media is "no longer in the periphery of executive and media pundits alike, Latinos have ensured U.S. sport mediascapes comprise a bicultural, binational, and bilingual ethos.... Bilingual media is as powerful as it is necessary."[31] How did we get to this point in time? It is by capturing the story of the life and career of individual broadcasters such as Orlando Sánchez-Diago that historians can begin to shed light on the account of how individual teams and announcers helped to usher in an era where Spanish speakers are valued by MLB, not just for the talent they bring to the field but also for the passion ingrained in them as fans of "our national pastime."

Notes

1. "Latins Like W.S. Broadcasts," *Sporting News*, November 7, 1940, 6.
2. Samuel O. Regalado, "'Dodgers Beisbol Is on the Air: The Development and Impact of the Dodgers' Spanish Language Broadcasts, 1958–1984," *California History* (Fall 1995): 280–289. Quote is on p. 283.
3. *Ibid*. This statistic is presented on p. 284. This was not the Dodgers' first attempt at reaching out to local Spanish speakers. In their last season in Brooklyn, the team scheduled to offer some games in Spanish. See "40 Brook Games in Spanish," *Sporting News*, March 20, 1957, 25.

4. See Arnoldo De Leon, Ethnicity in the Sunbelt: *Mexican Americans* in Houston (Houston: Center for Mexican American Studies, University of Houston, 2001), 98.

5. Stuart Shea, Calling the Game: *Baseball Broadcasting* from 1920 to the Present (Phoenix: Society for American Baseball Research, 2015), 251–259. Quote is from p. 253.

6. *Ibid.*, 253.

7. *Ibid.*

8. Author's interview with René Cárdenas, April 15, 2020. Copy in author's possession. See also Milton H. Jamail, *Venezuelan Bust, Baseball Boom: Andres Reiner and Scouting the New Frontier* (Lincoln, NE: Bison Books, 2008), 48–49.

9. For more information on this facility, see https://www.todocuba.org/esta-es-la-historia-del-hipodromo-de-marianao-la-meca-de-las-carreras-en-cuba/. Accessed on August 10, 2020.

10. Author's interview with Orlando Sanchez, April 9, 2020. Copy in author's possession.

11. For more information on the significance of arguments concerning baseball among Cuban men, see Thomas Carter, "Baseball Arguments: *Aficionismo* and Masculinity at the Core of *Cubanidad*," in *Sport in Latin American Society: Past and Present*, ed. J.A. Mangan and Lamartine P. DaCosta (London: Frank Cass, 2002), 117–138.

12. See Roberto Gonzalez-Echevarria, *The Pride of Havana: A History of Cuban Baseball* (New York: Oxford University Press, 1999), 65, 66, 246, 248. See also César Brioso, *Havana Hardball: Spring Training, Jackie Robinson, and the Cuban League* (Gainesville: University Press of Florida, 2015), 50.

13. Author's interview with Lynda Kroneman and Gemy Boss, April 21, 2020. Copy of interview in author's possession. See also Jamail, *Venezuelan Bust, Baseball Boom*, 49.

14. See "Colt .45 Games Will Be Broadcast in Spanish," *McAllen Monitor*, April 8, 1962; "Radio Chain for Houston Grows to 23," *Austin American*, April 6, 1962; "Cardenas to Air Colts Diamond Tilts," *Pampa Daily News*, April 6, 1962.

15. Jamail, *Venezuelan Bust, Baseball Boom*, 49. See also Shea, Calling the Game, 253–254.

16. "Domed Stadium Tours Started," *Odessa American*, April 18, 1965; Shea, Calling the Game, 254.

17. "New Astro Radio Loop Composed of Outlets," *Baytown News*, July 17, 1966.

18. "Astros Go Spanish, Si!" *Bryan Eagle*, July 17, 1966. See also Edgar W. Ray, *The Grand Huckster: Houston's Judge Roy Hofheinz, Genius of the Astrodome* (Memphis: Memphis State University Press, 1980), 279, 348, 387.

19. "Astro Latin Trip 'Better than Ever,'" *Marshall News Messenger*, January 29, 1967; "South of the Border Tour Pleases Astros' Group," *Austin America-Statesman*, January 30, 1967.

20. Author's interview with Fred Hofheinz, April 13, 2020. Copy of interview in author's possession.

21. "Spanish Broadcasts Help Astros Gain Popularity," *Tyler Morning Telegraph*, April 4, 1972.

22. Jill S. Seeber, "Hofheinz, Roy Mark," in *Handbook of Texas Online*, http://www.tshaonline.org/handbook/online/articles/fho87. Accessed on August 12, 2020.

23. Kevin Baxter, "The Sunday Profile: Wins and Losses: René Cárdenas Brought Baseball to Millions with His Pioneering Broadcasts in Spanish. Now, Shaken by Tough Times, He Clings to His Claim to the Hall of Fame," *Los Angeles Times*, June 18, 1995. See https://www.latimes.com/archives/la-xpm-1995-06-18-ls-14323-story.html. Accessed on August 12, 2020; Houston Astros, "René Cárdenas Biography," July 31, 2008. See http://www.mlb.com/hou/fan_forum/cardenas_bio.jsp. Accessed on August 12, 2020.

24. Author's interview with Rolando Becerra, April 27, 2020. Copy of interview in author's possession.

25. See http://www.houstontx.gov/planning/Demographics/docs_pdfs/Cy/coh_race_ethn_1980-2010.pdf.

26. Shea, *Calling the Game*, 257.

27. Author's interview with Rolando Becerra, April 27, 2020. Copy of interview in author's possession.

28. *Ibid.*

29. Author's interview with Lynda Kroneman and Gemi Boss, April 21, 2020. Copy of interview in author's possession.

30. See the following for more information on Canel: Bill Madden, "Canel's Voice Carries On," *New York Daily News*, September 18, 2005, https://www.nydailynews.com/archives/nydn-features/canel-voice-carries-article-1.621209; Luis Rodríguez-Mayoral, "Buck Canel: The Voice of 'Beisbol' throughout Latin America," *La Vida Baseball*, September 19, 2017, https://www.lavidabaseball.com/buck-canel-ford-frick-award/.

31. Both articles accessed on August 13, 2020. Jorge E. Moraga, "On ESPN Deportes: Latinos, Sport Media, and the Cultural Politics of Visibilities," *Journal of Sport and Social Issues* 42, no. 6 (2018): 470–497. Quotes are from pp. 490 and 492.

Amaury Pi-González

Jorge Iber

A brief mention in newspapers throughout the country in early June 1978 noted that the Oakland Athletics, a franchise that had recently been broadcasting their English-language offerings via a 10-watt facility located on the campus of the University of California at Berkeley (the signal was so weak that according to a historian who has written about the A's broadcasting history, it "barely carried as far as the Oakland-Alameda Coliseum"),[1] decided to increase their reach and offer Sunday home contests to Spanish-speaking aficionados on a 1,000-watt *emisora de radio* (radio station): KOFY.[2]

Behind the microphones for the green and gold would be Amaury Pi-González and Julio González. For the Cuban-born Amaury, this unique opportunity marked the beginning of a meandering 40-plus-year career in print, radio, and television that has seen him announce games *en Español* for not only the A's but also for the Giants, Mariners, Angels, the NBA's Golden State Warriors, and even, quite recently, select games for the NHL's San Jose Sharks (just how does one translate terms familiar to aficionados of the sport such as "biscuit in the basket" and "natural hat trick" into Spanish?).[3]

The transmissions by Amaury and Julio were not the Athletics' first foray into this market, as in 1968, Puerto Rican–born Victor Manuel Torres, a World War II veteran and Latino community activist with ties to the first Spanish-language station in the Bay Area, KBRG, approached Finley about the opportunity to reach this audience in the team's new domicile. This was a shrewd move by Finley, as Torres, a fan of the Giants from his early days in New York City, had previously approached the Stoneham family in the early 1960s to air games, only to be turned down due to that franchise's commitment to KSFO. Given that the region had a significant Hispanic population (with Oakland being around 8 percent and San Francisco at almost 10 percent, according to the 1970 census), Charlie knew an opportunity to make money when he saw it, even if he was not aware of the name of the actual language in which games would be broadcast. Torres announced games for the Athletics between 1968 and 1971 when, tragically, he was left a paraplegic due to a hit-and-run accident. This *pionero* (pioneer) of the baseball airways passed away in 1997 at the age of 76.[4]

The story of Amaury Pi-González ties into several aspects of the Cuban American story after the Castro revolution of 1959. Amaury was born on October 4, 1944, in Havana, the son of Joaquín Pi and Olga González. Joaquín was born in Spain, and as many of his countrymen did, he sought better opportunities in Cuba. Eventually, he owned his own plumbing business in the capital city. Olga worked as the enterprise's secretary and kept its books. There was another son born to the marriage, Joaquín Jr., also known as Jay, in 1952. During his childhood, as perfunctory among Cuban youths, Joaquín took Amaury to the Gran Estadio de La Habana to watch contests between the Habana Leones (Lions), Almendares Alacranes (Scorpions), Cienfuego Elefantes (Elephants), and the Tigres (Tigers) de Marianao. Amaury's recollections of those days are familiar to many who followed the Cuban league during the early 1950s. The association he argued, was "considered 'the league' in Latin America for American big-league players. Many players from that generation have told me that Cuba was the highest-paying professional league aside from Major League Baseball at the time."[5]

From an early age, Amaury's activities foreshadowed his career on the radio. Often, he would follow the legendary Felo Ramírez's lead, with a broom substituting for a microphone, and he would "broadcast" games in the family domicile. "I remember that in my patio in Havana I would grab a broom and turn it upside down and impersonate Felo…. [He gave his calls] great enthusiasm, in the Caribbean style there was always much zeal."[6]

After the revolution's "triumph," Joaquín and Olga faced the circumstances that most other business owners endured on the island—that is, their businesses, built with their own sweat and toil, were eventually "nationalized" to make it possible for Castro and his cronies to make the proceeds available (at least theoretically) to "the people." Shortly after this catastrophic event, Joaquín and Olga decided that the country's economic and political situation had become untenable and submitted Amaury to the auspices of the Catholic Church in a program that became known as Operación Pedro Pan (Operation Peter Pan), which, all told, brought approximately 14,000 Cuban children to the United States.[7]

Many of these individuals, with Yale University professor Carlos Eire being the most famous through his work *Waiting for Snow in*

Havana: Confessions of a Cuban Boy, wound up scattered throughout the nation.[8] A good portion of these Peter Pans ended up in locales where there were few other Hispanics. For example, after a stay in Miami, Dr. Eire eventually went to live in Bloomington, Illinois. Amaury was more fortunate than most of his Peter Pan brothers and sisters in that he was already familiar with South Florida, having visited what would become the Cuban American mecca in 1958. Additionally, he already had a relative, an aunt named Violeta, living in the city when he left his homeland for good in 1961. In an email exchange with this author, Amaury noted that his most prominent recollection of his flight to freedom via Pan American Airways was being surrounded by several Catholic clergymen (who were also being expelled from the country). The bitterness created by the revolution, and what was done to his parents' business, left an indelible mark on his disposition down to the present. The pride in being Latino, and Cuban American specifically, has always shone through in his work and commentary.[9]

Pi-González, who aspired to be an architect, had completed his education by the time he left his homeland. He attended Colegio La Luz (The Light School) for his elementary education and a military institution, Academia Militar del Caribe (Military Academy of the Caribbean) for his high school education. Although indicating that he wanted to work in facilities planning and construction, Amaury also stated in a recent interview that working as a broadcaster was also a possibility. Visiting with historian Adrian Burgos of the University of Illinois, Amaury recalled that is mother often caught him doing the "imitation of Felo [legendary Cuban broadcaster, Felo Ramírez]" noted previously.[10] In addition to living in southern Florida, Pi-González also had family in New York City and went back and forth between the communities until his brother and parents arrived in the United States in 1962 and 1964, respectively. One of his early memories of life in Miami was riding on buses that had signs designating "colored" and "white" seating sections in the still-segregated city.

Just as it had been in Havana, Amaury's life in his new city continued to revolve around baseball. One of the highlights of his time in the Magic City was spending time as a ball boy and batboy for the Baltimore Orioles (and getting to meet players such as Mike Cuellar, Brooks Robinson, and others) during the team's spring training days at Miami Stadium. Of course, this opportunity made him latch on to the Orioles as his "first" favorite team in the United States. "I will forever remember the players ... during those years.... I was on the field with them, and for me they were like gods.... The Orioles will always have a place in my heart."[11]

In 1966, at age 22, Pi-González was eligible for the draft and entered the army in Coral Gables, Florida. He served in numerous facilities during his hitch: Fort Benning in Georgia, Fort Lee in Virginia, and Fort Lewis in Washington State. Scheduled for deployment (to serve as a medic), he never went to Vietnam and received an honorable discharge in 1968. One of his recollections from his time in the military was the reticence of other Latinos he interacted with (mostly Puerto Ricans, as he recalls) to speak any Spanish, even within their own group.[12]

Although the GI Bill would have provided Amaury with many educational benefits if he so chose, he decided not to attend college. Instead, he went north and began to write columns covering both the Mets and Yankees for a Spanish-language publication based in Newark. In his endeavors in print, he came under the tutelage of Efraín Osorio, who headed that newspaper, *La Voz*, for many years. He also had the opportunity to review movies and even served as an extra on the *Jackie Gleason Show*. This post lasted for about one year and proved quite valuable, providing Amaury with enough background and a line on his résumé, which helped him continue working in sports news after leaving the East Coast.[13]

In July 1969, an old army buddy, Ed Martinez, suggested that Amaury follow him to the West Coast, particularly to San Francisco. There, he continued in the newspaper field, now covering the A's and the Giants for *El Bohemio* (which began publication in 1970 under the ownership of Fernando Rosado). In addition, he leveraged his status as a veteran to hire on as a stockbroker with Dean Witter at an office located in the Embarcadero Center. After several years of employment in both fields, Amaury took the audacious step to knock on Charlie Finley's door seeking the opportunity to broadcast on radio.[14]

With Charlie's blessing, Amaury began (what would be) his first run announcing for the team in 1978 and remained in place even after the A's sale to Walter A. Haas, Jr. (who would own the team until his death in 1995), through the end of the 1993 season. These years would feature some of the most frustrating but also memorable events in the history of the Oakland franchise. Amaury would be behind the microphone to call contests over KFYO during the nadir season of 1979 (the team finished 54–108 and drew approximately 307,000 attendees for their 81 home games), the threats by Charlie to sell the franchise to ownership groups in both New Orleans and Denver, the start of the "Billy Ball" era (in 1980, when the team finished 83–79), all the way through to the renewed glory years of 1988–1990, which featured (another) three consecutive visits to the World Series (as the team did in 1972–1974), and one more championship trophy in 1989 (the year of the Loma Prieta earthquake).

Not surprisingly, Pi-González's most vivid recollections for these years concern two incidents in the World Series: the triumph versus the Giants (a sweep), the temblor, and the crushing disappointment of the home run by Kurt Gibson against Dennis Eckersley the previous year, when the heavily favored A's lost to the Dodgers.[15]

In one of the few times that Amaury commented on the change of team ownership, in 1981, he was asked to discuss the differences between Finley and Haas regarding Spanish-language radio. Whereas Charlie was known to hassle over broadcasting rights up until the very start of a season, Haas was quite different. Pi-González, now with KIQI (as sports director) argued that "we had a contract with Charlie Finley, to carry a few games. But he was very difficult to work with. The difference this year was unbelievable—they recognized the need and helped us every step of the way." Even under these circumstances, the Spanish-language broadcasts carried only 15 games that season. The A's would not broadcast all their games in Spanish until the 1990 season (and that was with KRCX). Another aspect of these broadcasts featured Amaury interviewing A's manager (1986–1995) Tony LaRussa in Spanish (he is from the Spanish/Cuban/Italian area of Tampa, Florida, known as Ybor City).[16]

Although thousands of miles away from the land of his birth, Amaury continued to express concern (and inform people) about goings-on in Cuba. In 1980, as the Mariel boatlift was in full swing, he was part of an eight-hour marathon on San Francisco's Channel 14 on which he moderated a discussion about the cause of the exodus as well as helped raise money to assist the men and women fleeing Castro's gulag. This is just one example of Amaury's work in promoting causes relating to not only his fellow countrymen but all Latinos in the United States.[17]

By the early 1990s, Amaury began to expand into various aspects of Spanish-language broadcasting. While he continued to serve with the A's, he also worked as the sports anchor for KSTS in San Jose, and as the NBA season neared, he was also signed up to become the voice of the Golden State Warriors on KIQI. At this time, the NBA had five other teams, the San Antonio Spurs, Houston Rockets, Miami Heat, Chicago Bulls, and the Portland Trail Blazers broadcasting in Spanish.[18] Pi-González would serve in this capacity until the end of the 1997–1998 season. During these years, the team struggled, notching only one winning season and playoff appearance (1993–1994, when they lost in the first round of the playoffs). There was some disagreement concerning why the franchise decided to end its Spanish-language broadcasts. According to a 1998 report in the *San Francisco Examiner*, Amaury indicated that he was told that the program had lost money the two previous seasons. On the other hand, Warriors' director of broadcasting Dan Becker indicated that the effort was profitable, but the new ownership of KIQI could not clear enough airtime to accommodate the team's broadcasts. Either way, Pi-González was disappointed to see his run in basketball ended. "I don't think they [the

A young Amaury Pi-González behind the microphone for the A's for KBRG (courtesy Amaury Pi-González).

team's new ownership] were very concerned about the Hispanic audience, even though the latest census indicates there are 1.2 million Hispanics in the nine-county Bay Area." By the time that the Warriors ended their Spanish-language endeavors, the number of NBA teams with efforts in *Español* had doubled to one dozen.[19]

In addition to being the *voz* for the Warriors, Amaury also served in a similar capacity for the Giants between 1994 and 2006. During these years, he continued to speak out about Latino issues, helped establish a shrine in San Francisco to honor the contributions of the Spanish-surnamed on the major league diamond, and branched out into international broadcasts of MLB. One topic that concerned Amaury during these years was the perceived slight of Sammy Sosa during the 1998 season as he and Mark McGwire chased immortality for the single-season home run record. While acknowledging McGwire's greatness, Pi-González very publicly asked why Commissioner Selig was in attendance when the white player hit his 62nd home run yet was not present to witness the same feat by a Dominican. In 2000, he also noted that in previous years, Latino ballplayers had to be twice as good as a white athlete to gain any recognition or mention in the papers. Fortunately, times had changed.[20]

To shed further light on the contributions of Latinos to MLB, Amaury was part of a group that helped to establish the Hispanic Heritage Baseball Museum specifically to honor such athletes. One of the principal backers of this endeavor was Giants' great Orlando Cepeda. As of 2020, the hall does not yet have a permanent home in the Bay Area but does have traveling exhibits. Amaury serves as the current vice president of the organization. Last, during his time with San Francisco, Pi-González finally worked with his idol, Felo Ramírez, in 1998 and then called the 1999 National League Champion Series for the Caracol Network, which is based out of Colombia. Further, he has also shared the microphone with Jaime Jarrín and Eduardo Ortega during his career.[21]

Given all the work he does on the air and in the community, it should be more than enough to fill in a professional announcer's time. However, starting in 2003, Amaury took on an even more incongruous assignment: broadcasting contests for two teams simultaneously, by this feat joining the likes of Harry Caray and Jack Brickhouse in MLB history. In addition to continuing to work for the Giants, Pi-González would take off to Seattle and do Spanish-language games for the Mariners on KXLY. "I know most of the pilots on Alaska Airlines," he quipped in 2005. That season, he totaled more than 100 home games between the two clubs. Randy Adamack, vice president of communications for Seattle, noted that "his delivery is exciting and the enthusiasm he brings to the booth is great. It's something you can't teach." Amaury would continue with this hectic pace through the end of the 2006 season.[22]

The roller-coaster aspect of Pi-González's career continued after his stints with the Mariners and Giants. After the 2006 season, Amaury moved on to yet another team in the American League West: the Angels in Anaheim. He would work for them over the 2007 and 2008 campaigns.[23] Then, he returned to the Athletics for 2009 and 2010. Toward the end of that second stint with Oakland, Amaury was the subject of an interesting article by the *Wall Street Journal* which provided readers with a sense of the changing demographics concerning broadcasting baseball in Spanish. This essay noted that Amaury was taken off the air in the middle of the season (in July) by two local AM stations. The issue was not his abilities, but rather the fact that by the early 21st century, the main Spanish-language audience had changed dramatically. Whereas in previous decades the local fans (an estimated 1.5 million in the A's broadcast area by 2010) were primarily Mexican Americans who had grown up with baseball, the current populace was now mostly Mexican, Salvadoran, and Guatemalan, aficionados of soccer, not baseball. Additionally, the populace skewed much younger, while listeners of baseball on the radio skew older. The finances also were troublesome as "Latino radio networks increasingly cater to younger audiences, relying on syndicated talk shows and music rotations

... [that] cost next to nothing for local affiliates to program." Indeed, two stations that Amaury had previously carried A's Spanish broadcasts, KNAT and KLOK, switched to all-Vietnamese and Hindi-Punjabi formats during these years. The result was that Amaury broadcast his last game of the season shortly before he was inducted into the Bay Area Radio Hall of Fame. Also of note, he is the only Spanish-language broadcaster in this august entity.[24]

He would not be silent for long, as he then headed south, once again to broadcast with the Angels, though this time on television with Fox Sports Net West. He continued with the network between 2011 and 2017. By this stage of his career, Amaury had broadcast games in Spanish for every team in the American League West (Angels, Athletics, and Mariners), save the Texas Rangers (of course, also not including the Houston Astros, which joined the division in 2013). In the meantime, just to fill in some of his ample off hours in 2010, Pi-González also served as play-by-play announcer in Spanish for another NBA team, the Los Angeles Clippers.[25] Finally, he returned to his favorite and initial haunt behind the microphone, rejoining Oakland for a third stint starting in 2018.

Another aspect of Amaury's work deals with outreach to the community, particularly with the Bay Area's youth. In 2016, he noted that during his earlier employments with the Athletics, one of his favorite jobs was being part of an endeavor called A's Amigos, which brought schoolchildren and teachers to the Coliseum for individual contests. In his discussion with Franklin Otto, Amaury noted the significance of this work: "I speak to them about the importance of the game, and its history. This is what I most enjoy. Through the game of baseball, you can reach youths and open their eyes. [I emphasize to them the need to] stay in school, study hard, to treat their parents well, and follow the example of the players [who worked diligently to get to the majors]."[26]

As of the start of the 2020 season, Amaury was beginning his 43rd year as a broadcaster. Since the Athletics are a "small market team," he may not have the national recognition that a person such as Jaime Jarrín or Eduardo Ortega has. However, there are few people in the industry who can equal the quality, longevity, and experience of Amaury. He has, literally, done it all regarding Spanish-language radio (and TV) sports. He has also done something very few other announcers have attempted: broadcasting simultaneously for two MLB franchises. As a Cubano greatly influenced by the late, great Felo Ramírez, the announcer he mimicked in his Havana youth, Amaury can take pride in knowing that his idol is likely smiling down from above and listening to his call for Oakland.

Although Felo might not understand all the nuances when listening in on the San Jose Sharks in Spanish, he surely must be proud that

Amaury has broken down so many barriers for the next generation of Spanish-language sports announcers. As a way of summarizing how far he has come and how the industry has transformed, Pi-González recalled that the audience and *locutores* are now much more valued, as they should be, given the demographic changes that have taken place in the United States since the 1970s. "I worked in radio at a time when the Hispanic audience was quite insignificant, and businesses did not buy advertisements. I suffered greatly [with low pay], and I give thanks to God for my tenacity; I never gave in and threw in the towel." After more than four decades calling games, Amaury Pi-González has more than paid his dues and earned his place among the Spanish-language MLB broadcast legends.

Notes

1. Stuart Shea and Gary Gillette, eds., *Calling the Game: Baseball Broadcasting from 1920 to the Present* (Phoenix: Society for American Baseball Research, 2015), 179.

2. "A's Games in Spanish," *Journal News* (White Plains, NY), June 1, 1978.

3. For information on Amaury's work with the Sharks, see https://www.mlb.com/athletics/team/broadcasters.

4. See the following: Shea and Gillette, *Calling the Game*, 178–179; J.L. Pimsleur, "Obituary—Victor Manuel Torres, October 8, 1997," https://www.sfgate.com/news/article/OBITUARY-Victor-iManuel-Torres-2802699.php. Accessed on April 16, 2020. For population information, see http://www.census.gov/population/www/documentation/twps0076/CAtab.pdf.

5. Adrian Burgos, "La Vida Voices: Oakland A's Broadcaster Amaury Pi-Gonzalez," July 11, 2019. See https://www.lavidabaseball.com/la-vida-voices-amaury-pi-gonzalez/.

6. Franklin Otto, *Locutores Hispanos: Perspectivas desde las Grandes Ligas* (New York: Slingerland, 2016), 21.

7. For a primer on this story, see Yvonne M. Conde, *Operation Peter Pan: The Untold Exodus of 14,048 Cuban Children* (New York: Routledge, 1999).

8. Carlos Eire, *Waiting for Snow in Havana: Confessions of a Cuban Boy* (New York: Free Press, 2003). For a detailed examination of the experiences of Pedro Pan children, see Conde, *Operation Pedro Pan*.

9. Email from Amaury Pi-González to author, March 13, 2020. Copy in author's possession.

10. Burgos, "La Vida Voices."

11. Amaury Pi-González, "As the 2020 Season Opens: Your Favorite Baseball Team," July 22, 2020. See https://sportsradioservice2013.wordpress.com/2020/07/22/thats-amaurys-news-and-commentary-as-the-2020-season-opens-your-favorite-baseball-team/. Accessed on August 21, 2020.

12. Amaury Pi-González, interview with author, March 25, 2020. Copy of interview in author's possession.

13. *Ibid*. See also Burgos, "La Vida Voices."

14. For information on this publication, see https://www.mondotimes.com/1/world/us/5/316/14224.

15. Amaury Pi-González, interview with author, March 25, 2020. Copy of interview in author's possession. See also Burgos, "La Vida Voices."

16. Dave Cheit, "Happy, but Not Satisfied," *Berkeley Gazette*, April 21, 1981. See also "Around the Dial," *Sacramento Bee*, April 3, 1990.

17. "Cuban Freedom Telethon," *San Francisco Examiner*, May 3, 1980.

18. "Basketball in Spanish," *Napa Valley Register*, October 31, 1992; Bob Epler, "Seis Equipos de la NBA Transmitirán en Español," *La Voz Hispana*, October 25, 1995.

19. Jorge L. Ortiz, "Warrior Sign Off on Spanish Radio," *San Francisco Examiner*, October 22, 1998.
20. "Radio Team Says Sosa Slighted," *San Francisco Examiner*, September 16, 1998; Roberto Gonzalez and Paul Doyle, "Accent on Greatness," *Hartford Courant*, December 13, 2000.
21. Jorge L. Ortiz, "Shrine to Hispanic Players in Works," *San Francisco Examiner*, May 16, 2000. See also Burgos, "La Vida Voices."
22. George Estrada, "He Makes the Spanish Call," *Corvallis Gazette-Times*, August 4, 2005. See also Shea and Gillette, *Calling the Game*, 315.
23. See Angels Press Release, February 20, 2007, https://web.archive.org/web/20080108152453/http://losangeles.angels.mlb.com/news/press_releases/press_release.jsp?ymd=20070220&content_id=1808785&vkey=pr_ana&fext=.jsp&c_id=ana.
24. Joe Millman, "A Voice of Beisbol Is Benched," September 23, 2010. See https://www.wsj.com/articles/SB10001424052748703440604575495870425594224.
25. Leon Bedolla, "NBA Los Angeles Teams' Games Narrated in Spanish," November 29, 2010. See https://latinola.com/story.php?story=9092.
26. Otto, *Locutores Hispanos*, 153.

Uri Berenguer

Bill Nowlin

In the ranks of Spanish-language baseball broadcasters, Uri Berenguer stands out due to his relative youth. He turned 40 on May 11, 2022, but he already had 17 years as a full-time broadcaster under his belt after the completion of the 2019 season.

Even before he went full time in 2003 with the Red Sox Spanish Radio Network, as it was called at the time, Berenguer was described as "a pressbox veteran, a statistician for the sports radio station WEEI by age 13 who called his first game in Spanish at 17."[1]

His years behind the microphone place him 10th in tenure on the list of Spanish-language broadcasters, behind Juan Alicea, Ervin Higueros, Luis Mayoral, Enrique Oliu, Eduardo Ornelas, Eduardo Ortega, Amaury Pi-González, Óscar Soria, and Alex Treviño. One could say that it's a profession that can offer a lengthy career for those with the talent.

The path that he took to become the *voz* of the Red Sox, though, was a very unusual one. He took a path no one else would want to follow.

He was in the right place at the right time, not long after the Red Sox began to offer Spanish-language broadcasts to a growing Latino community in Greater Boston and New England.

First, let's look at Uri's road to Boston. He came to Boston because of cancer. Uri Berenguer was born on May 11, 1982, in Panama City, Panama. His father, Félix Augusto Berenguer, was director of pharmaceutical sales for the German firm Schering AG. His mother, Daisy Judith Ramos-Berenguer, had worked as a secretary at a doctor's office. They enjoyed a good life, though Uri's father had to travel throughout Latin America for his work and a couple of times to Germany. The couple's first child was a girl, Irana, born on April 23, 1979.

For someone so young at the time, Uri retains some vivid memories from Panama, where the family lived "in a small little neighborhood. I can remember some fun times, playing around, climbing trees and stuff like that." But he also remembers being in a cast after one of the first surgeries he had. "Someone made me a makeshift thing like a skateboard so that I could drag myself around. I dragged myself around the neighborhood. There was this little hill I used to go down."[2]

Uri was diagnosed with cancer in 1984. That's why his right leg was in a cast. The ultimate diagnosis was histiocytosis, a rare form of bone cancer. The family didn't know that at first. All they knew was that he was in pain. "The very first memory that I associate with my cancer was one night. I had been suffering. I was in pain, in my right leg. My bed was up against the wall, and I used to slap my leg against the wall, to try and numb it or find some kind of pain relief. I was crying, and I broke down and told him [his father] how much pain I was in. That's my first memory.

"I remember several treatments that I was put through that were horrific. I remember in the hospital being submerged into a tub of ice in an attempt to keep my fever under control. I guess I was having some awful fevers. Being held down in the ice.

"I had gone through multiple surgeries before I came to the U.S., several smaller surgeries ... even trying to scrape the tumor off my bone. I remember being in a cast that started on my hip and then went all the way down my right leg.

"I was living in the hospital—sleeping there—and I remember being put through some kind of class or course on how to brush your teeth. I had some ulcers in my mouth, and they thought I just wasn't brushing correctly. When I came to Boston it turned out that I had several different tumors in my mouth. I had a bunch of teeth pulled and miniature surgeries in my mouth."[3]

It came to the point that the doctors in Panama weren't sure how to proceed. When they discussed amputating his leg, Uri's parents looked farther afield, with his father inquiring through associates and colleagues in the medical community in Panama. It was recommended that he go to Boston and be treated through the Jimmy Fund Clinic at the Dana-Farber Cancer Institute.

On November 19, 1985, Uri and his mother, Daisy, traveled to Boston. It was the first time either had left Panama. Daisy spoke no English. More extensive surgeries followed—at least seven of them over time.

When they first arrived, they lived at the Howard Johnson hotel, the back lot of which was less than 100 yards from Fenway Park. "My very first memory of Fenway Park is one when I didn't know it was Fenway Park. We were looking out the window of the hotel and I remember seeing that green building. I didn't know what it was, and my mom didn't either. She said, 'I don't know. It must be some kind of factory or something.'

Fast forward 20 years later and that 'factory' was my practically my second home."

His doctor was Lindsay Frazier, whom he calls "my second mom." Although she works in the field of pediatric cancer, they formed a bond, and 35 years later, Uri is still her patient, through an exception that was granted.[4] He has had the same nurse from early days, too—Robin Griffey.

When the doctors did the first surgery, neither Uri nor his mother knew whether his leg had been amputated. As Red Sox broadcaster Joe Castiglione tells it, "When he woke up in the recovery room, he asked his mother whether his leg was still there. She told him yes, but she didn't really know until she lifted up the sheet on his hospital bed and saw for herself. The doctors had been able to save his leg and his life."[5]

Mother and son returned to Panama, but there was a relapse and they returned to Boston, with this time Daisy determined to stay until Uri was cured. They first stayed at the Ronald McDonald House, then got a place to stay in Brockton, and later in Dorchester.

Uri doesn't know when he first began chemotherapy. He was so used to being in the hospital that having another shot was routine for him. He had multiple operations on his right leg, with months and sometimes years between them. When he was six or seven, he says, he had a friend from Ohio named Veronica who was at the Jimmy Fund. "She passed away … and it was my first experience of losing a friend. That's when I knew I was in trouble."[6]

They were successful. Uri was even able to play sports in school. "They absolutely did miracle work. That's one of the things I was very proud of—never mind that I was supposed to die. I wasn't supposed to ever walk again. And in high school, I ran track, I played baseball. I played football. I've done the Boston Marathon a number of times. This all from a kid who wasn't supposed to have a leg."

The cancer Uri had didn't want to be beaten. There was the leg. There were the tumors in his mouth. And there was more. One relapse was due to a tumor in his spine, another for one on his jaw.[7] After two years of remission, when he was in the sixth grade, there was another relapse.

"I had a couple of brain tumors, a couple of tumors inside my skull. One of the worst tumor pains that I remember while here in the U.S. was in my ear. I think it was my left ear. Horrific, horrific pains. I remember on several occasions having to be transported from our apartment in Brockton, taken out on a stretcher and taken straight to the hospital because I was in horrific pain. The cancer tried to get me everywhere."

And then there was the cruel illusion of false hope when he thought he'd beaten it.

"You go through these moments of extreme, extreme joy—when you're told that you're cancer-free, when you're told that you're in remission from something you've been battling so long, it is amazing. 'Oh my God, I've reached it. I'm cancer-free.' You are quite literally in heaven.

"You're supposed to be in remission for five years before you're considered cured. The worst thing that happened to me is I was four years into it and then I had a relapse. That is the absolute worst thing you can go through. I had to go through that a number of times. A relapse is the absolute worst. You've already been through a bout with cancer. You've already beaten one tumor. You've already gone through surgeries. You've already gone through chemo. You've already gone through radiation. You've gone through this shit—and you've won. Then at four years, after you've built up your hopes for several months, and then you're told it's back. You're like, 'What the hell?'"

Finally, in 2000, he was declared cancer-free. And it's now been 20 years.

The year 2003 was his first as broadcaster, but he'd already been working at Fenway Park for six prior seasons. His first visit was in 1994, when he was 12. He was invited to visit Fenway after some of the Red Sox had visited him at the Jimmy Fund Clinic. The Red Sox already had a decades-long tradition of supporting the Jimmy Fund, dating back to the late 1940s and Ted Williams.[8] In 1953, it became the "official charity" of the Red Sox. In the Tom Yawkey years, the Jimmy Fund logo was the only bit of "advertising" permitted inside Fenway Park.

Joe Castiglione began broadcasting for the Boston Red Sox in 1983, working alongside Ken Coleman, who broadcast for the Red Sox from 1966 to 1989. Coleman was executive director of the Jimmy Fund from 1978 to 1984. Joe often volunteered to help at Jimmy Fund functions and in 1990, during former Red Sox second baseman Mike Andrews's more than 30 years as chairman of the Jimmy Fund, Joe took a position with the Jimmy Fund as their representative to the Red Sox. He organized events at Fenway Park and elsewhere and, about three times a year, would go with two or three Red Sox players to visit young patients at the Jimmy Fund Clinic. During the 1994 season, he went with catcher Damon Berryhill and another player or two and "met a 12-year-old boy with big eyes. He was being treated for histiocytosis.... I was introduced to him and was told that his name was Uri Berenguer. I instantly asked whether he was related to Juan Berenguer, also known as 'Señor Smoke,' a hard-throwing right-hander who had pitched in the major leagues for 15 years.... Uri said yes, Juan Berenguer was his uncle."[9]

There was the baseball connection. And Joe said that Uri had a certain "maturity" and "charisma" to him. "I asked him, 'Why don't you come to Fenway when you're finished with your treatments and watch from our booth?' He did and showed a real interest. We used to use him to get coffee and run stats and that type of thing. It wasn't every day, but he came several times. He was 12."[10]

Uri says, "I met Joe. He did his Joe thing. Joe knows everyone when it comes to baseball. He immediately made the link [to Juan Berenguer]. He got my information, maybe from my mom. He wanted me to come to the booth, to a game. The rest is history. I remember him making me feel special. Maybe a little more important than anyone else because of my uncle. I was very impressed with Joe."[11]

By age 14, he was an intern.

In the meantime, the Berenguer family had grown and reunited. Uri's younger brother Mark Howard Berenguer was born on February 27, 1990; he was named after two doctors who had treated Uri. His father, Félix, moved to the Boston area when Uri was around 10. He had been working in Panama to support the family. When he came to the United States, he had to join his wife in working at more humble occupations. She found work as a housekeeper. He didn't speak English and had difficulty getting a work permit. He had cleaned the church they attended to pick up a little extra cash and finally landed a position as a maintenance worker at the apartment complex where they lived. The couple adopted a fourth child, Jasmine, in 1995. Daisy Berenguer had also taken in foster children for a while, working for ABCD, a Boston governmental program associated with the Department of Children and Families. She took in Jasmine as an infant, only a few days old. After more than a year, the Berenguers had fallen in love with the little girl who had come from horrific circumstances and decided to adopt her rather than place her back in the system.[12]

"We developed a relationship over the winter," Uri said of Joe Castiglione. "By the time I was 13, I was going to the ballpark regularly. Not every day but regularly. By 14, they made me an intern. They had a college student, and I would intern every once in a while, filling in for their intern. Eventually, I became a full-time intern.

"The bulk of my work was really being a student of Joe. My responsibilities were to attend to him and Jerry Trupiano's needs. If one of them needed coffee or water during the game, I'd go get it. I was in charge of handing them the live reads during the innings. Keep the pitch count. I kept my own scorecard. Checked on certain information for them if I was asked to do so.

"But honestly, the bulk of the work, as I looked at it, was just to be a student of Joe. I got to the ballpark usually when he got there and just followed him around. Tag along.

"Go to the clubhouse. He introduced me to so many people—ballplayers, managers, club personnel.... Joe knows everyone. Joe knows everyone.

He's not a bad person to be associated with. Everyone loves him—more than love, everyone respects Joe. I really admired that. Still do. From really early on, I had the sense that he was showing me the ropes. I tried to pay attention to him, study him quite a bit. Being an intern wasn't really work. For me, it was fun. I got to be at the ballpark. The things I had to do for them were simple.

"The work really came in … what work was I going to give myself? Pay attention to what Joe does, how he prepares. How much he prepares, etc.

"At first, I wasn't doing it consciously, but early on—very early on—I might say from the first day I was at the ballpark for a full day with him—I felt that the thing he did was the greatest thing on earth. I don't know that at that age I had definitely decided 'That's what I'm going to be,' but I know that I considered it one of my top choices and I know that I wanted to be just like him. Was I doing so consciously? At a certain point early on, I did have that intention."[13]

Castiglione also introduced him to the Spanish broadcasters. Puerto Rican natives Héctor Martínez and Bobby Serrano had started broadcasting Red Sox games in 1988 for what was initially called the Red Sox Hispanic Radio Network.

The idea to begin Spanish-language broadcasting of Red Sox games seems to have sprung out of conversations between Red Sox employees Ken Carberry and Jim Healey. Carberry had been working for the Red Sox since 1979, initially hired as "Sherm Feller's backup announcer and handler." Feller was the longtime public address announcer at Fenway Park and a character. He needed to undergo some bypass surgery and Carberry became his backup. Carberry came from a family background in radio. His father had been a working DJ and Ken himself was studying radio at Curry College. He impressed enough folks at Fenway that when Feller returned, he was asked, "Why don't you stay and help him out and fill in when he needs it?" "So I did. Over a few years, I ended up becoming the control room supervisor. I stayed for several years and I ran that room—the video scoreboard and then the audio."[14]

Jim Healey had joined the Red Sox in 1975. While a student at Boston College, he had been the first general manager of the college radio station, WZBC-FM. He became the first marketing director for the Red Sox in 1979 and in 1985 was named broadcasting director. He became a vice president of the team in 1987. To the best of their shared recollections, sometime during and after the 1986 World Series, Carberry and Healey had begun talking about adding a Spanish-language broadcast to the array of Red Sox offerings. There had been a couple of Spanish broadcasters who had covered the Mets–Red Sox games during the 1986 World Series.

One of those broadcasters was Juan Alicea, one of the team for the "International Spanish Network, which carried the Mets 1986 and 1988 postseason play throughout the United States and Latin America."[15] "That's probably what first gave me that idea," Carberry recalled. "They were great guys. They were really super. They did a heck of a job. They put them in that booth or different booths. I think they may have broadcast from a camera sling—I'm not kidding—that was in front of us. They were cool guys—and you could hear them because the windows were open, and they were right in front of us on the camera sling. I had studied Spanish back then—my Spanish was a lot better than it is right now—so I enjoyed speaking to the guys. I thought this could be a pretty good idea, to put this thing together."

Healey says of Carberry, "He asked about doing it. It was something I'd been wanting to do but just didn't have the time or the ability to do it. He said he could put it together. He had a couple of guys in mind who would do the play-by-play and color. Ken hired them Héctor Martínez and Bobby Serrano. We developed a short contract. It wasn't much money. It was just to get it out there and try and tap into that market."[16]

Carberry's recollection meshes: "I just said, 'Boy, we should do a Spanish broadcast.' I'd been involved in radio, and I was doing some other stuff in radio, and I just thought it would be fun. So, yeah, I put it together with Jim Healey. I talked to him about the idea, and he loved it, so we put together a Spanish broadcast. Jim was certainly a major part of it for the Red Sox. He was my boss at the Red Sox. He had had the idea as well, so we talked about it. It may have been his idea first. We talked about it a lot, though. I did offer, 'I'd like to do it,' and he agreed."

"We only did home games for a while and some road games," Healey said. "I think they'd go to New York and do games from New York."

What might be called the Hispanic market in New England was by no means a large one in the late 1980s, but it was a growing one. "Not huge," recalls Carberry. "There were sections. We'd see it happening … not in Boston but in Chelsea. Lawrence. You had the Fall River/New Bedford area. You had Providence. You had Worcester. When I put together the network, that's how I put it together. To be in those cities as well as Boston. I had a radio station carry it in Boston. I had a radio station carry it in Lawrence. I had a radio station in Worcester. I had a radio station in Providence."

The broadcasts were not just confined to one radio station. It was a network right from the beginning. "I knew that it had to be a network in order to get the bodies, so we went right to those stations. The exact stations and the exact markets changed a little bit over the years here and there."

For the Red Sox, there wasn't much money at first, but Healey encountered no resistance. "Just the opposite. Everybody thought it was a great idea to do it. We just didn't want it costing us any money." It gave the team an entrée into the growing Hispanic community. The flagship station was WRCA, 1330 AM.

Alberto Vasallo III is president and CEO of the multimedia company El Mundo Boston. He was a student at Boston College at the time. His father had founded the media company and had run Radiolanda since 1975. "We had the games on our station," he says. "Part of the El Mundo world was also radio. WRCA, 1330 AM. We broadcast for like 18 hours a day. We had the radio station and a Limited Market Agreement, an LMA. We were also the flagship station." He recalls a reporter for the *El Mundo* newspaper. "She said, 'Hey, do you know these guys? Bobby Serrano, he's with the Boston Police. And Héctor Martínez.' My father knew Bobby Serrano. Bobby always had an announcer's voice, a very deep baritone voice. That's how I first heard they had been selected. I found out about it after they'd been selected." In time, Alberto developed a pregame show that kept the property of El Mundo. "And our on-air personality—J.P. Villamán—became so good at it that eventually I suggested that he go into the booth. And he worked out really well."[17]

But we're jumping ahead here. J.P. first became a full-time broadcaster in 1999. Bobby Serrano and Héctor Martínez worked, the two of them together, for 11 seasons, 1988–1998.

At first, the only games broadcast were home games—and not necessarily all of those. Particularly in the earlier years, Carberry explained, "We did not do all the games. We did select games. We'd usually do them from a radio station studio, one of the stations like WROL. Back then, my father owned WROL for a period of time. We did a lot of work with El Mundo. WRCA. We worked with El Mundo a lot, with the father and son."[18]

The broadcasters would watch the game on television and broadcast play-by-play over the radio. The practice is reminiscent of the early days of English-language radio broadcasts of baseball games. In the 1930s, a young Ronald Reagan, for instance, first developed a national audience by "creatively re-creating" Chicago Cubs games over radio station WHO—his information not provided by television (since it hadn't yet been invented) but from reading telegraphic accounts of the game transmitted from the ballpark.[19]

It was one thing to do home games, but for the first few years of Red Sox Spanish broadcasting, economic reasons prevented the broadcasters from going on road trips. This presented certain problems in that not all Red Sox games were available on television. "We did our road games from a radio studio, watching TV. Hey, you do what you can."[20]

There was beginning to be a little more attention paid to the fact that there were Spanish-language broadcasts. The *Boston Globe* may have been describing the first broadcast from Fenway Park itself, when it said, "The two Red Sox Spanish-language announcers … made their debut Friday night [May 18] at Fenway Park in the game against the Twins."[21] A month later, the paper said that "Polaroid and Pepsi have joined Anheuser-Busch as major sponsors."[22] The following week, there was a major feature article spreading over much of two pages. The stations were listed as WROL (950 AM), Boston; WCCM (800 AM), Lawrence; WACE (730 AM), Springfield; WLVH (1230 AM), Hartford; and WRIB (1220 AM), Providence. Jim Healey said, "This Hispanic market is a big market, an important market—and it's a market you don't have to educate. These people know about baseball."[23] There were nine other teams with Spanish-language broadcasts. The broadcasters talked at some length about the May 18 game. ("We went off the air a couple of times…. We didn't have the stat books and had to do them off the top of our heads. It was nearly a disaster.") And they talked about the difficulties of rendering sayings like "shoestring catch" in Spanish.

The *Globe* even published an editorial on July 5. Noting the team's "poor reputation in race relations for a long time," the paper praised the January hiring of Elaine Weddington as assistant GM and adding Spanish play-by-play in May as "a recognition by the Red Sox of the diversity of their fans and their community."[24]

An article in the January 23, 1991, *Boston Globe* said that radio station WVIB had carried the Spanish-language broadcasts of both the Red Sox–A's playoffs and the World Series. A *Globe* article in May said that the network embraced four stations during both 1990 and 1991: stations in Boston, Springfield, Lawrence, and Hartford.[25] That said, the English-language broadcasts were a far larger venture. WRKO was the flagship station, and the Red Sox Radio Network was "carried on more than 60 stations in New England."[26]

There was a little more scrutiny, too. As more major league ballplayers came from Latin countries, Bob Ryan asked in a November 1992 column, "Is it true that nobody in the entire Red Sox organization speaks decent conversational Spanish?"[27]

This was just around the time Bill Kulik had been brought in. "I was hired as a producer of the broadcast. That's how I started with it and then slowly but surely started to work my way toward being more than just a producer."[28]

Courting the Spanish-speaking audience was reflected as well by national enterprises such as HBO, which announced in the fall of 1993 that they would launch HBO en Español.[29]

For the 1994 All-Star Game, Red Sox Spanish broadcaster Héctor Martínez joined Tony Pérez on NBC, via secondary audio programming (SAP) "for the 25 percent of the nation [including Boston]" that had SAP.[30]

The Red Sox network had six stations in 1994—WROL and five affiliates.[31]

These were the years when Uri began to frequent the booth, becoming an intern, and often getting a ride home. "Joe [Castiglione] would actually drive me home. Most of the nights. Occasionally, my mom would pick me up. If Joe had something to do after the game or if it were a travel day, I would take the bus or train home."[32] Uri went on his first road trip at an early age. Joe Castiglione says, "I remember going to Tampa Bay and Atlanta with him. He was on the team plane. I remember he went jet-skiing with my daughter at Clearwater Beach. He would have been 14. He stayed with us."[33]

Throughout the 1990s, Uri continued to be treated for cancer. As noted, he endured seven surgeries over the years as well as chemo and radiation therapy before he was deemed cancer-free in 2000.

After Red Sox general manager Dan Duquette acquired Pedro Martínez from the Montreal Expos, Fenway Park blossomed with Dominican flags as fans saw Pedro put together arguably the best three-year stretch any major league pitcher ever had—in 1998, 1999, and 2000. Duquette knew what the Sox had in Pedro. The spontaneous and genuine excitement was welcome, and as early as mid–May, the *Globe* reported that WRCA, "the Red Sox' Spanish radio affiliate, is considering adding Pedro Martínez's road starts for the second half of the season."[34]

On May 4, 1998, the *Boston Globe* published a front-page sports section story titled "Martínez Brilla contra Texas." The story was entirely in Spanish; as an accompanying note explained (in both languages), "as a service to our Spanish-speaking readers, the Globe will run Red Sox game stories written in Spanish on days when Pedro Martínez pitches at home."[35]

Uri Berenguer was getting more involved, too, in 1998. "I was engineering and producing, and then by 16, I was hosting the pregame show." He'd do interviews in the clubhouse before the games and put them on the air. It was very unusual to be getting started in the business at such an early age. He agrees: "It was. It really was. I was thinking what a hot shit I was. I loved it. I really did. I fell in love with it very early on. I was on the radio! At 16, I was the host of a pregame show of a major league baseball team, for crying out loud.

"And then midway through that season, I was bold—I told Kulik, 'Hey, listen, I'd like to try an inning during the game broadcast with the guys.' They gave me a shot, and sure enough, I guess I did well enough that they gave me the opportunity to do the fifth inning. For the second half of the 1998 season, I was doing the pregame show and the fifth inning. Every game."³⁶

All this while he was finishing high school at Boston Latin Academy. He was a member of Latin Academy's baseball, football, and track teams. That was quite an accomplishment for someone who had only come to Boston due to his mother's determination to try and save his leg from amputation. Joe Castiglione shared a memory of a time he went to see Uri play football: "When he was a senior at Boston Latin Academy, the game was in West Roxbury. This big kid scored—twice his size—and Uri hit him. He was called for unnecessary roughness. I always teased him about the fact that he was half the kid's size."³⁷

Sometime around 2000, the agreement between the Red Sox and the Carter Radio Network was up for renewal. Bill Kulik outbid Carter, and the Spanish Béisbol Network (SBN) was born. The bidding was a sum into six figures.³⁸ One of the things Kulik wanted to do was to expand and in more ways than one. The broadcasts had for the most part been weeknight home games, with the occasional road trip—50 games a season.³⁹ Kulik, ambitious as was Dan Duquette, wanted to cover all 162 games—although this didn't necessarily mean going on the road with the team. Just as home games had been broadcast from the studio at El Mundo and from other locations, so, too, could away games. The games were all televised now, so a "remote" broadcast could be set up almost anywhere. They set up a studio in Fenway Park and—in a practice that still continued through the 2023 season—road games are often done from an otherwise-empty Fenway.

Come the pandemic in 2020 and through the first month-plus of the 2021 season, all the English-language television broadcasts—home and away—were done from remote locations.

Héctor Martínez had departed after the 1999 season. Bobby Serrano stayed on through 2001, joined in 1999 by J.P. Villamán, a Dominican.

Kulik lined up sponsors such as Heineken, Dunkin' Donuts, and Western Union. Caliente 1330, owned by the Vasallos, was the flagship station. The broadcast team he put together for 2001 added Adrián García Márquez, whom SBN had hired away from Oakland "where he broadcast the A's games in Spanish. He also does Wednesday night baseball for ESPN."⁴⁰ García Márquez was Mexican, so the broadcast team was one Puerto Rican, one Dominican, and one Mexican. Kulik said the local Latino community was 41 percent Puerto Rican, 16 percent Dominican, and 19 percent Central American. He envisioned the possibility of network affiliates in both the Dominican Republic and Puerto Rico.⁴¹

As it happens, during the season, subscribers to MLB.com were able to access the Red Sox broadcast. The 2001 Red Sox team had Pedro, "Super Manny" (Manny Ramírez), Jose Offerman, and others. García Márquez brought a new style to the broadcasts with a heavy dose of player nicknames, which caught on with both listeners and the players themselves.[42]

Kulik himself did some of the play-by-play and made the broadcasts less formal. "I quickly realized that Spanglish wasn't such a bad thing," he said. "I wasn't broadcasting to Bogotá, Colombia. I was broadcasting to Lowell. It was different, so 'un batazo a jardin izquierdo'—it didn't really matter if I said, 'un batazo a left.' Everybody knew what I was saying. The dawning of it came in two senses. Number one, I was in Walmart and there was a mom, a grandmother, and a granddaughter all walking along. The little girl went running up to a doll and said, 'Mira, Mami! Mira, Mami! Compre eso. Es on sale.' And all three of them knew what she was talking about. 'Es on sale'? What is 'Es on sale'? They all knew what she was saying. I realized from that moment, I don't need to have perfect Spanish. 'Un batazo a left'—if it sounds hipper and smarter and tighter, say 'Batazo a left.' Don't worry about it. Just go with it."[43]

As a cancer survivor and someone associated at least part time with the Red Sox, Uri made a few on-air appearances promoting various fundraising events. Team president John Harrington was also a Dana-Farber trustee. He joined with Joe Castiglione and Professor Roger Giese, director of Northeastern University's Environmental Cancer Research Program, to help secure Uri a scholarship to attend Northeastern University beginning in the fall of 2001. Among the courses he took was Joe Castiglione's course in broadcast journalism. Another of Professor Castiglione's students who later became a Red Sox broadcaster was Don Orsillo.[44]

In January 2002, Major League Baseball approved the sale of the Boston Red Sox to new owners.[45]

The four-station SBN did broadcast all 162 games in 2001, and the network grew to eight stations heading into 2002, with WLYN (1360 AM, in Lynn) as the flagship. García Márquez was so popular that he was hired away by TeleFutura, a new channel on Univision.[46] Replacing him were two others—Luis Tiant and Juan Báez. Tiant joined the Red Sox broadcast team for the 2002 and 2003 seasons. Báez had become popular in the Dominican with a couple of years of winter baseball broadcasting under his belt. He worked only the 2002 season.

There was another broadcaster with a similar name—Juan Óscar Báez. He had begun a sports talk radio show in Boston in 2001. He hosted the pregame show starting in the second half of the 2004 season and joined full time in 2005. He had reportedly played in the Yankees system, reaching as high as Double A.[47]

New Red Sox vice president of public affairs Dr. Charles Steinberg helped expand community efforts, building on the team's first Latino Night at the ballpark in 2001.

In addition to WLYN, the network included AM stations in Brockton (WMSX, 1410), Framingham (WKOX, 1200), Lawrence (WHAV, 1490), Worcester (WORC, 1310), Providence (WRIB, 1220), Hartford (WPRX, 1120), and Bridgeport, Connecticut (WBRG, 1110).

The year 2003 was Uri Berenguer's first year on-air as a full-time regular. He'd done the pregame show and the fifth inning since 1998 and had become a staple in the booth in 2002 as an engineer, but now—just 19 years old for the first few weeks of the season—he was a full-fledged member of the broadcast team, handling the play-by-play with J.P. and Luis Tiant as analysts.

Battling cancer for as long as he had, he had become a determined young man. "I took the attitude that nothing is going to stop me. I'm going to succeed. And if I can't do it for myself, I'm going to do it for my mom."[48]

Uri was also quick to credit "Papa Oso"—J.P. Villamán: "I would say that the one who influenced me the most was my first broadcast partner, J.P.—J.P. Villamán. To this day, J.P. is hands down the most energetic talent I've ever been around. I would tell you that J.P. was not the guy you would go to for baseball information or knowledge. But he could make a ground ball in front of the home plate umpire sound exciting. To him, everything was … ecstatic.

"He absolutely influenced me. I think I learned over the years to bring it down a notch. In my opinion, anyway, not everything is a grand slam. And shouldn't be, especially when you do 162 games over the year and you're a one-man broadcast. But you know what? Every game does have its exciting moments. Every game does have its exciting plays. And Latinos aren't afraid to show that."[49]

It was in 2003 that SBN audio was added to all New England Sports Network (NESN) telecasts through the SAP feature.[50]

Doing a Remote Broadcast

What is it like doing a "remote"? Uri explained, "It's much harder to do. Much harder than doing a game live. As a broadcaster for 20 years now, I've done a lot of remote broadcasts—even recently—and they're much harder to do. When you're at the ballpark you can rely on all your senses. It's not just what you see. You sense everything around you. The atmosphere. I've been at the ballpark many times when I'm broadcasting a game from the ballpark…. I've done West Coast games when the team's on the West Coast and I'm at Fenway Park, broadcasting the game. The game starts at 10:00 p.m. our time. I don't get out of the ballpark until 3:00 a.m. As a broadcaster, it's more challenging.

"I enjoy the challenge a little bit more because … if you told me there was a baseball game going on at Fenway Park an hour from now, I can do the game. It's second nature to me right now. [For a home game] I don't need much prep. I don't need any prep, really. I'll get there and for at least one game, I can absolutely wing it. I can wing it. But when you're not there live at the game, there's a lot more work that goes into it. Baseball's a very slow game. There's a lot of time to fill. My job is not only to bring the action to my audience; I have to inform them. I have to bring the play-by-play. I have to entertain them. It's my responsibility. When I think of my audience, most of them are just getting off work and what they want is an escape from reality. I have to provide them with at least three hours of fantasy world."

When on the road, it's more work. "There's a lot of prep that goes into it. When you're not there [and doing a remote], there's a lot of imagination that goes into it. The cameramen are very good nowadays, but they're not as good as my eyes. Sometimes there's a foul ball hit, and I don't know how far or where it went. I have to judge it by the reaction of the audience, the reaction of the players, the umpires. As you do it more and more, you learn how to pick up things. You learn how to pay attention real closely. You learn how to be a real student of the game. You can't rely on just what you see on camera or on TV.

"The Spanish broadcast has gone through a lot of cuts in the last two or three years. In 2018, I didn't do any West Coast trips. We've cut a lot of travel in recent years. I've done quite a bit of those remote broadcasts."[51]

By no means is it just the Red Sox who do remotes, Berenguer explained. He does all the home games from the Spanish broadcast booth on the fifth level at Fenway Park, but he says, "Very rarely do I have any Spanish broadcaster show up at Fenway. It has happened. But more often than not, the visiting team's Spanish broadcaster is not with the team."[52]

Improvements in technology have helped. There are often multiple feeds. Not being present but trying to describe the fullness of the game can be challenging. "Some of the hardest things are if there's an argument, or something going on with an umpire, that I may not have been privy to because the camera was not on the umpire. Or there's a play and the camera's not on them right away. The worst thing that happens is when they're showing some graphic or something—showing some clip—and you hear the crack of the bat. I'm not listening to the broadcast. They might be showing a clip of an old game or something like that. Next thing you know, they come back to live TV and the guy's on first base. What I've learned to do is to keep multiple broadcasts on the monitors. I'll watch the away team's broadcast. I watch the home team broadcast. I'll have MLB Gameday up at all times. I'll have ESPN Statcast up at all times. Nowadays with social media.... If you were to watch me do a broadcast, you would see me with maybe up to five screens in front of me."[53]

The 2004 World Series and the Years That Followed

In 2004, the Spanish-language broadcasters worked the two Red Sox–Cardinals World Series games in Saint Louis, coming home on the team charter with an exuberant front-office staff and later receiving a world championship ring to celebrate the first World Series win the Boston Red Sox had enjoyed in 86 years. Berenguer now has four such rings, including 2007, 2013, and 2018.

In early 2005, however, J.P. Villamán was killed in a car accident on his way home in the early morning hours of May 30 after returning from a weekend series at Yankee Stadium. It became Uri's task to take over from the vibrant personality who had been behind the Spanish mic for eight-plus seasons.

Alberto Vasallo recalled the relationship that had developed between the two. "He was 'Robin' to J.P. as Batman. Then J.P. passed away, and over the last years Uri's been the official voice of the Sox and he's become very ... his brand, personality ... they relate him to the Red Sox because he's been doing it his whole adult life."[54] At the time, Uri was shaken badly. J.P. had been "a rock in Berenguer's life—a partner, friend, and mentor."[55] It was already a difficult time; Uri's mother, Daisy, had been diagnosed with breast cancer and was fighting her own—ultimately successful—battle. Just a few weeks earlier, Uri had run his first Boston Marathon, said to be the first former Jimmy Fund patient to have run the 26-mile, 365-yard race.[56]

Óscar Báez joined the broadcasts and Bill Kulik added some play-by-play as well. It was J.P. who had bestowed on Kulik the moniker "El Gringo Malo." During one of J.P.'s pregame shows in 2003, when Sammy Sosa got suspended for a corked bat, Kulik was producing and J.P. was taking listener calls, defending Sosa. Kulik punched up a sound effect he had on the board, Tom Hanks in *A League of Their Own* saying, "There's no crying in baseball." J.P. responded, "Ah, es el gringo malo!" The next caller said, "Quiero hablar con el gringo malo." The second caller said the same thing. "In that moment," Kulik said, "I realized I have a persona that they like. In sports, you can argue and disagree, but people like that argument." He started doing more on-air work. Kulik moved over to the Philadelphia Phillies after the 2007 season.[57] Since then, he's the lead man on the Phillies' Spanish-language broadcasts. He says, as was the case in Boston, "They don't know my name, but they know my nickname. They all know me as the gringo malo."

Over the wintertime, Berenguer joined Gil Matos hosting a 9:00–11:00 p.m. nightly sports TV show on Univision New England.[58]

In 2005, he had also begun a daily show on XM Satellite Radio, *Solamente Pelota*. "XM radio was really good for me," he says. "That's when my career really did start to 'take off.' It was a good show. It was a national show. Every day, Monday through Friday—the show was 3 to 7, and then I would pretty much trade microphones and do the Red Sox play-by-play. During the baseball season, I was literally on the air Monday through Monday. There were no weekends off."[59] When he wasn't doing the XM show, he was doing Red Sox play-by-play. Others handled the Red Sox pregame show.

By 2007, WROL was the flagship again and there were seven affiliates reaching Massachusetts, Connecticut, Rhode Island, and New Hampshire.

Óscar Báez remained Berenguer's partner through the 2014 season. Bill Kulik, however, decamped to Philadelphia after 2007, though he kept producing the broadcasts in Boston through 2013.

There was one point when Berenguer's schedule became too busy. The network was busy, and so was he. In 2009, he was "selected as an announcer for MLB Network of the Caribbean World Series played in Mexicali, Mexico from February 2 to February 7."[60] And the SBN was busy as well. In 2010, with a new flagship station (WWZN, 1510 AM), they would again cover all 162 games, but also "once again broadcast all 12 games of the Caribbean World Series live to cities across the United States."[61]

On August 6, 2010, Berenguer joined Jade McCarthy as cohost of a nightly television show, *NESN Daily*, which aired seven nights a week at 11:00 p.m.[62] There were a number of shows he had to miss. And after the economic crash which began in the latter half of 2008, budgets were tighter. "We ran into some financial problems," said Kulik, "and Oscar was doing a lot of games on his own." The television pairing didn't work well and the last *NESN Daily* show with Uri was on November 11; McCarthy began to do the show solo. The "chemistry" hadn't been right. Executive Vice President of Programming Joel Feld said, "I think you have to keep in mind that this was Uri's first television opportunity in a leading role. I think he's got an enormous amount of talent. Our job is to match his talents and abilities to fit our needs."[63]

Uri Berenguer was not listed in the *2011 Red Sox Media Guide*. The only broadcaster listed was Óscar Báez, with assistance from Bill Kulik only. Now the company was called Spanish Béisbol Productions. But, says Kulik, Uri was in fact there and working the broadcasts. The economics were becoming more marginal, though. "Every year we dropped about $100,000 to where we were down to around $200,000 to $300,000. It was getting worse and worse and worse and by 2013 it had hit rock bottom. The

Uri Berenguer chatting with Rafael Devers at Fenway Park (courtesy Marly Rivera).

Red Sox took over the broadcast and decided to go with a one-man show, that one-man show being Uri."[64]

In the meantime, Berenguer had begun to build a family. A friend, Jason, introduced him to Jackie, a student getting her master's at Boston College in Hispanic literature and culture. She was working at Best Buy to make ends meet. Uri explains, "I hate to admit it, but I was definitely a playboy. I went through my phase of doing all right with the ladies. Jason says to me one night, 'Dude, there's this girl that I work with at Best Buy. She's looking for a career. She wants to do something in media. She wants to do it in Spanish. I just happened to mention, "Oh yeah, my buddy Uri is the Spanish broadcaster with the Sox."'" Jackie interned with Berenguer and the Red Sox for the full season of 2006.

Although they never married, Jackie became mother of two children with Uri—in May 2021, Logan was 10 years old, and Julian was 7. Given that schools were closed for in-person learning during the pandemic, Uri was able to help them with remote learning, a whole new challenge. Uri and Jackie had separated in August 2018 but have an ongoing cooperative relationship in child-raising. As he says, "Absolutely. We have to." Of Colombian descent, Jackie was born in the United States. She works as a high school Spanish teacher. Given her responsibilities teaching, the boys spent maybe 75 percent of their time with Uri. When the school year ends, it will probably go back to 50-50.

After 2013, the Red Sox took over the Spanish-language broadcasts themselves. Beginning in 2014, Uri Berenguer became a Red Sox employee, not a Spanish Béisbol Productions employee.

Through the 2019 season, WCEC in Methuen (1490 AM/103.7 FM) was the lead station.

The internet, of course, offers a far greater reach than terrestrial radio ever could. As far back as 2005, it was noted that J.P. Villamán had "fans as far away as Costa Rica, Venezuela, and Spain" who heard him on satellite. "They would sometimes call into his pregame show, which pleased Villamán enormously."[65]

Berenguer himself had a fan club—overseas. "The wildest thing that I've experienced over the last five or six years—I have my own little fan club. It was started in Spain, of all places. You wouldn't think of Spain as a baseball country. It's not. It absolutely is not. And if they want to listen to my broadcast, they're staying up … they're starting at one o'clock in the morning to listen to it. They dubbed it Uri Berenguer Nation. They've sent me T-shirts and stickers and a whole bunch of stuff. They've come to Fenway Park once a year from Spain. I meet with them. I've taken them out to dinner. It started as a group of five buddies. They just fell in love with my broadcast, and it's grown to—last I was told—it's over 60 some-odd people. All over Spain. They get together once a month to listen to my broadcast together and discuss the status of the team, my broadcast, etc."

The main man behind the fan club is "Luisma" (Luis Manuel Cagigal Calvo) from Errentería—near San Sebastián. He was a music photographer, a road manager for some bands in Spain, and worked in the music business. As of 2020, he has been working as a mailman, riding a motorbike.

"I don't know why, but I always liked baseball," Luisma said in a 2020 interview. "When I was a kid, I used to play baseball at school or summer vacations. Nothing serious."[66] He started following baseball through MLB.TV around 2010 and discovered Uri's feed in 2014. He had grown up following Boston Celtics basketball in the time of Larry Bird, Ainge, McHale, Parish, and Dennis Johnson and finally made a first visit to Boston in 2013.

For five seasons in a row, through 2019, Luisma and a few friends made a pilgrimage to Fenway Park and met up with Uri. The last time the group came, Luisma had a surprise for Uri—he was sporting a tattoo on his arm reading, "Uri Berenguer Nation," along with another reading, "Entering Fenway."

Unfortunately, 2019 was the last season that Uri Berenguer broadcast for the Red Sox. That June, there was a domestic dispute that resulted in him being suspended from his work. Nilson "Junior" Pepén took over in his absence, while the suspension was in effect. Given the worldwide COVD-19 pandemic and the truncated 2020 baseball season, it was a long time before Major League Baseball got back to Berenguer. He finally heard from them in December 2020 and was told that he was being given a one-month suspension, without pay, retroactive to September 2019. He was also asked to participate in a counseling program. This was, one can see, well over a year after the fact.

He then contacted the Red Sox to ask about reinstatement for the 2021 season, but "the very next day, the Red Sox called me and told me that they had decided that I would not be coming back for the 2021 season."[67] Nilson Pepén handled the Spanish broadcasts during the 2020 and 2021 seasons. The likelihood of Berenguer returning is uncertain. One might surmise that the more time passes, the less likely it may be. "Do I hope I could come back? Yeah, absolutely, I love my job, But at the moment, they have told me that I would not be welcome back for the 2021 season, and that was that. I got all my stuff. All my stuff is out of my booth."[68]

The actual incident was a physical altercation between Berenguer and another man with whom Uri's ex, Jackie, became involved. Whatever charges were initially filed were dropped. The case was dismissed. Charges might have been pressed against all involved, but it was essentially a "he said/he said" situation. Berenguer is forthright in acknowledging, "I was both the victim and the aggressor. I was definitely an aggressor, and I was definitely a victim. It was an ugly day. It was a real ugly day."

That said, the incident caused him to lose the position he grew up in, the profession he loved. The MLB suspension was for a month. He admits to feeling let down by the Red Sox. After decades involved in Red Sox broadcasts, he felt like—as he put it, for lack of a better term—the "red-headed stepchild." He said, "I was always passionate about my job, and I have no problem saying I was damn good at my job." One shouldn't "judge someone by a still picture. Part of one day." It is, he acknowledges, "their prerogative. It doesn't mean I'm not disappointed by the way they dealt with it."

While his priority has been his sons, he has started to do some other work. "I launched a podcast and I've been developing that slowly and surely. I'm also right now in the very beginning of talks with another professional team to provide them with a Spanish broadcast. That's very early talks. We have meetings going. We'll see where that goes. As soon as I have anything to say, I'll let you know."

The *3 Leches Sports* podcast can be seen at https://www.youtube.com/channel/UC3WBi01FbBUv_FudyvnSm3Q.

Cancer is never far from his mind, though, Uri explained, "Cancer has a hold on me to this day. Parents, we worry about everything about your kids. When your kid has a cold or has a stuffy nose or has a cough, you think, 'Oh, he has a cold. No big deal.' Well, that's not the case with me. When my kids have a fever, I'm scared shitless. I can't sleep. I literally do not sleep. It could just be a cold, but I don't know that. Until I know it's nothing more than a cold, I'm scared shitless. Does my kid have cancer? That's a really crappy feeling. I can't be a quote-unquote 'normal parent.' I'm this parent on edge because I know my history with cancer."[69]

Notes

1. *Boston Globe*, August 7, 2005.

2. All direct quotations come from a series of author interviews with Uri Berenguer in April and May 2020. Uri added another memory: "I remember my very first day of preschool. My mom walking me there. Me being so excited. I had just gotten a yo-yo. I didn't know any of the kids and I was keeping to myself. I remember standing in a doorway. The kids were in a playground, the yard in back of the school. I remember swinging it forward and it came back, and I caught it. I remember feeling it was so cool, and some of the kids actually seeing me do it. Of course, I could never do it again after that. That was a moment of icebreaking. I started making some friends."

3. Author interview with Uri Berenguer, April 25, 2020.

4. For an article on Dr. Frazier and her patient, see Saul Wisnia, "Special Bonds," *Paths of Progress* (Boston: Dana-Farber Cancer Institute, Spring/Summer 2007), 25, 26.

5. Joe Castiglione, *Can You Believe It?* (Chicago: Triumph Books, 2012), 219.

6. Bill Griffith, "Walking Example of Jimmy Fund's Work," *Boston Globe*, August 3, 2002, 78.

7. Griffith, "Walking Example of Jimmy Fund's Work."

8. See Saul Wisnia, *The Jimmy Fund of Dana-Farber Cancer Institute* (Charleston, SC: Arcadia, 2002). See also the forthcoming book, still in manuscript form, "Ted and Jimmy," the story of Ted Williams and the Jimmy Fund by Bill Nowlin. The bonds between the

Jimmy Fund and the Red Sox continue. In April 2016, Larry Lucchino became chairman of the Jimmy Fund. Lucchino is the president/CEO emeritus of the Boston Red Sox..

9. Castiglione, *Can You Believe It?* 219.
10. Author interview with Joe Castiglione, May 4, 2020.
11. Author interview with Uri Berenguer, April 16, 2020.
12. The only one in the family who is not a U.S. citizen is Uri. Both parents became citizens. Mark was born in the United States. "My oldest sister, Irana, she's now married and has five kids. I'm the only one who's not actually a citizen. I am a legal resident. I just have not yet become a citizen." It's something he has intended to do, but with two children of his own and his other responsibilities, it's just something he has not done.
13. Author interview with Uri Berenguer, April 16, 2020.
14. Author interview with Ken Carberry, April 23, 2020.
15. "Mets Broadcasters," MLB.com. See https://www.mlb.com/mets/team/broadcasters. Accessed on May 8, 2020.
16. Author interview with Jim Healey, April 22, 2020.
17. Author interview with Alberto Vasallo III, May 6, 2020.
18. Author interview with Ken Carberry, April 23, 2020.
19. See, for instance, Curt Smith, "Ronald Reagan: The 'Great Communicator' Advanced from Sports Announcer to the Oval Office," *Sports Broadcast Journal*, September 7, 2019, https://www.sportsbroadcastjournal.com/ronald-reagan-the-great-communicator-advanced-from-the-broadcast-booth-to-the-oval-office/. Accessed on May 8, 2020.
20. Author interview with Ken Carberry, April 23, 2020.
21. Jack Craig, "Daly Has Inside Track," *Boston Globe*, May 20, 1990, 47. The article mentioned Hector Martinez on play-by-play and Bobby Serrano as analyst, noting a five-station network which Ken Carberry "optimistically estimates" an audience of 500,000.
22. Jack Craig, "CBS Shuffles Its NFL Pairs," *Boston Globe*, June 26, 1990, 40..
23. Fernando Gonzalez, "The Boston Red Sox … Now en Español," *Boston Globe*, June 28, 1990, 41..
24. Editorial, "The Other Red Sox Gains," *Boston Globe*, July 5, 1990, 10. Weddington was "the first woman, and one of too few blacks, to have made it to such a position in major league baseball."
25. Jack Craig, "Cup Brims with Promise for SportsChannel," *Boston Globe*, May 14, 1991, 31.
26. Susan Bickelhaupt, "WRKO Plans to Extend Its Reach," *Boston Globe*, August 31, 1991, 77.
27. Bob Ryan, "Some More Leftovers," *Boston Globe*, November 28, 1992, 69.
28. Author interview with Bill Kulik, May 4, 2020.
29. Susan Bickelhaupt, "Howie Carr's Back, and HDH Has Him," *Boston Globe*, October 1, 1993, 66.
30. Jack Craig, "Baseball Banks on Star Power," *Boston Globe*, July 3, 1994, 43.
31. Jack Craig, "Baseball Banks on Star Power."
32. Author interview with Uri Berenguer, April 16, 2020.
33. Author interview with Joe Castiglione, May 4, 2020.
34. Howard Manly, "Cordero Talk Boosts Spanish Media," *Boston Globe*, May 22, 1998, 98.
35. Tito Stevens, "Martinez Brilla contra Texas," *Boston Globe*, May 4, 1998, 45. Stevens wrote these stories regularly through 2003. Diego Ribadeneira wrote a number of such Martinez stories. And Uri Berenguer became a published author with one game account of his own on p. 74 in the July 2, 2002, *Globe*: "Martinez Poncha 14 en Otra Victoria."
36. Author interview with Uri Berenguer, April 16, 2020.
37. Author interview with Joe Castiglione, May 4, 2020.
38. Author interview with Bill Kulik, May 4, 2020. The English-language rights were understandably far larger. An article in the May 12, 2000, *Globe* suggests that WEEI was paying about $5 million a year for Red Sox radio rights, but the Red Sox were looking for $35 million for a seven-year deal.
39. The figure 50 comes from Bill Griffith, "Sox and Fox Proving to Be a Fine Marriage," *Boston Globe*, March 30, 2001, 95.

40. Griffith, "Sox and Fox." Garcia Marquez had previously done pregame and postgame broadcasts for the San Diego Padres.
41. Griffith, "Sox and Fox."
42. Bill Griffith, "Spanish Telecasts Are Round-Trippers," *Boston Globe*, July 13, 2001, 86.
43. Author interview with Bill Kulik, May 4, 2020.
44. "Joe Castiglione," Massachusetts Broadcasters Hall of Fame, http://www.massbroadcastershof.org/hall-of-fame/hall-of-fame-2015/joe-castiglione/. Accessed on May 10, 2020.
45. One account of the sale is Bill Nowlin, *Tom Yawkey: Patriarch of the Boston Red Sox* (Lincoln: University of Nebraska Press), 409–412.
46. Bill Griffith, "Beloved Voice a Throwback," *Boston Globe*, March 15, 2002, 103.
47. *2006 Boston Red Sox Media Guide*, 650.
48. Griffith, "Walking Example of Jimmy Fund's Work."
49. Author interview with Uri Berenguer, April 16, 2020.
50. Bill Griffith, "NESN: Teeming with Conflicts," *Boston Globe*, March 28, 2003, 117.
51. Author interview with Uri Berenguer, April 16, 2020.
52. Author interview with Uri Berenguer, April 20, 2020.
53. Author interview with Uri Berenguer, April 20, 2020.
54. Author interview with Alberto Vasallo III, May 6, 2020.
55. Bill Griffith, "Tragedy Has Taken Air Out of SBN Booth," *Boston Globe*, June 3, 2005, 30.
56. Frank Litsky, "A Mother's Stubbornness Provides a Reason to Run," *New York Times*, April 18, 2005.
57. Author interview with Bill Kulik, May 4, 2020. The Gringo Malo adds, "I think we and J.C. Romero are the only two who own World Series rings from '07 and '08. We both were with the Red Sox in '07 and we both moved over to the Phillies in '08."
58. Clea Simon, "Program Brings Cultural Factor of Spanish-Language Sports Coverage," *Boston Globe*, February 23, 2006, 80.
59. Author interview with Uri Berenguer, April 20, 2020.
60. *2009 Boston Red Sox Media Guide*, 618.
61. *2010 Boston Red Sox Media Guide*, 526.
62. The *Globe* ran a story announcing the cohosting plan in July. Chad Finn, "Casting NESN in a New Light," *Boston Globe*, July 16, 2010, C2.
63. Chad Finn, "Berenguer Is Out of the Mix," *Boston Globe*, November 12, 2010, C3.
64. Author interview with Bill Kulik, May 4, 2020..
65. Franco Ordóñez, "Last Farewell for Voice of Medias Rojas," *Boston Globe*, June 4, 2005, B1, B5.
66. Email from Luisma, June 19, 2020. He notes a website in Spanish where Spanish baseball fans usually write about baseball: https://www.beisbolmlb.com. He himself has written some articles, one among them this 2017 article about a visit to Fenway Park: https://www.beisbolmlb.com/fenway-park-solo-hay-uno/. Accessed May 14, 2021.
67. Author interview with Uri Berenguer, May 12, 2021.
68. Author interview with Uri Berenguer, May 12, 2021. Uri did not work for the Red Sox for either the 2022 or 2023 seasons.
69. Author interview with Uri Berenguer, April 25, 2020.

Luis Rodríguez-Mayoral

Lou Hernández

A well-known title line from a poem written by 19th-century Puerto Rican writer and activist Lola Rodríguez de Tió says that *Cuba y Puerto Rico son de un pájaro las dos alas* (Cuba and Puerto Rico are two wings from the same bird). It could be said that Luis Rodríguez-Mayoral genealogically epitomizes this cultural bond between the two nations.

"I was conceived in San Antonio de los Baños, Cuba, while my father, who was a U.S. Army officer, was stationed at a Cuban militia air base there," revealed Rodríguez-Mayoral. "I was born in Ponce, Puerto Rico, December 16, 1945, shortly after my father was transferred to Puerto Rico. My mother was a native of Ponce; she came from a very well-known family. My father came from Vega Alta, about 25 miles west of San Juan."[1]

And so began an incredible baseball journey for Rodríguez-Mayoral that would lead him through not only the sports Halls of Fame of several countries but also through the highest halls of global power and circles of widest cultural importance in the world, not to mention the lofty achievement of broadcasting over 2,000 major league games and authoring several books.

Born to José Rodríguez Vega and Marvi Mayoral Goyena, Luis was the middle of three children. Older brother José preceded him by two years, and younger sister Lourdes arrived ten winters afterward.

It was at an early age in his birth country that Luis first experienced the transformational moment that would lead him on, as he put it, "a mission from God in baseball." He pinpoints the life-changing event, at age six, this way: "A few days before my father left to serve in the Korean conflict (1951), he took my brother and I to a ball game at [estadio] Paquito Montaner in Ponce. As soon as we scaled the incline leading to the seats, I saw the players practicing on the field, and I felt like my spirit got away from my physical being, and it was a joy that I cannot describe. My love for baseball was born that day in Ponce."[2]

The young Luis spent his first 10 years happily in Puerto Rico, before his father's profession resulted in some uprooting of the family, first to Panama and then Seattle, Washington. In August 1956, two years after returning from Korea, José Rodríguez Vega was restationed to Fort Gulick in the former Panama Canal Zone. Rodríguez Vega assumed an instructor's post with the camp's military police.

Like countless others of his time and age, Luis tuned into ball games and collected trading cards. "I started listening to major league baseball in Panama on the Armed Forces Radio," wrote Luis in his autobiography, as he continued to nurture his special affinity for the game. "At night, I would listen to 'La Voz de los Estados Unidos de América' [Voice of America Radio] for long stretches. I also liked to read, and I spent a lot of time in the library. I read newspapers from the States. They were dated, maybe a week old, but they provided information on the major leagues and its ballplayers. I expanded to reading biographies on the skillful players—Ted Williams, Babe Ruth—whenever I could. I was always searching for knowledge about baseball, particularly on the big league level."[3]

Like many teen fans, he followed some players more closely than others. "My idols were [Luis] Aparicio and Beto Ávila," Rodríguez recollected fondly. "There was Clemente, Vic Power, Miñoso, oh, Miñoso—he had his uniform number retired by the White Sox 37 years ago *today*. So it was mostly Latin players, but I was well aware of the greatness of Henry Aaron, Mickey Mantle, and Warren Spahn was a favorite player of mine, too."[4]

As a teenager, Luis possessed an innate ability to recognize the sometimes-harsh realities of life that burdened some people more than others. "Playing in the Pony League in Panama, we would use Mount Hope Park," recalled Rodríguez-Mayoral. "We would play at certain times and then the black kids would play, having a different schedule apart from us. There did not exist segregation within the military but there was latent segregation between the civilian population of Americans and Canal Zone workers."[5]

It was from these types of civic observations that Rodríguez-Mayoral developed personal doctrines of humanitarianism that guided his life forward. "Interestingly, while I was in Panama, you could cross a bridge and it would take you from the Canal Zone, where we lived, into the republic of Panama," he stated. "I saw a big area of commerce with people from all over the world. Stores and businesses from as far away as Japan and China. It made me realize that we we're not the center of the universe. I realized then that the world belongs to everyone. And that's how I first developed my pro–Latin sentiments."[6]

After finishing middle school, Luis started high school but was forced to move after his first year when his father received a transfer notice to Seattle in November 1959. "I was sad to leave Panama," reflected Rodríguez-Mayoral, "where, among other things, my 'Latin Americanism' was born and where I was exposed to unfamiliar cultures."[7]

In Seattle, Luis continued his upper grade education at Queen Anne High School and followed his favorite sport through the *Game of the Week* broadcasts, headlined by Dizzy Dean. Although some of his adolescent years were spent abroad, Luis was able to return to Puerto Rico while still in his teens and graduate from high school and then attend the University of Puerto Rico. That's because in September 1960, his father decided to retire from the military and reestablish his home on his birth island. The family rented a car to take them from Seattle to Charleston, South Carolina, to catch a flight to their native land. During the trip, Luis remembers catching several games of the 1960 World Series on the car radio, with Roberto Clemente getting hits in every game.

The family settled in the Santa Rosa ward of the city of Bayamón, not far from San Juan, in 1962. The same year, a nearly 17-year-old Luis unexpectedly ran into Orlando Cepeda at the Mall de Santa Rosa. One of Luis's idols, the future Hall of Famer considered the encounter as the start of a decades-long friendship that has spanned two centuries. Cepeda affirmed as much in his back-cover blurb for Rodríguez-Mayoral's 2002 book, *Mi Vida ... Más Allá de un Sueño*:

> I've known Luis-Rodríguez-Mayoral for some 40 years. His love of baseball has allowed him to succeed and at the same time provide value to all Latin Americans inside and outside of this great game.[8]

Coincidentally, another native major leaguer and fellow resident of Santa Rosa further nudged Luis along his baseball-drawn path. "Julio Navarro lived three streets away from where we did," Rodríguez-Mayoral attested. "He drove a white Chevy Impala. Julio was the first professional player that understood my love for the game and my desire to broaden its reach. Julio and his wife Haydée became like a second set of parents to me. It was through Julio that I met other big leaguers, such as José Pagan, Héctor Valle, Dagoberto [Bert] Campaneris and Nino Escalera, to name a few."[9]

Although it was his "out-of-body experience" as a six-year-old boy that kindled his love affair with baseball, a closer person-to-person contact, years later, actually set in motion Luis Rodríguez-Mayoral's extraordinary multipurposed, lifelong relationship with the game.

As a 19-year-old on leave from the U.S. Coast Guard Reserves, Rodríguez-Mayoral found himself flying home to Puerto Rico. "On the flight from Miami to San Juan," related Luis, "a heavy-set man with white hair and deep voice is sitting in the seat next to me. It turns out he was Howie Haak, one of the first big league scouts to go into Latin America. And I asked him about the ring he was wearing, and he said it was the 1960 Pittsburgh Pirates world championship ring. And we talked. Pancho Coimbre came up. Haak knew him. Coimbre was a scout for the Pirates. My grandparents, through their connections, knew Coimbre and his family."

"Howie and I became friends first. You have to remember at that time, within the baseball culture of Puerto Rico there were few people that spoke English. Whenever Howie came to Puerto Rico, I hung out with him for four or five days. I was his cultural bridge."[10] (Rodríguez-Mayoral began learning English as part of the curriculum in Catholic grammar school in Ponce and broadened its use while in Panama and Seattle.)

Thanks to the Haak-Coimbre connection, Rodríguez-Mayoral received an invitation for a dream encounter with Puerto Rico's most recognized athlete. In the winter of 1965, the 20-year-old accompanied the Pirates' scouts to Roberto Clemente's home in Río Piedras. "I was a college student," said Luis. "I'll never forget. We were on his balcony in the San Agustín development and you could see from Carolina to old San Juan. A beautiful view. We were there for about half an hour. I was in awe. From the time I shook his hand, I sensed a great affinity existed between us."[11]

It took several years after the initial chance meeting with Haak, however, for Rodríguez-Mayoral to latch on to his first major league job. Naturally, it was with the Pittsburgh Pirates. In 1972, the Pirates hired him as a scout for all players, native and foreign, in the Puerto Rican Winter League.

The early '70s were a pivotal period for the baseball enthusiast. Two years earlier, through the Pirates, Rodríguez-Mayoral established the first Día del Pelotero Latinoamericano. It was the beginning of an annual, on-field recognition of Latin American major leaguers, all of them emceed by Rodríguez-Mayoral. Prior to this, a few big-league franchises had honored their outstanding Hispanic ballplayers individually, on occasion, but Latin American Baseball Player's Day became the first cultural recognition of Hispanic players as a group throughout the major leagues. "My original thinking behind the concept was to highlight contributions to the game by Latin ballplayers, which even then started to become richer and richer, and always being aware of the tough time transitioning they had," specified Rodríguez-Mayoral. "From an early age, 16, 17, I was aware of the hardships and prejudices Hispanics in the game encountered in the 1950s and '60s."[12]

Inspired by his admiration of Orlando Cepeda and Roberto Clemente, the idea was born during a summer day in 1970, at the Atlanta home of a Rodríguez-Mayoral friend, Dr. Ángel Guardiola. At a party, which hosted Atlanta Braves' Hispanic teammates Cepeda, Tony González, Felix Millán, and Gil Garrido, the 20-something Luis formalized his plans to pay tribute to what he felt was an underappreciated segment of major league baseball. Rodríguez-Mayoral eternally extends his gratitude to then-Braves vice president, Dick Cecil, for supporting and designating September 6, 1970, as the inaugural event date.

The Ponce native also attributes the eventual success and longevity of the initiative to backing he received from the start, which came from the top. "It would not have been possible without the blessings of [Commissioners] Bowie Kuhn, [Peter] Ueberroth, [Bart] Giamatti, [Fay] Vincent, and marginally Selig, Bud Selig," admitted Rodríguez-Mayoral. "My dear friend Bobby Maduro introduced me to Bowie Kuhn at the 1971 Caribbean Series. Maduro practically took me by the hand to meet Kuhn. I always had ideas to make the game more internationally appealing. Bowie Kuhn understood me. He gave his approval for the Latin American Baseball Player's Day to continue.

"Kuhn then introduced me to Ueberroth. Giamatti, I had already met because he was National League president, so that transition was smooth. And Fay Vincent I met through Giamatti, even though his tenure in office was short. Peter O'Malley [Dodgers owner] was another person who was always in my corner. Those guys deserve much of the credit for allowing me to contribute to the game the way I contributed to it."[13]

As Luis was launching the forerunner to today's Hispanic Heritage celebrations that virtually all MLB teams promote, he took a step toward greater personal growth in the sport he loved. Rodríguez-Mayoral began radio broadcasts of big-league games to his home country. "From 1971 to 1982, I did about 800–850 games from the States to Puerto Rico by way of four stations," said Luis. "They were all through independent producers based in Puerto Rico. We did mostly Northeast coast games. Yankees, Mets, Orioles, Boston."[14]

The fourth annual Latin American Baseball Player's Day, held at Fenway Park, July 21, 1973, was a significant and special one for the young Hispanic ambassador. Rodríguez-Mayoral had received consent from Bowie Kuhn to honor an individual Hispanic player during the event with a named Roberto Clemente Memorial Award. (Not to be confused with MLB's renamed Commissioner's Award to the Roberto Clemente Award in the same year.) On a drizzly afternoon, Rodríguez-Mayoral honored his boyhood idol, Luis Aparicio. "The Minnesota Twins were in town," remembered Rodríguez-Mayoral. "Three hours before the field ceremony,

I met Tom Yawkey, Red Sox owner. He received me in his office, wearing a white shirt and his ubiquitous suspenders. He told me, 'I want you, during your ceremony, to give Aparicio his [commemorative] 500th stolen base." (A few days earlier, Aparicio had become the first Hispanic player to steal as many bases in the major leagues.)

"Seconds before I handed Aparicio the base, my mind flashed with images of myself as a 14-year-old traveling through Chicago in my parents' car. We had stopped for gas, and I asked someone what that big building was in the distance. He answered that it was Comiskey Park ... home of the White Sox, I thought, team of Luis Aparicio. And I recalled myself as a ballplaying youngster in Panama, listening to White Sox games, over the Armed Forces Radio, with Luis Aparicio at short. And then in 1983, I visited Aparicio at his home in Maracaibo. Luis married a Puerto Rican woman, Sonia Llorente. Standing up for Aparicio at his wedding was best man Buck Canel."[15]

Aparicio was elected to the U.S. Hall of Fame in 1984, the first Venezuelan to be enshrined there. Canel was awarded his own Cooperstown corner in 1985, as the first Hispanic Ford C. Frick recipient. It came five years after his death. The Argentine-born Canel's placement, at the time, would not have been possible without Luis Rodríguez-Mayoral. Luis conveyed the unique story in this manner: "In 1936, Buck Canel was the first Hispanic media rep to cover the Cooperstown Hall of Fame inaugural. The only Latino who covered the event. Canel was friends with one of my mother's relatives, Radamés Mayoral, who was the longtime play-by-play man of the Ponce Leones of the Puerto Rican Winter League. Canel had broadcast in Puerto Rico for a few years.

"But I first ran into Buck Canel during my initial MLB broadcasting years to Puerto Rico. It was in 1972, a couple of days before the All-Star game in Atlanta. I was in the press box and looked to my left and there he was. I introduced myself and we hit it off. And until the day of his death, he was my closest connection to major league baseball. He was like my grandfather, in a way, and I was his grandson. We had a great, great relationship. I was happy to honor Canel at the tenth Latin American Baseball Player's Day at Yankee Stadium (July 3, 1979).

"When the first Ford C. Frick Award was presented in 1978, I said to myself, Canel needs to be considered. From 1978 until 1983, '84, I campaigned for Buck Canel. By myself, from Puerto Rico, I wrote letters, I made phone calls. I called Bowie Kuhn. And in 1985, Canel was named the award's recipient. In fact, the official photo the Hall of Fame shows of Canel was supplied by me. Canel is cropped out, but it was a photo taken along with Al Rosen, then president of the Yankees, and myself. No one else had a good photo of Buck Canel. Incredible but true. The PR guy from the Hall of Fame asked me if I had a good photo of Canel. I said yes and I sent it to him."[16]

As if that were not enough, when the Hall of Fame could not locate Canel's widow, they turned to Rodríguez-Mayoral. Apparently, following Canel's death in 1980, his widow, Colleen, had sold their home in Croton-on-Hudson and relocated to rural North Carolina. The intrepid Luis tracked her down, and she and her grandchildren were able to attend the induction ceremony.

The scouting job with the Pirates lasted until 1978. Luis then followed up in a similar capacity for two years with the Chicago White Sox. And after his independent MLB broadcasting role ended in 1981, Luis took on front-office jobs in the Puerto Rican Winter League. He had one-year stints as general manager with the Arecibo and San Juan teams in the mid-'80s. He stayed on as a club administrator with San Juan into the new decade.

The 46-year-old Rodríguez-Mayoral then received a call from a new major league ownership group that would lead to cementing his historic place as a Hispanic broadcast journalist and baseball history maker. He clarified: "When George Bush bought the Texas Rangers, the team did not have personnel to deal with the number of Hispanic players. Bush's office, probably John Blake, the Rangers' PR man, called me in Puerto Rico in February of 1992. I was with the Puerto Rican representative in the Caribbean World Series in Hermosillo, Mexico. I returned his call when I got home. I ended up traveling to Fort Meyers during spring training and was offered the job. I was hired to be assistant public relations director of the Texas Rangers. I was the first liaison; now every team has a Latin liaison to the players."[17]

As a result of his new job, Rodríguez-Mayoral was forced to leave his position with *El Vocero,* a daily newspaper in Puerto Rico for which he had covered major league baseball since 1974. The newspaper also reached 16 U.S. cities with large Hispanic populations. As he was settling into his new post, Luis was invited to speak at Harvard University's John F. Kennedy School of Government on April 24, 1992. The following month, Soviet leader Mikhail Gorbachev spoke from the same podium as Luis.[18]

The first Puerto Rican executive in the major leagues soon expanded his duties, which delivered an increased but welcomed workload, according to him. "In 1993, something came to pass with the announcer doing the Spanish radio broadcasts, and he could not fulfill his duties. The Rangers knew I had experience doing broadcasts, and so Blake asked me to take it on, with the title of director of Spanish broadcasting. I said, of course, I'm here to work. So I continued to do the transitioning work with the players and the PR work with the Hispanic community. With the broadcasting of games, my day began at eight in the morning and ended at two in the morning. I was the play-by play man. I did close to 1,200 games for the Rangers from 1992 to 1999, plus three post-seasons."[19]

It's worth remembering that the Rangers of the 1990s boasted a Murderers' Row of Hispanic superstar talent. Pudge Rodríguez, Juan "Igor" González, José Canseco, and Rafael Palmeiro were all teammates with the Texas club. "I knew all of the great Hispanic players on the Rangers like they were my little brothers," added Rodríguez-Mayoral. "By the way, I'm the one that started the 'Papi' thing in MLB. I know it stuck with David Ortiz, but you verify it with Juan González, I used it first, and then others began using it."[20]

Rodríguez-Mayoral was not only an older brother figure to some of the Rangers' players; he was also a cultural educator. In 1993, while traveling on Rosa Parks Boulevard in Detroit, near Tiger Stadium, he had to explain to González and Pudge Rodríguez who the civil rights igniter was and why she merited such a significant street in her name. He promised one day that they would meet her. Five years later, Rodríguez-Mayoral met Reverend Jesse Jackson at a luncheon in Dallas. Through Jackson's connections, Rodríguez-Mayoral was able to attend a ceremony honoring the 85-year-old Parks the same year. Luis took the two Ranger ballplayers with him. "She was in a wheelchair," he later transcribed. "'What are you, men of baseball, doing visiting me?' she asked in a low voice. 'I've known about you since I was a boy in Panama.'"[21]

His tenure behind the microphone, and all other duties with the Rangers, ended in 1999, as Rodríguez-Mayoral decided to transition to an alternative posting as Latin American liaison with the Detroit Tigers. Rodríguez-Mayoral held the job for two years, during which his only child, a daughter named Eukaris, graduated from the University of Texas at Arlington in 2000.

In 2001, Rodríguez-Mayoral visited his former boss, who had himself transitioned to an elevated posting in the nation's capital. "When I was with the Rangers," illuminated Luis, "George Bush would go to my office, put his feet up on my desk, lean back on the chair, and talk. He usually wore cowboy boots, jeans, and a regular shirt. We would talk three times a week for about an hour. The Rangers had their offices in a building right next to the stadium. I walked from the office to the ballpark.

"I was invited to the White House in 2001, April 16. Accompanying me was [Indians outfielder] Juan González and Puerto Rican congressman from New York José Serrano, who served as our guide. There is a little curved passageway into the Oval Office. President Bush greeted us there;

he kissed my bald pate. The get-together at the White House was supposed to last 10 minutes. It lasted an hour and 15. Unexpectedly, Vice President Dick Cheney also joined us. I remember González asking the president to halt the U.S. bombing exercises on Vieques.

"I was invited a second time [to the White House] in 2007, and the same thing occurred as far as duration. A scheduled short meeting stretched out over an hour. George Bush is *buena gente*, a good guy."[22]

Multiple invitations to the White House are a rarity for most citizens. For the spiritually minded son of the Island of Enchantment, he views such occurrences as part of the "divine design" of his life that was laid out for him. "Doors miraculously opened for me," he humbly spoke. "I did not open any doors. That is why I say God has paved all the major league roads and baseball boulevards I have traveled. How else could a person like me, with my background, have been able to accomplish so much?"[23]

Luis and his former Texas Rangers boss, President George W. Bush. Juan González is on the right (collection of Luis Rodríguez-Mayoral).

Rodríguez-Mayoral's front-office position with the Tigers was his last with major league baseball. In 2005, Rodríguez-Mayoral was touted as co-grand marshal to the Puerto Rican Day Parade in New York. One of the largest parades in the country, Luis shared the marshalling honors with reggaeton artist Daddy Yankee.

In 2013, the Puerto Rican Sports Hall of Fame recognized their native son's overall contribution to the sport; Rodríguez-Mayoral shared the induction honors with former Yankees outfielder turned musician Bernie Williams. Rodríguez-Mayoral's Halls of Fame accreditations began in 1991 with the Ponce Sports Hall of Fame and the Monterrey-based Mexican Hall of Fame. They augmented in 1999, through the Latin American International Sports Hall of Fame in Laredo, Texas, and the City of Bayamón in 2014.

His current personal biography states that he continues to author articles, grant interviews, and conduct conferences on MLB. Rodríguez-Mayoral settled permanently in northeast Texas, after relocating to the United States for his employment with the Rangers three decades ago.

However, his perspective on residency has evolved with age to coincide with his deep sense of purpose. "Almost half of my experience has elapsed away from the island where I was born," analyzed the septuagenarian. "Therefore, I cannot define home as a place. Home, to me, is a state of mind from where I have given the best every day while attempting to help humanity on a mission assigned by God, particularly by way of baseball and journalism."[24]

Notes

1. Phone interview with Luis Rodríguez-Mayoral (LRM), May 8, 2020.
2. *Ibid.*
3. Luis Rodríguez-Mayoral, *Mi Vida ... Más Allá de un Sueño* (Fort Worth: Sprint Press, 2002), 16. LRM also developed a diverse love of music during these formative years, inspired in large part by his father's record collection. Among Luis's favorite singers were Latin preeminents Lucho Gatica, Toña la Negra, Celia Cruz, Ruth Fernández, Bobby Capó, and Benny Moré. He also developed an appreciation for the U.S. musical genres of the period, headed by the likes of Elvis Presley, Paul Anka, The Platters, Roy Orbison, Brenda Lee, Buddy Holly, and Ritchie Valens, among others. Holly's widow, Maria Helena Santiago, is a native of Juana Díaz, Puerto Rico, and resides about 10 miles from Arlington, Texas, LRM's current residence. In the past, he has spoken with her at length and says she has never lost her love for her native island.
4. Phone interview with LRM, May 8, 2020. The Chicago White Sox retired Minnie Miñoso's uniform number on May 8, 1983. The Mother's Day ceremony was attended by Hall of Famer Monte Irvin and Baseball Commissioner Bowie Kuhn, among others. U.S. president Ronald Reagan sent Miñoso an engraved silver plaque. LRM attended, less than two days after presiding over the annual Latin American Baseball Player's Day at Dodger Stadium.

5. Rodríguez-Mayoral, *Mi Vida*, 17.
6. Phone interview with LRM, May 8, 2020.
7. Rodríguez-Mayoral. *Mi Vida*, 18.
8. *Ibid.*, back cover.
9. Follow-up phone interview with LRM, May 21, 2020.
10. Phone interview with LRM, May 8, 2020. Ponce-native Francisco "Pancho" Coimbre was considered Puerto Rico's best baseball player of the first half of the 20th century. An outstanding contact hitter, he played throughout the Caribbean basin and in the U.S. Negro Leagues.
11. Follow-up phone interview with LRM, May 21, 2020. A year prior, LRM was working as a guide and counselor for the Puerto Rican branch of the American Camp Association. One day, the leader of the camp asked his young counselor to accompany him to the airport to pick up someone, the son of his mother's best friend, he said. It turned out to be Cassius Clay. The pair spent five hours with the boxing titan as Clay visited with the kids in the camp.
12. Phone interview with LRM, May 8, 2020.
13. *Ibid.* LRM has photos with all of the mentioned commissioners and O'Malley. Included in the shot with the Dodgers owner is Tommy Lasorda and player Pedro Guerrero.
14. *Ibid.* The stations were WAPA-Radio, WIAC-Radio, Radio Aeropuerto, and Radio San Juan. His partners during those years were Terry García, Josué González, José Santiago, and Eugenio "Gino" Guerra. LRM's most memorable broadcasts include Roberto Clemente's 3,000th hit (9/30/72); uniform retirement days of Clemente, Minnie Miñoso, and Nolan Ryan (4/6/73, 5/8/83, and 9/15/95, respectively); inaugural game of the Ballpark in Arlington (4/11/94); and first interleague game (6/12/97).
15. Luis Rodríguez-Mayoral, "Luis Aparicio: Orgullo de Venezuela e Inmortal del Béisbol," Bèisbol101.com, April 16, 2020, https://www.bèisbol101.com/2020/04/luis-aparicio-orgullo-de-venezuela-e-inmortal-del-bèisbol/. Eventually, more than 200 players were recognized in ceremonies over 24 years. Following Roberto Clemente's death, the celebrations were topped off with the individual naming of a Hispanic player to receive the Roberto Clemente Memorial Award (RCMA). The first RCMA recipient was Luis Aparicio in 1973, with Benito Santiago bestowed the last in 1993. LRM could not continue the celebrations after that year due to his broadcasting commitment with the Texas Rangers, and the festivities, as established, were discontinued.
16. Phone interview with LRM, May 8, 2020. LRM's album of photos with Hall of Fame–honored broadcasters include Canel, Felo Ramírez, Vin Scully, Ernie Harwell, Jaime Jarrín, Bob Prince, Tom Cheek, Joe Garagiola, and Tony Kubek.
17. Phone interview with LRM, May 8, 2020.
18. Gorbachev's speech occurred on May 15, 1992. In 1998, LRM was asked to be part of the White House's Affirmative Action Committee under President Clinton.
19. Phone interview with LRM, May 8, 2020. LRM's broadcast partners were Mario Montez, Mario Díaz Orozco, and J.J. Pérez.
20. Phone interview with LRM, May 8, 2020.
21. Rodríguez-Mayoral, *Mi Vida*, 88..
22. Phone interview with LRM, May 8, 2020.
23. *Ibid.*
24. Rodríguez-Mayoral, *Mi Vida*. Promotional press booklet, 2019, back cover.

Héctor Molina

Juan Jose Rodríguez

Familiar.

Written or spoken—in Spanish or in English—that single word illustrates one of the truly defining characteristics of Héctor Molina's broadcasting career. Throughout the three decades in which Molina's voice has entered the homes of Chicago sports fans, his skill to create familiar, close-knit connections with his broadcast partners and his expansive audiences has been a focal point of his career. Even "expansive" hardly tells the full story, as Molina's trajectory has paraded him across three marquee franchises in the Windy City and has bestowed four championship rings on him.

Just as sports fans in Chicago and around the world have embraced Molina's commentary for many years, Molina feels a similar connection to the millions who tune in. Upon returning in 2012 for his second stint broadcasting White Sox games, Molina simply revealed, "It really feels like coming back home."[1]

Chicago is Molina's current place of residence, but a trip from Chicago to his original hometown of Barceloneta in Puerto Rico would require a five-hour flight and an additional 40-mile drive upon landing. Founded by the Spanish in 1881—the last such town in Puerto Rico—the municipality was so named by Bonocio Llenza Feliú because of the joyous memories it conveyed of his own hometown of Barcelona in Spain.

Located more than 2,000 miles away from Chicago, Barceloneta does possess a much closer connection to Molina's present-day occupation than distance can reveal. Well before he would call a single or a home run, he began his career working as the morning DJ for Radio Borinquen (WBQN, 1160 AM), a local news and talk radio station in Barceloneta.

"The idea of working as a DJ never passed through my mind until a neighbor of mine—Juan Félix Ruíz, who was a Spanish teacher—bought a reel-to-reel recorder and decided to try it out with the kids in the neighborhood," Molina said.[2]

That initial impetus prompted Molina to consider exploring his interests a bit further. An avid fan of horse racing, Molina stumbled upon the idea of recording his "call" of an imaginary horse race. After doing so, he shared the recording with Ruíz, who was extremely impressed. Ruíz asked Molina, who was only 12 years old at the time, if at some point he would like to work in the radio industry. Molina responded that he would, but the conversation ended there.

"If a Spanish teacher was surprised with the diction and creativity of a 12-year-old boy," Molina said, "the idea [of working in radio] was constantly turning in my head. In high school, I belonged to the drama club, and that helped with my diction and helped to eliminate my fears of speaking in front of an audience."

After graduating from high school, Molina moved to New York with his uncle and 10 cousins—his parents doing the same a year later—and he once again began taking drama classes because, quite simply, "I had been bitten by the acting bug. I wanted to be an actor."

Those desires hardly changed. But his plans nonetheless did.

After turning 18 years old, Molina was drafted as part of a mandatory recruitment to serve with the United States Army in Vietnam—where he spent the next 14 months as the radio operator for the lead sergeant—an experience he still to this day labels "painful but positive at the same time."

"I learned that wars do not solve anything; they only make a few rich and tyrants of many," Molina recalled. "I learned that all human beings have the right to a life of peace, to a better quality of life that cannot be achieved with bullets or bombs."

At the conclusion of his time in Vietnam, Molina enrolled at Universidad Católica in Puerto Rico, which he chose over St. Edward's University (Austin, Texas) and New York University. "I wanted to study in my own language [Spanish] and return to the island," Molina said. He became involved in some local community service programs, and the itch to continue speaking in public arose once again. This time, he accepted a role as the master of ceremonies for various events but only as an unpaid volunteer.

This led to his more focused consideration of working in radio. However, that idea once again was put on hold.

Shortly after Molina had married his wife, Iraida, in 1972, he left once again to serve in the military, this time with the United States Navy at the Great Lakes (Great Lakes, Illinois) and Roosevelt Roads (Ceiba, Puerto Rico) Naval Stations.

Molina did not travel far to continue his education, opting to venture roughly two hours southwest of Barceloneta to San Germán, home to the main campus of Interamerican University of Puerto Rico. Molina graduated in 1977 with a degree in sociology, a major inspired by his time in Vietnam.

"[My time in Vietnam] totally defined who I wanted to be in the future," Molina said. "My years in college, my experiences in Vietnam and [my major in] sociology changed my way of seeing the world and its inhabitants."

Upon having completed his service with the army, Molina returned to work with the United States Post Office in Manhattan, where he had been prior to his time in Vietnam. However, after his graduation from Universidad Interamericana, he shifted industries and accepted a role as a substitute teacher at a Puerto Rican high school named for former governor Jesús T. Piñero. He remained at the school until a position arose with the Department of Social Services. During this time, he discovered an opportunity to try a radio-focused role, which manifested itself after a fundraising event for cancer patients.

"The owner of the radio station suggested to me that I 'try out' as a DJ, and I accepted," Molina said. "He told me to go to the radio station when I had time to do some demos and record commercials. He liked me and suggested an unpaid 'internship' in which I would learn how to use the console and train on how to use the microphone. Finally, after a month, they offered me the shift from 6:00 p.m. to 10:00 p.m., which included assisting during the sports segment from 6:00 p.m. to 7:00 p.m. with the sportscaster and professional storyteller Luis Antonio Dávila. I learned a lot with him and with my trainer, Rafael Serrano—ironically also a Spanish teacher—who taught me what radio was and how to use it as an instrument for good."

Molina finally left his job with Social Services when the radio station offered him a permanent job from noon to 6:00 p.m., a job with more money but also more adventure and more travel. A sudden change brought Molina to Los Angeles when the need for social workers became prevalent with the crisis of the Mariel in Cuba in the early 1980s. Already married and with three children, Molina said of his decision to relocate, "I didn't think twice" as the position offered more money and substantial benefits. The joy didn't last long as his position was eliminated shortly after Ronald Reagan was elected president in the early 1980s. Molina and his family were in the process of moving west, but his absence of employment halted the relocation.

In what would ultimately become a pivotal inflection point in his life, Molina elected to pay a trip to Chicago to reconnect with well-regarded radio producer Elias Díaz y Pérez, who had once offered Molina a job while Molina was in the midst of his radio work in Puerto Rico. Having a sister already living in Chicago, Molina desired to relocate and be closer to family, so he asked Pérez for his help in finding an opportunity to prove himself in the Windy City. A role for hosting a morning news segment became available, and Pérez offered to help Molina get started in what became the resumption of Molina's "adventure" of working in radio.

"Elias Díaz y Pérez was one of the people to whom I am most grateful for the opportunity he gave me. After I had spent three months with the news, his morning DJ resigned for money reasons, and I became the full-time morning announcer. I was able to bring my family, and the adventure began again."

The shuffling continued after Molina left to oversee the news for a newly launched 24-hour radio station in Chicago (WOJO-105 FM). Upon his departure, Molina tearfully looked his boss in the eye and said goodbye, to which his boss responded with this reassurance: "I have never had a more responsible person working for me than you. You deserve it [this new opportunity], and these doors will always be open for you."

After spending two more years working in the news and hosting a public service program, Molina and his family moved from Evanston to downtown Chicago, and he became the morning announcer from 1987 to 1994. These steps continued to bring him closer to the baseball diamond. When Molina's boss became a news executive at WOJO and thereby lost his side job as a baseball commentator for Cubs games, he recommended Molina as his replacement.

Molina's dream of breaking into the world of sports had finally become a reality.

During his time with WOJO, Molina worked as an analyst for Bears games for the 1987 and 1988 seasons, which he believes helped to spark—and subsequently boost—his popularity among fans in Chicago. In 1992, the Chicago White Sox and the Chicago Bulls agreed to broadcast their games together for the next five years, and in 1994, Molina resigned from his role with the morning show on WOJO to broadcast both teams' games on a more permanent basis, including the regular season and playoffs.

"I enjoyed the 'Beatles' experience when I did all the Chicago Bulls games [regular season and playoffs]," Molina said. "Four rings are the visual witness of that fabulous experience with Michael [Jordan], Scottie [Pippen], and the gang."

In 1998, the Caracol Network and ESPN joined forces to bring the broadcast of the World Series to Latin America. Having already called playoff games for the Bulls, Molina made his baseball playoff and World Series debut to broadcast the Yankees-Padres matchup in the Fall Classic.

"I got the call from Armando Talavera in New York, and I couldn't believe it," Molina said.

Molina had finally hit a home run with this opportunity. His hard work and dedication had gotten him this far; his voice and joyous spirit carried him the rest of the way.

A recent conversation with Chicago White Sox radio play-by-play broadcaster Len Kasper validated this idea and cemented the notion of Molina's overwhelmingly positive and approachable spirit.

"I just know that he loved baseball and people ... he's magnetic. He's got a magnetic personality and that's what always stuck out to me more than anything else."[3]

Kasper also noted that one of his few regrets throughout his illustrious career is not continuing to learn Spanish after high school and college, especially the more nuanced elements of the language.

"In Héctor's case, I see him a lot now," Kasper said, "and I really want to listen to some of his calls. And I wish I didn't have to get to a translation

Hector Molina with another Chicago broadcast legend, Harry Caray (courtesy Hector Molina).

just to see exactly what he's saying because the calls themselves are just ... they give you goose bumps."

Due to the Covid-19 pandemic that impacted the 2020 and 2021 MLB seasons in countless ways—including the reduction of fans present at stadiums and reduced travel opportunities for broadcasters—Molina called many of the games without a color commentator by his side. His current broadcast partner, Billy Russo, has worked as the team's Spanish radio color analyst since 2012, but he also works for the team as the manager of Spanish communications in addition to serving as a translator for the team's Spanish-speaking players, positions he has held since 2015. Thus, even though there has been a clear and distinct physical disparity between the seasons when Molina and Russo have stood side by side and those more recently when Molina has stood alone, Kasper has hardly noticed a shift in Molina's body language and demeanor from his neighboring booth.

"He's got a ton of energy from the first pitch till the last, and I always appreciate—you can tell from the minute you meet him—that he loves baseball and he loves being at the ballpark," Kasper said. "I have so much fun at the ballpark that you want to be around people who feel the same way you do, and a lot of people do, but there are certain special people [for whom] you can tell: This is not a job. In Héctor's case, it's totally genuine. It's never forced—he loves being around the sport as much as I do—and that matters to me. I like him even more because of that—I feel like we're kindred spirits."

Asked if he had a favorite game or memory of his time alongside Molina, Russo replied, "I don't think I can pick just one. Every day with Héctor is entertaining. It can be because the game is a very exciting game, and even [when the game might not be] as good as we were expecting, there's always something in the booth with him that you know that you're going to enjoy that day. And it can be a comment about the game, it can be a comment about how his day is going, a comment about his family ... There's always something that makes you smile."[4]

Kasper added, "I love his voice and the energy of his calls, but for me it's more about the person—he's such a memorable person because he lights up a room everywhere he goes. He's just got this great laugh, and I could just hear him tell stories for hours. He's just one of those people—when he walks into a room, you just feel good, he makes you feel good about life."

Kasper is hardly the only recipient of those good feelings. Recalling the start of his partnership with Molina, Russo noted, "We didn't have that chemistry that you build through the years. So our first time working together, he had a particular style, and I had a different style—he's been doing this here for a very long time and I was used to calling games in

Venezuela, so it's a little different. And when you're doing this for the first time with a new person, you try to get to know him. Especially with him being the play-by-play, I was trying to figure out ... how to mesh with his narrative. But he made that transition pretty easy, and we would talk during the breaks [to coordinate transitions]. It was an honest exchange on how to improve our work and how to make it very smooth and really professional."

Russo also senses a relation with Molina that stretches well beyond their occupation. "To me, not just because of the age gap, but he's like a relative—like an uncle or something like that. We have that kind of a relationship, and he brings that to the booth. There's always a teaching moment because we always try to explain things to the audience and even sometimes to ourselves."

"And he did it just because that's the way that he is," Russo added. "He doesn't have an ego, and that's huge. And I think that's one of the things that made us click right away."

Russo has learned plenty during his time alongside Molina, but he is far from the only one who has done so. Molina has been an integral mentor for many, including the legendary White Sox manager Ozzie Guillén—who, as Russo noted, is "a guy that is loved in Chicago"—and Guillén's son, Ozzie Jr. "Héctor knew him from when [the elder] Ozzie was playing ... Héctor used to call the games with Chico, and he traveled with the team. They [Molina and Guillén] created a strong bond, and I remember Ozzie telling me, 'He's one of the best.'"

Russo went on to continue lauding Molina's mentorship abilities. "One of the first things I knew about Héctor, and this came from Ozzie Jr.," he said. "'He was my teacher. He taught me how to call games, he taught me how to be on radio. And that was very good.' Those two [Guillén Sr. and Jr.] hold Héctor in really big regard. They really respect him, they really like the job that he does, and they listen to him. When Ozzie Jr. used to do games with Héctor, Héctor usually would give him advice about radio, work, and sometimes even about life and how to take advantage of the situation that he was in."

"And that's something that Ozzie Jr. would always remember."

A closer look at Molina's on-air tenure reveals a similar love for the game and for life as a whole. Kasper, a decorated broadcast professional who had worked as a play-by-play broadcaster across 22 seasons for three MLB teams—including 16 seasons for the crosstown-rival Cubs—before joining the White Sox in 2021, pointed out that a broadcaster's personality is one of the key traits that separates "the all-time greats" from their peers. According to Kasper, Molina fits squarely within that upper echelon of talent.

"This is what I like about every great broadcaster: He is himself on the air, and it's the same off the air—there's no act. And the all-time greats generally are who they are all the time, and that's the best compliment I could ever give anyone. And when I can hear Héctor and see him and then I talk to him off the air, he's the same exact person."

Personality is far from the lone element that Molina maintains. Russo pointed out that one of the most valuable lessons that he has learned from his time working with Molina is the importance of consistency, especially over the course of a 162-game regular season. "You always have to keep the rhythm all the time—you can't be too high, you can't be too low, you [have to be] in the middle, and that's a key," Russo said. "During those exciting games, during those walk-off games or even when your team is getting beat badly, you have to be in the middle. And that's not an easy thing to do."

That same person, Russo explained, has been characterized throughout his career by a "colorful" approach to his work, featuring his well-known lines of "Lo retrataron de cuerpo entero" (The batter was caught frozen) after strikeouts by White Sox pitchers and his signature "Sayonara, baby" after a White Sox home run.

"One of the things that makes Héctor the great play-by-play [broadcaster] that he is is that he knows the story of the game, and then he knows when to mix that knowledge with the game situation," Russo said. "And those are things that make listeners excited."

Listeners' excitement when listening to Molina stems from more than just his popular one-liners. His familiarity with Chicago sports and the market as a whole has aided in his overly positive reception from White Sox fans.

"He knows what the listeners like to listen to because he knows the market," Russo said. "I was new here, so there were some words that I would say that wouldn't connect with the audience. Even during specific situations in games, we would discuss that 'this is called this way in Venezuela' or 'this is called this way in Puerto Rico' and then we would explain that situation on air, and that would add to the broadcast and make it more entertaining."

"It really didn't take us long to blend, and I think it was easy and that in a big measure was because of him."

Whether Molina is on the air or off the air, Kasper said, "he's just a very popular person at the ballpark because he always greets you with a smile on his face. I was once told that you should broadcast with a smile on your face, and Héctor obviously learned that at a very young age because he does it to this day incredibly well."

Notes

1. Chicago White Sox, "Se Habla Béisbol," *Inside the White Sox*, March 30, 2012. https://whitesoxpride.mlblogs.com/robin-e64eb67ea3fb.

2. Héctor Molina, interview by author, August 31, 2021. Going forward, any quote from Mr. Molina is drawn from this interview.
3. Len Kasper, interview by author, August 13, 2021. Going forward, any quote from Mr. Kasper is drawn from this interview.
4. Billy Russo, interview by author, August 26, 2021. Going forward, any quote from Mr. Russo is drawn from this interview.

Tony Oliva

César Brioso

Growing up on his father's farm in rural Cuba during the 1940s and 1950s, Tony Oliva didn't have a television. But his family did have a radio. And every winter, Oliva would listen to announcers describe the baseball exploits of stars such as Camilo Pascual and Orestes "Minnie" Miñoso as they played in the Cuban League. "That was the biggest entertainment we had, especially for me because I'm from the countryside. I was raised in the countryside," Oliva said. "In Cuba, there was a very good league. Cuban baseball was like the big leagues here [in the United States]. It was the best baseball in Latin America at that time.... The league was very good. The competition was very good."[1]

Oliva rooted for Cienfuegos, one of the four teams in the league along with Habana, Almendares, and Marianao. Like Oliva, Cienfuegos pitcher Pedro Ramos, who played 15 seasons in the majors with the Senators, Indians, Yankees, Phillies, Reds, and Pirates, was from Pinar del Rio. "In Cuba, the most popular teams were Habana and Almendares. And then Marianao and Cienfuegos," Oliva said. "But my team was Cienfuegos. My dream was that someday I would play baseball in Cuba with the Cienfuegos team.... I never played in any type of organized baseball or anything. I only played in the countryside. But I felt so good about myself; I believed I could play in the Cuban League because I thought I could hit against any pitcher."[2]

Oliva never imagined he would instead play in the major leagues, much less become an eight-time All-Star in 15 seasons with the Minnesota Twins. And despite the myriad roles he has played with the Twins organization—player, first base coach, batting coach, minor league hitting instructor, marketing, and community relations—Oliva also never imagined he would become the Twins' Spanish-language radio analyst. "I've done a little of everything," Oliva said. "And when they asked me if I would like to do it, I never say no. It's good to always leave the door open and try to learn other things and see if you can improve yourself. So, I said yes.... It's been a very good experience—from baseball player to doing something I never thought I would do. In this world, you never know when you have an opportunity."[3]

The latest phase of Oliva's 63-year association with the Twins organization began with a historic one-off broadcast on July 28, 2002. Oliva and guest play-by-play announcer Edgar López, who was the Spanish-language voice of the Texas Rangers from 2000 to 2003, called a game between the Twins and Toronto Blue Jays on KCCO-AM 950, the first Minneapolis–Saint Paul radio or television station to carry a Twins game in Spanish in what was then the franchise's 41-year history.[4] López and Oliva's broadcast mimicked the English-language coverage on sister station WCCO-AM 830 and included taped pregame interviews with Latino players, scores and promos throughout the day, and a postgame show that included player-of-the-game awards and highlights.[5] The Twins won 4–0 as Johan Santana struck out 13 in eight innings and Torii Hunter went three for four with a home run.

López "was well-prepared and quite glib as he described the action on the field," Herón Márquez Estrada wrote in his coverage of the broadcast for the *Minneapolis Star Tribune*. "He drew out of Oliva numerous stories about his playing days with the Twins and in the minor leagues. Oliva seemed a little nervous at first, mentioning that he hadn't done broadcasting. But as he described 12-hour rides in prop planes, and how the 2002 Twins seem to be living a dream season, the three-time American League batting champion seemed to ease into his new role."[6] Asked if he had any doubts about announcing the first time, Oliva said with a laugh, "Yes, the first and the second and the third and the fourth."[7]

In making the franchise's first foray into Spanish-language broadcasting, Twins officials pointed out that Minnesota's Hispanic population had more than doubled since 1990, with census figures showing the number of Minnesotans who identified themselves as Hispanic growing from about 54,000 in 1990 to about 143,000 in 2000, a 166-percent increase.[8] "With the way the Hispanic population has boomed, and with the influx of Latin players on our team," said Brad Ruiter, the Twins' then-director of communication, "we figured it would be a natural fit to do something like this."[9] The Twins produced no more than four Spanish-language broadcasts per season from 2002 to 2005, with the team flying in a play-by-play announcer for each game. In 2005, Oliva became a mainstay on the broadcast, which included eight games in Spanish. "The experience has been fantastic," Oliva said. "We started with 2 games a year ... and now we do 50 games a year, every Sunday and Tuesday. But I'm still a rookie. I feel like a rookie. My partner is very good. Alfonso Fernández, he's the boss, right?

Tony Oliva on the air for his beloved Minnesota Twins (courtesy Minnesota Twins).

Like I said, I'm a rookie, [but] I'm defending myself. I feel a little more comfortable now. Who would have thought that I would be part of the [broadcast] in Spanish?"[10]

Fernández joined Oliva in 2006, and the Spanish broadcasts increased to 13 games in 2007, 26 games in 2008 and 2009, and to the present level of 50 games in 2010. Games can be heard at Twinsbeisbol.com. Previously, Fernández had done Spanish broadcasts for the Minnesota Timberwolves, Minnesota Vikings, Los Angeles Clippers, Los Angeles Lakers, and Los Angeles Rams. "This was my first baseball team," Fernández said. "It's been a tremendous change because baseball is slower. It's more knowledge and, above all, it has many rules, many secrets: how to pitch, how to hit, how to field, how to stand in the batter's box, how to deal with a closer, how to deal with a starter, if it's a lefty, if it's a right-hander, the way pitchers throw. There are many things to learn, and practically for me in 14 years, I'm still a rookie. Every day, every broadcast, I learn more and I learn more from Tony because he knows it all."[11] Fernández says calling Twins games has "been a totally beautiful experience" and says working with Oliva "has been a blessing for the 14 years that we completed the past year [2020]." He says Oliva has improved "enormously" as an analyst.

Oliva's passion is evident in his calls. Andrew Halverson, the Twins' director for broadcast, said one of his favorite Oliva calls came when Jim Thome hit a 10th-inning, walk-off, two-run home run to give the Twins a 7–6 victory against the Chicago White Sox on August 17, 2010. As Fernández is calling the shot, Oliva is heard yelling, "It left the stadium! Yeah, yeah, yeah, yeah, yeah! Incredible! Incredible! That is incredible! That ball completely left the stadium!" It's a great example of Oliva's energy and passion in the booth, Halverson said. "Sometimes he forgets he's working in a broadcast," Fernández said. "He gets emotional like a ballplayer when the team wins or somebody hits a home run, when somebody hits a double, a triple, drives in an important run to tie the game.... And when the team loses, he gets down. That's when he forgets that he's a broadcaster, and he reacts like a ballplayer."[12]

Considering his humble origins, Oliva has had some remarkable opportunities in baseball. One of five brothers and five sisters, Oliva grew up on the family farm in Entronque de Herradura, a small village about 25 miles east of the capital of Pinar del Rio Province. The one-square-mile farm included sugarcane plants, orange, mango, grapefruit, banana, and avocado trees and a baseball field built by his father, Pedro. Oliva started playing baseball at age seven, playing on Sundays after church. By age 19, he was playing for an amateur club from nearby Los Palacios.[13] But Oliva's dream of playing in the Cuban League never came to fruition in the aftermath of Fidel Castro's 1959 revolution as Castro's communist regime barred professionalization of all sports in Cuba in 1961. "For me, it would have been a dream to play in the Cuban League so my father and my family could have seen me play, and my brothers, my friends, you know?" Oliva said. "Because I played here [in the United States], nobody in Cuba knew what kind of ballplayer I was because ... I played in the countryside in Pinar del Rio. If they had seen me play, they would have been surprised because they would have said, 'Where did this come from?' My first year in the minor leagues I batted .400 and I had never played anywhere. For me, it would have given me tremendous pride to have played in Cuba so Cuban fans would have been able to see me play in Cuba."

Instead, Oliva's baseball future awaited in the United States. As the Cuban League conclude its final season in February 1961, Twins scout Joe Cambria signed Oliva that same month. Papa Joe, as Cambria was known in Cuba, is credited with signing as many as 400 Cuban baseball players from the 1930s to the 1950s. Roberto Fernández Tápanes, who had played 10 seasons in the Washington Senators and Reds' farm systems, played on the Los Palacios team with Oliva, with Fernández and Oliva batting third and fourth, respectively. Fernández, whose final season in the minors came with the Class AAA Havana Sugar Kings in 1957, recommended Oliva to Cambria.[14] "He [Fernández] asked me if I would like to play professionally," Oliva said. "And I said, 'Well, I don't know what 'professionally' is, but if my father lets me, I'll go.' And they talked with my father, and my father said yes. Then Fernández brought Joe Cambria, and he saw me play once and he signed me. I was very happy that I had the opportunity to sign and also that Fernández Tápanes saw me play and he thought I had what it took to be a ballplayer."

Oliva's signing did not come without discrepancies regarding his given name. Is it Antonio or Pedro? And his date of birth—1938, 1940, and 1941—have appeared in official records at different times. Oliva biographer Thom Henninger wrote in his 2015 book that Oliva was born Pedro Jr., on July 20, 1938, the third of 10 children.[15] Oliva first appeared in a Twins media guide in 1962 as Antonio "Tony" Oliva with the same 1938 date of birth. But the following year, he was listed as Pedro "Tony" Oliva with a July 20, 1940, date of birth. And the Twins' 1964 guide gave his date of birth as July 20, 1941. Cambria likely fudged Oliva's birth date to make Oliva younger—a common practice among foreign-born players at that time. And Oliva's wife, Gordette, essentially confirmed that in a 2011 interview. "That's the way the scouts did it then," she told the *Minneapolis Star Tribune*. "The thought was if a team felt it had a younger player, they were most likely to keep him."[16] Federal naturalization records from the U.S. District Court in Minneapolis show Pedro Tony Oliva becoming a U.S. citizen on December 15, 1971, after his name was "changed by Decree of Court from Pedro Oliva-Lopez, as part of the Naturalization."[17]

In his 1973 autobiography, penned with *St. Paul Pioneer Press* writer Bob Fowler, Oliva recounts how, after signing with the Twins, he had to use his brother's birth certificate in order to secure a passport to enter the United States: "The problem was that I didn't have a birth certificate and couldn't get a passport without one. My older brother, Antonio, had one but I don't remember why … he had one, so I borrowed it. That seemed like the thing to do; he didn't need it, and I did."[18] But now, Oliva insists that wasn't the case. "I never used my brother's passport or anything like that," he said recently. "I've repeated that a thousand times to people. Those are tales. I came here legally with my passport correct and my age correct. All that was something that wasn't true. But I've said it very clearly to people. For 20 years, I've been repeating the same thing. Sometimes when people ask, I tell them write whatever you want, but this is what happened. If you want to write it, fine. And if not, write what you want."[19] Oliva acknowledged that "when they signed me, I didn't know what I was signing" but says "my complete Cuban name is Antonio Oliva López, Oliva for my father and López for my mother."[20]

After signing, Oliva was to report to Fernandina Beach, Florida, for the final two weeks of spring training in early April. On April 9, Oliva and 21 other Cuban players flew from Havana to Mexico City, where they were to acquire visas to enter the United States. But a bureaucratic snag stranded the players in Mexico for 11 days, during which time the Castro regime repelled the April 17 Bay of Pigs invasion, an ill-fated attempt by CIA-trained Cuban exiles to overthrow Castro. By the time Oliva and the other players made it to Florida, only three days of spring training remained. Florida gave Oliva his first experience with the racism of the Jim Crow South. The Black Cuban players were not allowed to stay in the town's only hotel and had to take up lodging in the home of a local African American woman.[21] Oliva played in only four exhibition games, going 7 for 10 but struggled in the field. At the end of camp, 11 Cuban players were assigned to the minor league camp, but Oliva was one of 11 who were released. Returning to Cuba was not an option with U.S.-Cuba relations severed. So Cambria interceded on Oliva's behalf, lobbying Phil Howser, the general manager of the organization's Class A team in Charlotte, North Carolina. Howser eventually managed to get Oliva a spot on the Class D team in Wytheville, Virginia.[22]

In 64 games in his first professional season at Wytheville, Oliva batted .410. He followed that up in 1962 by hitting .350 in 127 games at Charlotte, earning a September call-up to the Twins. In 1963, Oliva hit .304 with 23 home runs and 74 RBIs at Class AAA Dallas–Fort Worth, earning another September call-up. Oliva arrived in Minneapolis to stay in 1964 and led the American League with 217 hits and a .323 average. He clubbed 32 homers and drove in 94 runs, earning American League Rookie of the Year honors. He won two more American League batting titles in 1965 (.321) and 1971 (.337) and led the American League in hits in five of his first seven seasons. Despite a pair of knee surgeries for torn ligaments in 1966 and '67, Oliva's career could hardly have gone any better during those years.

Off the field, Oliva had to adjust to the cultural differences in the United States, navigate a new language, and cope with the separation from his family in Cuba. But those personal struggles became less daunting after a chance encounter in the spring of 1964 led to a lifelong relationship. Gordette DuBois, a 17-year-old from Hitchcock, South Dakota, was on her senior class trip in Minneapolis and staying at the Hotel Maryland, the same hotel where Oliva lived at the start of his rookie season with the Twins. She and her classmates were in the lobby looking for autographs after attending a Twins game when she met Oliva. "Tony came in," Gordette said, "and Tony being Tony, even though he could only say 10 words in English, he still came right up to all us kids and signed our pieces of ripped up paper that we gave him to sign."[23] Oliva asked for her phone number and the two began dating after DuBois moved to Minneapolis to enroll in a business school. Their first date was dinner with her parents when they moved her to Minneapolis. "My parents fell in love with him the first time they met," Gordette said.[24] Tony and Gordette were married in South Dakota on January 6, 1968, a time when interracial marriages were controversial. "Truthfully, it was never an issue in my hometown once people met Tony,"[25] Gordette said. "Who doesn't love Tony?" The marriage would produce three children: Anita, born in 1969; Pedro, born in 1970; and later a son named Ricardo.

Although Oliva's personal life was proceeding well, an injury in 1971 changed the course of his playing career. In a game against the Oakland A's on June 29, Oliva sustained torn cartilage in his right knee after diving for a ball off the bat of Joe Rudi. The injury to the same knee that had required two prior surgeries caused him to miss almost 30 games and required surgery in September. He played only 10 games in 1972. Oliva played four more years before retiring after the 1976 season but was never quite the same. He did, however, benefit from the introduction of the designated hitter rule in the American League in 1973, and Oliva smashed the first-ever home run by a DH as he homered off A's pitcher Catfish Hunter in the first inning of the April 6 season opener. "If it hadn't been for the injuries, I would have batted much more," Oliva said. "After that began with all the [injury] stuff, I had to DH. My legs bothered me so much I couldn't play very much.... I give thanks to God that I was able to play all the years that I played, do all things I did, and I'm very content with that."[26]

Oliva finished his career with a .304 batting average, 1,917 hits, 329 doubles, 220 home runs, and 947 RBIs. He was named to the American League All-Star team in eight consecutive seasons (1964–71) and received MVP votes every year from 1964 to 1971. In 1991, the Twins retired No. 6 for Oliva—the franchise's third player after Harmon Killebrew and Rod Carew to be so honored. And the Twins unveiled a large bronze statue of Oliva at Target Field in 2011. During Oliva's 15 years on the Hall of Fame ballot (1982–96), he never came close to receiving 75 percent of the vote among members of the Baseball Writers' Association of America that is required for induction. His best showing on the ballot—47.3 percent—came in 1988. But he narrowly missed out in the 2014 Golden Era ballot, getting 11 of 16 votes (68.8 percent) from the committee—one vote shy of the number needed for induction.

Having come so close, Oliva believed he would reach the Hall of Fame one day. "I think yes. I think yes," he said in 2020. "The last [ballot], I missed by one vote."[27] Oliva's confidence was vindicated seven years after the 2014 vote when he and fellow Cuban baseball legend Orestes "Minnie" Miñoso were voted into the Hall of Fame by the Golden Days Era

Committee on December 5, 2021. Miñoso had died in 2015, but cameras from Bally Sports North captured the moment Oliva received his call from the Hall of Fame as he was surrounded by cheering family and friends at his home. "It's a special time, special for me and special for my family and special for Cuba," Oliva told the regional sports network. "It's so beautiful to be able to be here, talk to you guys, hear you guys. I knew sooner or later I was going to be in the Hall of Fame, but I wanted to go in while I'm alive and then be able to speak to you people and thank everybody."[28]

Notes

1. Author interview with Tony Oliva, June 11, 2020.
2. Interview with Oliva.
3. Interview with Oliva.
4. Brian Murphy, "Viva los Twins! Sunday's First Local Minnesota Twins Radio Broadcast in Spanish is 'a Natural Fit' for the Team and Hispanic Community," *Saint Paul Pioneer Press*, July 27, 2002, 1A.
5. Herón Márquez Estrada, "Twins Go to Bat for Hispanic Fans: In a First for Minnesota, Sunday's Game Was Broadcast in Spanish, a Nod to the Growing Hispanic Population," *Minneapolis Star Tribune*, July 29, 2002, 1A.
6. Márquez Estrada, "Twins Go to Bat for Hispanic Fans."
7. Interview with Oliva.
8. Márquez Estrada, "Twins Go to Bat for Hispanic Fans."
9. Murphy, "Viva los Twins!"
10. Interview with Oliva.
11. Author interview with Alfonso Fernández, June 29, 2020.
12. Interview with Fernández.
13. Thom Henninger, *Tony Oliva: The Life and Times of a Minnesota Twins Legend* (Minneapolis: University of Minnesota Press, 2015), 1–3.
14. Henninger, *Tony Oliva*, 4.
15. *Ibid.*, 1.
16. Patrick Reusse, "A Legend Rooted in Minnesota," *Minneapolis Star Tribune*, April 8, 2011, 10C.
17. Naturalization Index, Minnesota, 1930–1988. Records of District Courts of the United States, Record Group 21. National Archives at Chicago, Illinois. Ancestry.com.
18. Peter C. Bjarkman, "Tony Oliva," in Peter C. Bjarkman and Bill Nowlin, *Baseball's Alternate Universe: Cuban Baseball Legends* (Phoenix: Society for American Baseball Research, 2016), 312.
19. Interview with Oliva.
20. *Ibid.*
21. Henninger, *Tony Oliva*, 5.
22. Bjarkman, "Tony Oliva," 313.
23. Henninger, *Tony Oliva*, 29.
24. *Ibid.*, 29.
25. Reusse, "A Legend Rooted in Minnesota."
26. Interview with Oliva.
27. *Ibid.*
28. César Brioso, "Opinion: Tony Oliva, Orestes 'Minnie' Miñoso Finally Get Hall of Fame Vote They Deserved," *USA Today*, December 7, 2021, 4C.

References

Bjarkman, Peter C., and Bill Nowlin, eds. *Baseball's Alternate Universe: Cuban Baseball Legend*. Phoenix: Society for American Baseball Research, 2016.

Henninger, Thom. *Tony Oliva: The Life and Times of a Minnesota Twins Legend*. Minneapolis: University of Minnesota Press: 2015.

Jorge Jarrín

Scott Melesky

Jaime and Jorge Jarrín have been a pioneering and powerful force together in the news and sports world over the past combined eight decades. The father and son team both have received many awards and accolades for their coverage of sporting events and news-breaking happenings. Through the historical eyes of broadcasting, the Jarríns' careers seem to have paralleled each other. For Jorge Jarrín, his path to greatness in the broadcast and journalism field was a different one than that of his Hall of Fame radio-announcing father Jaime. Jorge's journey has culminated in bringing him to the same hallowed grounds in the radio booth at Dodger Stadium where he is highly respected in the sports and Latino communities in his 38 years in the broadcasting field. His son Stefan was a former professional baseball player in the Los Angeles Dodgers' and Philadelphia Phillies' minor league systems in 2011 and 2012. The Jarríns' contribution to baseball has continued for three generations.[1]

During his college years at Pepperdine University, Jarrín showed a stronger interest in television and the theater than sports. He did get a taste of the excitement of being part of a successful sports environment during the Waves men's basketball team finish in the second round of the 1979 NCAA men's tournament in a close 76–71 loss to then number two UCLA at Pauley Pavilion during Jarrín's senior year.[2] Pepperdine was led by men's basketball coach Gary Colson, who had a 34-year career rebuilding college basketball programs at Valdosta State (GA), New Mexico, Pepperdine, and Fresno State. Jarrín was not announcing games yet but was impacted by Colson on campus.[3] He would be the first athletic figure who would have a positive impact on Jarrín's life. "I loved Pepperdine and am so proud of what they accomplished when I was there. I was more of a fan then, but I got to learn from Coach Colson. He was a great guy," Jarrín said. "Besides being the men's basketball coach, he taught tennis and physical education at the school, and I took both of his classes. I learned a lot from him. He was a great coach and teacher."⁴

After graduating from Pepperdine with a bachelor's in theatre arts in 1979,⁵ Jarrín initially did not follow in his father's footsteps to the broadcast booth to cover the Los Angeles Dodgers. He was fully aware of his sports pedigree but said he wanted to pursue other interests after graduating from college. "I was always around [broadcasting] with my father, and it was in my DNA," Jarrín said. "Initially, I did not pursue it and it was not one of my career goals. I was pursuing working in entertainment."⁶

In his first job out of college, Jarrín began his career in the television entertainment industry. He worked at NBC Studios as a page for two years. In this prestigious industry position, which is the longest running position in NBC history, Jarrín would join the likes of Ted Koppel, Willard Scott, and Regis Philbin as people who started as pages and developed into successful broadcasters and television personalities. In his duties as a page, Jarrín would get experience in public relations, marketing, development, and television production. He would also serve as a tour guide to the fans of the network for an hour-long tour of the studios. He admitted that the daily interactions that he had with the fans and tourists at the studio would build up his confidence and would make him more comfortable behind the microphone years later.⁷

Jarrín would move up the TV studios ladder from being a page to working backstage on the award-winning and prestigious *Johnny Carson Show*.⁸ Jarrín's work at NBC led to his being hired as the public relations manager at the Los Angeles Coliseum in 1984.⁹ He would return to the sports world as he began working for the Los Angeles Olympic organizing committee. This famed facility would host the opening and closing ceremonies and the track and field competition as it did in 1932. The 1984 Summer Olympics in Los Angeles was a historic and popular olympiad.¹⁰

It was the first Summer Olympics held in the United States since Los Angles hosted it back in 1932. The Games of the XXIII Olympiad is considered to be one of the most successful Summer Olympics of the modern era. It made profits of $250 million and was highlighted by the United States Olympics team who earned 83 gold medals and 174 overall medals, the most earned since the 1968 Summer Olympics in Mexico City, Mexico, when they earned 45 gold and 107 overall medals. Carl Lewis tied Jesse Owens's record of winning four gold medals in track and field set back in the 1936 Summer Olympics in Berlin, Germany. Edwin Moses won his second Summer Olympics gold medal in the 400-meter hurdles and continued his win streak of 105 straight races.¹¹ The U.S. men's basketball team led by future NBA Hall of Famers Michael Jordan, Patrick Ewing, and Chris Mullin and coached by three-time NCAA men's basketball champion coach Bob Knight earned the U.S. men's basketball team's eighth overall Olympic gold medal.¹² It was an amazing two weeks for the city and Jarrín was in the midst of it all. He excelled in his role during the Olympics which would lead to his first full-time announcing job at KABC.

One year later, when Jarrín visited his father at a game at Dodger Stadium, he was approached by Bud Furillo. Los Angeles was still captivated and excited by the Summer Olympics held a year earlier and people wanted to continue to talk about it and celebrate it. Furillo was a host of a sports talk show on KABC and invited Jarrín to be a guest on the show and reflect on his experiences at the 1984 Summer Olympics. Jarrín's description of the action and experiences in the previous year's Olympics on the show were so descriptive and impressive that then–KABC AM 790 president and general manager George Green invited Jarrín to audition for the traffic report position that Kelly Lange left vacant to take a news position.¹³

Although he did not have any experience doing traffic reporting at the time, Jarrín auditioned for the position and was hired two weeks later. He underwent chopper training for two weeks at KTRK-TV in Houston, Texas, before returning to Los Angeles. The training would be more than sufficient as Jarrín would stay at KABC for 26 years as "Captain Jorge." He worked a daily grueling schedule from 5:15 a.m. to 10:00 a.m. and 4:00 p.m. to 6:00 p.m. doing morning and late-afternoon traffic news segments from Jet Copter 70 with pilot Aldo Bentivenia. Jarrín also provided coverage for Spanish station KLAX-FM, which made him the only Southern California broadcasting personality to work in two different languages.¹⁴

"I really enjoyed my time as Captain Jorge," Jarrín said. "In this position, I wanted to be able to tell folks traveling the safest ways to get home and tell some jokes to make their drive home easier. I wanted to be informative and provide them with the most accurate and up-to-date information."¹⁵

Jarrín became a city favorite as a traffic reporter and was respected and beloved for his information and humor. Besides making listeners' drive to work a pleasant experience, Jarrín worked to make sure his listeners and viewers were safe driving on the freeways.

Jarrín excelled as a news journalist in covering the 1992 Los Angeles riots, 1993 and 1996 Malibu brush fires, and a hostage situation on the freeway while he was patrolling the skies as a traffic reporter.¹⁶

"During the LA riots, I got a firsthand look at the 25 fires as they were being lit and when trucker Reginald Denny was attacked. LA looked like a war zone out of Beirut, Lebanon, and I saw the LAPD pulling back from the rioting and the National Guard coming in," Jarrín said. "People were getting pulled and dragged out of their cars and being attacked and beat up. I felt it was my job to keep the listeners safe and to tell them not to go to this area. I had a 360-degree panoramic view to report on the riots which helped me inform the listeners and viewers which places to avoid driving because they were too dangerous places to be in."[17]

For his excellent news coverage of these events, Jarrín was honored by his peers and the city of Los Angeles. In 1993, the Associated Press awarded four top awards to him and KABC for reporting on the 1992 Los Angeles riots. The Associated Press also awarded Jarrín for his live coverage of a highway patrol pursuit and hostage situation. In 1993, Jarrín was also awarded the Golden Mike Award for Best Live Coverage of a Late Breaking News Story in 1993, given by the Southern California Radio and TV News Association. The City of Los Angeles honored him with an Outstanding Contributions as an Excellent and Accomplished Broadcaster award.[18]

"It was an honor to receive these awards," Jarrín said. "It was very humbling, and I am appreciative of them. [As for my coverage,] I just wanted to make sure my viewers and listeners were safe and keep them from driving in any dangerous areas and situations."[19]

Jorge was the second Jarrín to give award-winning coverage to political civil unrest in Los Angeles. In 1965, Jaime covered the Watts riots and the funeral of President John F. Kennedy. He would also follow in his father's footsteps in the sports broadcasting world.[20]

While at KABC, Jarrín stayed connected with his father's sports broadcasting lineage. He contributed to the daily sports show in between his traffic reports. Jarrín also worked with former major league player Jose Mota on DirecTV's *Major League Baseball Game of the Week*. These games were broadcasted all over Latin America. Mota, the son of former major league star Manny Mota, played two years in the MLB and is currently the Dominican play-by-play announcer for the Los Angeles Angels telecasts on Fox Sports West/Prime Ticket and KCOP and is the Spanish radio color commentator for the Angels on KWKW. Jarrín said he learned so much about the intricacies of the game with his coverage with Mota.[21]

"I really enjoyed working with Jose on the DirecTV game of the week," Jarrín said. "He is so knowledgeable, sharp, and intelligent about the game. I was learning as a sports analyst and I asked him questions that fans would about the game. Jose would give great and detailed answers about the insights of the game which made calling the games with him very special."[22]

By 2004, Jarrín was back into baseball full time when he was hired by the Dodgers to be the manager of radio broadcast sales and Hispanic initiatives. In his 11 years at the position, Jarrín expanded the Dodger Radio Spanish Radio network from 30 games in 2004 to the full 162-game slate in 2015. Jarrín has made an impact in the reporting field that transcends baseball and has helped the Latino community with his work and initiatives.[23]

"The Latino community is a very hardworking and loyal community," Jarrín said. "They really started supporting the Dodgers during Fernando [Valenzuela] mania; we had at one point 10–15 million Latino listeners to Dodger games [in 1981]. They have a really strong energy, and it is an honor to serve them. I wanted to do my very best to get as many Dodger games available to the Latino community and I am very proud that we were able to accomplish that."[24]

The Latino community is one that is near and dear to Jarrín. He is of Ecuadoran descent and said he was taught the importance of community by his father and late mother, Blanca. His deep respect for the Latino and the Los Angeles communities has led him to work and lead different foundations with his father and independently.

"My mom always told me to never take anything for granted and always count your blessings and be humble," Jarrín said. "She always told me to never forget where you came from, and I haven't forgotten. My father taught me a lot about the Latino community. They are very hard working and loyal. We have always wanted to help our community. It is very important to me to give back and support the community."[25]

Philanthropy has defined Jarrín's life since graduating from Pepperdine University in 1979. Over the past 40 years, Jarrín was a partner for the RLR/Jarrín Agency and was active in the Latin Business Association, the Oscar De La Hoya Foundation,[26] the Lucy Pet Foundation,[27] the Ronald McDonald House of Pasadena, Stillpoint Family Services, and the Pepperdine University Latino Advisory Council. He is one of the leaders in the Jaime and Blanca Jarrín Foundation.[28]

The foundations that Jarrín has led, supported, and partnered with include Alta Med Health Foundation, the Los Angeles Regional Food Bank, and Los Defensores, a Los Angeles–based legal service company. For many years,

Jorge Jarrín on the air for the Los Angeles Dodgers (courtesy Jorge Jarrín).

Jarrín organized and hosted the annual Jorge Jarrín Golf Classic. Since November 19, 2019, Jorge has helped host the Jaime and Blanca Jarrín Foundation Golf Classic with his father. The Jarrín foundation's proceeds from the golf tournament have gone to health care for more than 30,000 needy families and have donated $60,000 to the Los Angeles Regional Food which has served 11.9 million families during the pandemic.[29]

"I have been able to work with my dad on the Jaime and Blanca Jarrín Foundation [for late mom, Blanca]," Jarrín said. "We raised $60,000 for 268,000 meals [for 11.9 million families]. We are living in really tough times and it is important to help all the people that are going hungry right now. We also want to make sure that the community gets proper legal help when they need it. Our foundation has helped families with food and also have provided financial aid for law and journalism students. We have worked with Defensores, which helps thousands of people with legal questions. We always want to be there and help the community."[30]

In addition to helping increase the Dodgers' expansion of their Latino fan base as a leader in broadcast sales, Jarrín was also an active member in the Dodger broadcast team. In 2012, he worked with Manny Mota to broadcast Dodger games on Fox Deportes and Sportsnet LA. Jarrín also cohosted *Dodger Talk* with former player and manager Kevin Kennedy and David Vassegh.[31] Mota is a 20-year major league veteran. He has played for the Giants, Pirates, Expos, and Dodgers, was an All-Star in 1973, and helped the Dodgers win the 1981 World Series. Mota set the record for pinch hits with 150 career on September 2, 1979. The record lasted 22 years until Lenny Randle broke it on October 7, 2001. Mota also coached the Dodgers from 1980 to 2013 and earned another World Series ring in 1988.[32] Kennedy managed the Texas Rangers from 1993 to 1994 and the Boston Red Sox from 1995 to 1996.[33] Vassegh is a Dodgers reporter for MLB Network and the host of *Dodgers Talk* on AM 570. He has been reporting on LA sports since 1998 and is a graduate of Cal State University–Northridge.[34]

"I was so fortunate to work with each of these amazing men," Jarrín said. "We all had great chemistry together which made working with all of them a pleasure. Manny Mota is a legend. Roberto Clemente was one of his friends. He held the all-time pinch-hitting record for over two decades. He is so respected, and I learned a lot from him. Kevin Kennedy has experience as a player, manager, and front office. He is extremely knowledgeable about the game and breaks it down so easily when he is explaining it to you. David Vassegh was great to work with. He was very professional and absorbed everything about the game."[35]

After completing 29 years in the broadcasting business, Jarrín would make history and join his father, Jaime, in the broadcast to call games together in 2015. The Jarríns are the only father-son Spanish broadcasting duo in Major League Baseball. Jarrín said he was very excited and happy when Dodger management approached him about joining his father to broadcast Dodger games together on the radio. He was happy to finally work with his father and see him every day at Dodger Stadium.

"In 2015, I was asked to work with my dad which made us the first father and son broadcasting team, which has been so cool to do," Jarrín said. "My father is a legend and a pioneer. He has been broadcasting baseball for 62 years. It is great to come into work and see him every day at the ballpark. I am very happy and really have enjoyed working with him."[36]

Even though Jarrín said he respects his father's talent and experience very much, he has worked on his announcing style and personality to be distinct from his father's.

"My father is the last of an [era] of the classic and great announcers," Jarrín said. "All those great and legendary announcers like Vin [Scully] have retired. My father has that booming and distinct voice when he calls the games. He has such a great style, but I try to have my own style that is distinct from his," Jarrín said. "Skip Caray, Jon Miller, and Dan Shulman are more of the announcing style that has influenced me. They all have a down-to-earth and folksy style which I try to show when I am announcing a game."[37]

Jaime (left) and Jorge Jarrín (courtesy Jorge Jarrín).

Although his announcing style differs from his father's, Jarrín said he takes his father's announcing tips and philosophy very seriously and respects and abides by them. In 2016, he was recognized by the Southern California Sports Broadcasters Association as the top Spanish radio analyst in Los Angeles.[38]

"My father is so talented. When he started radio broadcasting, he had to translate in real time what Vin Scully was saying in English into Spanish for his Latino viewers. He was like a United Nations official translator translating a foreign head of state's speech," Jarrín said. "He also instilled in me the hard-core bedrocks of journalism of always knowing the who, what, where, when, and why of every game you are broadcasting."[39]

Jarrín has seen a bevy of successful historic and championship teams during his time as a journalist in Los Angeles. From his time at KABC to his current broadcasting duties for the Dodgers, LA has made the World Series three times and qualified for the postseason 13 times.[40] Out of all those playoff teams, three Los Angeles Dodgers teams have stood out to Jarrín in his almost four decades of covering news and sports.

"The 1988 team was a very special and gritty team," Jarrín said. "It was incredible what they accomplished against the Oakland A's that year [beating them in five games to win the World Series]. What Kirk Gibson [walk-off pinch-hit home run off American League save leader and future Baseball Hall of Fame Dennis Eckersley] in game one was amazing, but people forget how dominant Orel Hershiser was during that entire postseason. It was a great Dodgers team. The 2017 team was another very special team. They had so many offensive and defensive weapons with Clayton Kershaw, Justin Turner, Cody Bellinger, and Adrian Gonzalez, to name a few, and it is so unfortunate what we know what happened [the Houston Astros admitted stealing signs to cheat to win the 2017 World Series], but that was a great team to cover. The 2020 Los Angeles Dodger team is very special as well and has the capabilities to accomplish some very big things this season. I really enjoy covering them."[41]

Jarrín said he has also enjoyed watching and talking to some of the all-time greats in Major League Baseball over the past 36 years. Two players who Jarrín really enjoyed interviewing were Baseball Hall of Fame and New York Yankees all-time saves leader Mariano Rivera and three-time All-Star and 1988 Cy Young Award winner Orel Hershiser during his broadcasting career.

"It was a thrill and an absolute honor to cover Mariano Rivera's last game [September 27, 2013—Tampa Bay Rays 4 at New York Yankees 0] for Fox," Jarrín said. "I was sitting next to him surrounded by other reporters and interviewed him. It was an unbelievable scene having my interview being recorded and having all those reporters writing down my questions and Mariano's answers to them. It was an unbelievable moment. It was a great game to be working at."[42]

Hershiser has become a colleague and close friend to the Jarrín family. He has been calling Dodger games as a color analyst for the past eight years, and Jarrín said he has enjoyed talking and working with him throughout the years.[43]

"Orel Hershiser was a terrific pitcher and has done so much for the game," Jarrín said. "He helped the Dodgers win the World Series back in 1988 and set the MLB record for 59 consecutive scoreless innings pitched in 1988. He has always been great to talk to and he has become one of my closest friends. He has such an amazing understanding and knowledge of the game. The way he can describe the speed of a fastball and how to throw it is amazing. It is so great to talk to him."[44]

The Covid-19 pandemic has changed the world in many ways since many countries and cities went into lockdown in March. It has had a strong effect on the 2020 Major League Baseball season as well. The season was shortened from 162 games to 60 games, making it the shortest regular season since 1878. The virus has also affected how the games are being called. Broadcasters can no longer travel with the team to road games. Many now have to call it at home or in the home stadium, drastically changing their access to the game and how they call it.[45]

"Covering the games in the pandemic era is very different and challenging from calling games in person in the booth before the pandemic," Jarrín said. "In the booth, everything is in front of you and you make the decision and the approach in calling the game. In the pandemic era, you are covering the game off the TV screen and is reliant on what the TV truck shows, it is hard when they interview a player or manager live during the game and the screen disappears or goes split screen. You also have to be careful of replays to not get them mixed up with the live action. It's a completely different way of calling the game. You don't have the control or access when you are at the stadium in person to call the games."[46]

One thing that has not changed is how Jarrín has enjoyed calling games with his father for the past six years. Jorge stepped down from his role as a Dodger broadcaster in 2020 and his father retired in 2022. Jorge said that he appreciated working with his father and is in awe of what his father accomplished in calling the Dodgers for over six decades.[47]

Notes

1. "Stefan Jarrín, Philadelphia Phillies," *Roto World*, August 18, 2020, https://www.rotoworld.com/baseball/mlb/player13255/stefan-jarrin.

2. "1978–79 Pepperdine Waves Roster and Stats," *Sports Reference*, August 19, 2020, https://www.sports-reference.com/cbb/schools/pepperdine/1979.html.
3. "Gary Colson," *Coaches Data Base*, August 19, 2020, https://www.coachesdatabase.com/gary-colson.
4. Jorge Jarrín interview, August 5, 2020.
5. Erik Squire, "Looking Down from Great Heights," Pepperdine University, February 7, 2002, 6, https://pepprdine-graphic.com/looking-down-from-great-heights/.
6. Jarrín interview..
7. NBC Universal, "NBC Universal Page Program," May 7, 2007, 5, https://www.page-program.nbcunicareers.com.
8. Squire, "Looking Down from Great Heights," 7.
9. Ken Baxter, "Eyes on the Road," *Los Angeles Times*, August 13, 1998, 10, https.//www.latimes.com/archives/la-xpm-1998-aug-13-ca-12567-story.html.
10. Los Angeles Coliseum, "Coliseum History," August 19, 2020, 1, https://www.lacoliseum.com/coliseum-history/.
11. Tim Dahlberg, "A Red, White and Blue Olympics in Los Angeles in 1984," August 10, 2020, 4, https://abcnews.go.com/Sports/wireStory/red-white-blue-olympics-los-angeles-1984-72286872.
12. USA Basketball, "Games of the XXIIIrd Olympiad," June 10, 2010, 4, https://www.usab.com/history/national-team-mens/games-of-the-xxiiird-olympiad-1984.aspx.
13. Baxter, "Eyes on the Road," 11.
14. Squire, "Looking Down from Great Heights," 8.
15. Jarrín interview.
16. Squire, "Looking Down from Great Heights," 9.
17. Jarrín interview.
18. Squire, "Looking Down from Great Heights," 10.
19. Jarrín interview.
20. Les Carpenter, "The Remarkable Story of the Latino Vin Scully," *The Guardian*, September 15, 2016, 12, https://www.theguardian.com/sport/2016/sept15/jaime-los-angeles-dodgers-announcer-vin-scully.
21. MLB.com, "Dodger Broadcasters," August 10, 2020, 20.
22. Jarrín interview.
23. MLB.com, "Dodger Broadcasters," 21.
24. Jarrín interview.
25. *Ibid*.
26. Squire, "Looking Down from Great Heights," 11.
27. KABC Eyewitness News, "Dodgers Jaime Jarrín Supports the Lucy Pet Foundation, a Low Cost Pet Clinic on Wheels," February 27, 2020, 2, https://www.msn.com/en-us/news/us/dodgers-jaime-jarrin-supports-the-lucy-pet-foundation-a-low-cost-pet-clinic-on-wheels/ar-BBZLJDqa.
28. MLB.com, "Dodger Broadcasters," 22.
29. Bill Plunkett, "Jarrín Foundation Will Donate to LA Regional Food Banks," *Orange County Register*, May 4, 2020, 5, https://www.ocregister.com/2020/05/04/jarrin-foundation-will-donate-to-la-regional-food-bank/.
30. Jarrín interview.
31. MLB.com, "Dodger Broadcasters," 22.
32. Rory Costello, "Manny Mota," December 2018, 40, Society for American Baseball Research, https://sabr.org/bioproj/person/manny-mota/.
33. Kevin Kennedy, "50 Years of Baseball," August 19, 2020, 5, Kevin Kennedy Baseball All Access Membership, https://www.kevinkennedybaseball.com/.
34. Engage, "David Vassegh," August 19, 2020, 1, https://www.letsengage.com/talent/davidvassegh.
35. Jarrín interview.
36. *Ibid*.
37. *Ibid*.
38. MLB.com, "Dodger Broadcasters," 23.

39. Jarrín interview.
40. MLB.com, "Dodgers Postseason Results," August 10, 2020, 1, https://www.mlb.com/dodgers/history/postseason-results.
41. Jarrín interview.
42. *Ibid.*
43. Joseph Wancho, "Orel Hershiser," November 12, 2018, 25, Society for American Baseball Research, https://sabr.org/person/orel-hershiser/.
44. Jarrín interview.
45. *Ibid.*
46. *Ibid.*
47. *Ibid.*

Pepe Yñiguez

Scott Melesky

Over the past 60 years, Los Angeles has had some of the most heralded and experienced Latino broadcasters calling baseball and football in the radio field. René Cárdenas and Jaime Jarrín were the first two Latino broadcasters to cover major team sports in 1958 and 1959 with the Los Angeles Dodgers. Pepe Yñiguez has continued to add to this great legacy as he enters his 31st year as a Spanish-language sports broadcaster in both baseball and football. He is third in experience on the Dodgers broadcasting team between Jaime Jarrín and Rick Monday. Yñiguez has proven and demonstrated that he is a very versatile radio show host and sportscaster. Yñiguez's radio career includes coverage for 28 years for the Los Angeles Dodgers and three seasons for the then–Los Angeles Raiders of the National Football League. He also did international and national baseball work from 1997 to 2005 in addition to his duties with the Dodgers.[1]

As a child born in Mexico, Yñiguez loved baseball. The country has an incredible tradition in baseball. Since 1925, the Mexican League has showcased countless talented baseball players including Baseball Hall of Famers Josh Gibson, Satchel Paige, Roy Campanella, James "Cool Papa" Bell, Martin Dihigo, Monte Irvin, Ray Dandridge, and Willie Wells and future Major League Baseball superstars Leo Najo, Bobby Ávila, Angel Castro, and Mel Amada. Yñiguez wanted to be a part of this great baseball tradition in Mexico and also had aspirations of playing in the major leagues in the United States.[2]

Yñiguez was a die-hard Los Angeles Dodgers fan and bought a shirt of the team which he wore proudly around his town. He idolized Dodger and Hall of Fame announcer Jaime Jarrín and the late René Cárdenas. He loved the way they called and described the Dodger baseball games that he listened to on his radio. They were so descriptive and informative and fueled Yñiguez's desire for the game.[3] His dream was to play baseball, and at 16 years old, he began to pursue it and played semipro baseball in Monterrey, Mexico, in 1976.

"I have always loved baseball," Yñiguez said. "I followed it as a kid, and I wanted to play in the major leagues. I was good enough to play in the semipros when I was only 16. I was young and wanted to be a big-league ballplayer."[4]

Yñiguez made an immediate impact on the team with his hitting and fielding in the outfield. His youth and versatility in the game helped draw early interest from the Houston Astros manager Bill Virdon and first base coach and scout Tony Pacheco. Previously, Pacheco managed the Colombian national team that won the 1965 Amateur World Series and the Latin team that won the 1972 World Baseball Classic. He would also sign future Houston Astros superstar César Cedeño to his first Major League Baseball contract.[5] Yñiguez was playing strong and was being scouted by Pacheco until a hamstring injury suffered during a game ended his budding baseball career.

"I was playing really well, and I loved playing the game," Yñiguez said. "I knew the Astros were interested in me, but I didn't want to have the surgery. I wasn't the same player anymore after the injury, but I still wanted to continue to stay involved in baseball."[6]

Yñiguez moved to the United States in 1977 and contacted his idol Jaime Jarrín before he entered broadcast school. He was enthusiastic and energetic about the field and asked Jarrín how to succeed in the sportscasting business. Jarrín was happy to help Yñiguez and talked to him at length about how to "get your foot in the door" in the broadcasting business. Yñiguez took his idol's advice and enrolled at the Columbia School of Broadcasting in North Hollywood, California.[7]

Yñiguez excelled in his time at the college and was hired by KWKW 130 AM Los Angeles after graduation. He was excited about his new job opportunity and was one step closer to his dream of working for the Dodgers. The radio station carried the Dodgers' Spanish radio rights since 1958, when the Dodgers moved to Los Angeles, California, from Brooklyn, New York (Stewart, 2007). During Yñiguez's time at KWKW, he would work in sports programming and host local shows and perform various duties as a disc jockey at the station.[8]

Yñiguez's talent and hard work at the radio station did not go unnoticed from Dodgers management who followed his work intently at KWKW. After a few years at the radio station, Dodgers vice president of communications, the late Tom Hawkins, made contact with Yñiguez while he was working at the radio station. Hawkins, a former basketball star with Notre Dame and one of the original Lakers in the NBA, previously worked at KABC radio, KNBC-TV, and KHJ-TV and was familiar and impressed with Yñiguez's skills as a radio broadcaster.[9] Hawkins was now working as vice president of communications under then–Dodgers owner Peter O'Malley and wanted to hire Yñiguez on the Dodgers' radio broadcasting team. The then–California Angels were interested in Yñiguez broadcasting games for them. Hawkins did not want the cross-town rival to steal Yñiguez away, so he had him do an impromptu audition of calling a taped game for one inning before having him meet with O'Malley.

"Tommy Hawkins was so influential in getting me the job with the Dodgers," Yñiguez said. "Tommy did so much for the Lakers and Dodgers and for sports in general. He was really excited about my announcing and had me practice in the hotel calling an inning on television before we went to Dodger Stadium to see Mr. O'Malley. He was very impressed on how I called baseball games and hired me on the spot. I loved the game of baseball and told Mr. O'Malley that and he hired me. I had offers from the Angels, but my dream was to always work for the Dodgers and I have been there ever since."[10]

Yñiguez joined the Dodgers in 1992 and hosted *Central Deportiva* and *Hablando con los Dodgers*. His knowledge and precision about the Dodgers and baseball were popular with the fans, and both shows became instant hits locally.[11]

"I really enjoyed hosting *Central Deportiva* and *Hablando con los Dodgers*," Yñiguez said. "They were pre-pregame and post-postgame shows. They were an opportunity to get me closer to the Dodgers and their fans. It was fun and a great opportunity."[12]

While working for the Dodgers as a radio host, Yñiguez branched out from baseball and was part of the broadcast team with Jorge Berry to provide Spanish radio broadcasting coverage for the storied then–Los Angeles Raiders franchise of the National Football League from 1992 to 1994. The Raiders have won three Super Bowls in five total appearances during his coverage of the team; Los Angeles won 26 games over three years and made two postseason appearances.[13] He got to travel with the team across the country and formed a friendship with the Raiders Hall of Fame owner, the late Al Davis.

"Mr. Davis was always so nice to our broadcasting team," Yñiguez said. "We traveled with the Raiders on the road, and he always gave us the best of everything. He always told me he would get us whatever we needed when we were calling the games."[14]

Unlike baseball, Yñiguez never played football and marveled at the differences between the two sports. The play, the coverage, and the fans were all vastly different from what he experienced covering and playing baseball, but he enjoyed his time with the Raiders.

"Covering football was so different than covering baseball in every way," Yñiguez said. "The game and the fans were different. In baseball, you have a smaller crew covering the game and you are doing more work than the broadcast. In football, the crew is bigger and you have more help from people during the broadcast. The travel was also very different. We traveled all over the country; we went to New York, Green Bay, to name a few. We had to fly in bad weather and covered games in places where it was very cold, but I had a great time covering pro football."[15]

Yñiguez said he also enjoyed covering the many superstars and legendary coaches in the NFL including future NFL Hall of Famers Joe Montana, Dan Marino, John Elway, Brett Favre, Troy Aikman, Jim Kelly, Emmitt Smith, Michael Irvin, Tim Brown, Bruce Smith, Howie Long, and the late Junior Seau, and head coaches the late Don Shula, Jimmy Johnson, and Art Shell.

"I had the pleasure of covering some of the greatest football players and coaches in the game," Yñiguez said. "Joe Montana and John Elway had incredible arms. They really could throw the ball. I got to see Brett Favre play in Green Bay. The talent was unbelievable. The Raiders had a great team. Howie Long was my favorite player to watch. He was so smart, strong, fearless, and a true warrior. Howie was Superman and the toughest man that I ever saw play the game. Tim Brown, Raghib 'Rocket' Ismail, Chester McGlockton, and Jeff Hostetler were all such great players for the team."[16]

A highlight for Yñiguez in his coverage of the Raiders was a 33–30 overtime game over the Denver Broncos on January 2, 1993, at the Los Angeles Coliseum. The Raiders were down 17 points twice in the game before Jeff Hostetler completed a third down pass to Alexander Wright for a four-yard touchdown to force overtime, and Raiders kicker Jeff Jaeger won the game with a 47-yard field goal. The Raiders' win would send them to the 1993 American Football Conference playoffs where they would be eliminated by the Buffalo Bills in the divisional playoffs.[17]

"I really enjoyed covering the Raiders [in 1993]," Yñiguez said. "Their win over the Broncos was an amazing game to call. Hostetler's throw to Wright was unbelievable. The Raiders would not give up on that game. The crowd was so loud and wouldn't let the Raiders lose that game. They had to win this game to make the playoffs. The way they won the game against a tough rival was incredible. It was a very special game to be involved in."[18]

Being a part of the Raiders radio broadcasting team for three years made Yñiguez an even more popular figure with fans in the Los Angeles area. During baseball season, excited Raiders fans would call in to *Central Deportiva* and *Hablando con los Dodgers* and ask him questions about the Raiders before and after Dodger games.

"The Raiders fans were so excited and passionate in LA," Yñiguez said. "It was funny when they called me during my Dodger shows to ask questions about the Raiders and to want to talk Raiders football. I would politely tell them that these shows were about the Dodgers, not the Raiders. They would laugh and apologize to me. The Raiders fans were so dedicated and loyal."[19]

Unfortunately for Yñiguez and Los Angeles football fans, the Raiders would move back to Oakland in 1995, thus ending his three-year run calling the team after he chose not to follow the team to Oakland. His broadcasting baseball career would begin to move him out of the talk shows and into the broadcast booth in 1997. René Cárdenas had a bout of bronchitis, and Yñiguez teamed up with legendary announcer Jaime Jarrín, which fulfilled a lifelong dream of Yñiguez. It would be a reunion 20 years in the making, when he consulted Jarrín about how to be successful in the broadcasting field before he enrolled at the Columbia School of Broadcasting. Yñiguez made the trip to New York with Jarrín to cover the Dodgers' three-game road trip against the New York Mets on April 16, 1997.[20]

"It was a great game to call," Yñiguez said. "René wasn't feeling well, and I was ready for the game. I have always looked up to him and admired both René and Jaime Jarrín and it was an honor to be working with him in that game. Pedro Astacio pitched a great seven innings for the Dodgers, and Wilton Guerrero and Eric Karros homered for Dodgers and they beat the Mets 5–2. It was a great game that I will never forget."[21]

Yñiguez's knowledge and enthusiasm in calling that game got the attention of fans and media alike. In the May 1, 1997, edition of the *Los Angeles Times*, reporter Kevin Baxter wrote, "Yñiguez was animated and excited, describing the most mundane plays in a way that pulled listeners into the action."[22]

The knowledge and insight about baseball that Yñiguez brought to the broadcasting booth got him attention from major television and radio networks across the country. His workload would quickly increase after his coverage of the Dodgers versus Mets game in April 1997. In addition to his Dodger broadcasting duties, Yñiguez was hired by Fox Sports International and began calling more games. His network debut was with former baseball players Dennis Martinez and Tito Fuentes, and the trio called the 1997 All-Star Game in Cleveland and the Caribbean World Series. They also all worked together to call the World Series from 1997 to 2005.[23]

"Calling the 1997 All-Star Game was an incredible experience," Yñiguez said. "To see that much talent on the field at one time was amazing. I was also fortunate to work with Dennis and Tito. They were great players and broadcast partners. They were both so knowledgeable and added so much to the game. Getting to call eight World Series in a row was an honor. The first World Series that I covered in 1997 was a true classic when

Florida upset Cleveland. The 2004 World Series when the Boston Red Sox defeated the Saint Louis Cardinals to win their first World Series in 86 years was a tremendous series to be at. You saw history being made in front of your eyes. The 2005 World Series when the Chicago White Sox won their first championship since 1917 was also exciting to work at."[24]

With Cárdenas retiring in 1998 and moving back to Houston, Texas, Yñiguez was able to earn the coveted announcing position with Jaime Jarrín on KTNQ 1020. They would work together until 2014 when Jaime's son Jorge would join his father in the radio booth. Yñiguez moved to SportsNet LA where he teamed with former Dodgers pitching star Fernando Valenzuela, and they have been working together the past five years.[25]

Yñiguez is a consummate professional and is respected by his fellow radio broadcasters in the Los Angeles Dodgers organization. Former KTNQ-20 Dodgers broadcaster Jorge Jarrín said he was grateful for all that Yñiguez has done for the Dodgers and the sport of baseball with his professional and diligent work.

"Pepe has been calling games for over 25 years and has that great distinct Latino voice that fans love," Jorge Jarrin said. "He is very experienced."[26]

Yñiguez said he has been humbled to work with two respected men in the Dodgers organization in his 26 years with the team and looks forward to working with Valenzuela every game.

"I love my job and I love working for the Dodgers," Yñiguez said. "It is such an honor and a thrill to be working for them after all these years. I learned a lot from Vin Scully and Jaime Jarrín. They are both great announcers and nice guys. Jaime has been great to work with and helped me when I was younger to get in the business. For years, Jaime worked by himself. It was great to work with him and I learned a lot from him. I also enjoy working with Fernando. He was a great pitcher for the Dodgers and knows so much about the game. He is very experienced about the game. I love his insights and knowledge which really adds to the games that we cover together. It is fun calling games with him."[27]

During his 32 years in the radio business, Yñiguez has called some great and exciting games in the team's history. In the hundreds of games that he has called for the Dodgers, a few select games have stood out in his memory. He said he feels fortunate to have been part of many record-breaking and historic wins that have added to the Dodgers' championship tradition.

"I have been calling Dodger games since 1997 and have seen some incredible games at Dodger Stadium and on the road," Yñiguez said. "One of the most dramatic games I ever called was when the Dodgers clinched the NL West Division on the last day of the season when Steve Finley hit a walk-off grand slam to beat the Giants 7–3 on October 2, 2004. It was such an important game and it was won in such dramatic fashion. The crowd was so energized and did not want to leave Dodger Stadium after the win. Another incredible game that I covered was on September 18, 2006, when the Dodgers hit four home runs [Jeff Kent, J.D. Drew, Russell Martin, and Marlon Anderson] in a row off future Hall of Famer Trevor Hoffman, and Nomar Garciaparra would hit a walk-off home run in the 10th inning to beat the Padres 11–10. Before this happened, it looked like the Dodgers were going to lose badly, but they came back to win in dramatic fashion. It was an unbelievable game to call. I also enjoyed working Clayton Kershaw's and Josh Beckett's no-hitters in 2014. Those two no-hitters were also very special to call."[28]

Yñiguez said he is a student of the game and history of baseball. He has played the game and covered countless Baseball Hall of Famers and superstars over two-plus decades as a radio broadcaster. In his three decades involved in the game, only two players and five baseball teams have stood out to him in his life in sports.

"I know I didn't get the opportunity to cover these two baseball players, but they are two of the greatest baseball players of all time," Yñiguez said. "They are Babe Ruth and Pete Rose. I have studied the game of baseball for many years and Babe Ruth could do it all in pitching and home runs. He changed the game and is my all-time-favorite baseball player. Pete Rose also was an incredible baseball player. I never saw anyone play the game the way Pete Rose did. He was always hustling and is the all-time hit leader. The best teams that I ever saw play were the 1975 and 1976 Cincinnati Reds teams. They were 'the Big Red Machine' and so many Hall of Famers and great players in Tom Seaver, Johnny Bench, Tony Perez, Pete Rose, Dave Concepcion, and George Foster. They won two World Championships. I was also very impressed with the 1977, '78, and '81 Los Angeles Dodgers. Those were also great teams and had so much talent. In those late-1970s teams, you had Steve Garvey, Ron Cey, Davey Lopes, and Dusty Baker and Fernando Valenzuela on the '81 team. Those are my favorite players and teams in baseball."[29]

The Covid-19 pandemic has changed the world we live in and has affected Yñiguez in the way sports shows are presented and how games are covered. When the baseball season was delayed in May, Yñiguez, Jaime Jarrín, Jorge Jarrín, and Alanna Rizzo shared hosting duties for the first ever Dodgers Latino Zoom Party. It drew 11,000 viewers, but it was a different format and style from shows that Yñiguez hosted in the past.[30]

"On May 20, we had our first ever Zoom meeting for the Latino fans," Yñiguez said. "It was great. We had Fernando Valenzuela, Adrian Rodriguez, Kiké Hernández, Julio Urías, Brusdar Graterol, and Edwin Ríos.

Eleven thousand fans tuned in, and I hosted it with Jaime, Jorge, and Alanna. It was fun and great to do, but it was harder to navigate the questions with all the guests and hosts. It was a fun time but a very different way of communicating."[31]

Calling live sporting events has also been a unique and different challenge for broadcasters and reporters across the country. In baseball, announcers are either covering the game from their house remotely or covering it at their team's home stadiums. Live interviews on the field with players and managers before and after the games have been replaced by remote Zoom meetings. This type of coverage has strictly altered how they are calling the game and the action that they see from their television monitor or live action from an empty stadium.[32]

"The pandemic has really changed everything in the world," Yñiguez said. "Sports is no different. When we cover games now, it is so quiet and strange without the fans. I really miss the fans' energy and excitement during the games. It really is different without them. When we do road games, we are in the broadcast booth in Dodger Stadium and can't travel on the road with the team. Instead of calling the action live, we have to go by and rely on the TV monitors, which limits what we can see and that we have no control over. It really makes the situation difficult in calling the game and has affected the way we see and broadcast the games to the fans."[33]

Even though recent times have been difficult for the world, Yñiguez said he has been very grateful and thankful of the support that he has gotten from the Latino community through his 29 years in radio broadcasting as they supported his shows and listened to the games that he has called. They sent him sympathy cards when his late-wife, Margarita, passed away from cancer in 2006.[34] They have become family to him and made his dream of becoming a Dodger radio broadcaster more exciting and fulfilling.

"The Latino community has always been very important to me," Yñiguez said. "They have supported me in everything that I have done. I go into and live in the community a lot and I interact with the fans. They are very supportive, passionate, and excited and it makes me enjoy the games I call even more because of their support."[35]

Notes

1. MLB.com, "Dodgers Broadcasters," April 1, 2020, 37, https://www.mlb.com/dodgers/team/broadcasters.
2. "Mexican League," Baseball Reference.com, August 20, 2020, https://www.baseball-reference.com/bullpen/Mexican_League.

3. Cary Osborne, "Pepe Yñiguez Keeps Wife's Memory with Him Every Day," *Dodgers Insider*, September 6, 2016, 6
4. Pepe Yñiguez interview, August 10, 2020.
5. "Tony Pacheco," Baseball Reference.com, August 10, 2020, https://www.baseball-reference.com/bullpen/Tony_Pacheco.
6. Yñiguez interview.
7. Osborne, "Pepe Yñiguez Keeps Wife's Memory," 7.
8. *Ibid.*, 8.
9. The Press Enterprise Staff and News Service Reports, "Tommy Hawkins Played for Lakers, Worked for Dodgers, Passes at 80," The Press Enterprise, August 16, 2017, 12.
10. Yñiguez interview.
11. MLB.com, "Dodgers Broadcasters," 38.
12. Yñiguez interview.
13. "1993 Los Angeles Raiders Players and Statistics," *Pro Football Reference*, August 11, 2020, https://www.pro-football-reference.com/teams/rai/1993.htm.
14. Yñiguez interview.
15. *Ibid.*
16. *Ibid.*
17. "1993 Los Angeles Raiders Players and Statistics."
18. Yñiguez interview.
19. *Ibid.*
20. Kevin Baxter, "A Format Change with Laughter," *Los Angeles Times*, May 1, 1997, 18.
21. Yñiguez interview.
22. Baxter, "A Format Change with Laughter," 19..
23. MLB News, "Dodgers to Hold Zoom Part en Español," May 21, 2020, 6, https://www.mlb.com/news/dodgers-hold-zoom-party-en-espanol.
24. Yñiguez interview.
25. Eric Stephens, "Jaime Jarrín & Jorge Jarrín Are New Dodgers Spanish Radio Team," Truebluela.com, January 30, 2015, 2.
26. Yñiguez interview.
27. Jorge Jarrín interview, August 5, 2020.
28. Yñiguez interview.
29. *Ibid.*
30. MLB News, "Dodgers to Hold Zoom Part en Español," 7.
31. Yñiguez interview.
32. Jorge Castillo, "Pandemic Will Create a Whole New Way to Broadcast Dodgers Games," *Los Angeles Times*, July 18, 2020, 4.
33. Yñiguez interview.
34. "Osborne, "Pepe Yñiguez Keeps Wife's Memory," 9.
35. Yñiguez interview.

3. Newer Voices

Francisco Romero

Jorge Iber

A recent article on one-half of the Houston Astros' current Spanish-language broadcast team, Francisco Romero (along with former MLB catcher Alex Treviño), compared the announcer's career with that of legendary soul singer James Brown (known as the "Hardest Working Man in Show Business"). The reason for this association is due to the many jobs (often simultaneously) Romero has held since beginning his time in televised news/sports.[1] Indeed, there have been occasions, just as with Amaury Pi-González, when Romero has broadcast for more than one MLB squad at the same time. In a career that now spans more than two decades, Francisco has also been the Spanish-language *voz* of teams from his alma mater, the University of Arizona, as well as the Cardinals' (football) franchise.

His path to the broadcast booth began in Nogales, Sonora, Mexico, in 1969. Francisco's father, who was an American citizen, worked north of the border (as a miner in the Tucson area) and would travel back and forth. By 1981, his parents determined that the time was right to remain in the United States with their six children. As a 12-year-old in a new country (though the family did visit Arizona regularly while still living in Mexico), the young Romero had yet to learn much English. As a baseball fan, however, he was already an afficionado of the Dodgers, particularly following with great interest the burgeoning phenomenon known as "Fernadomania" through the voice of Jaime Jarrín. While playing baseball with one of his brothers that summer, Francisco heard some news that would change his life: the Dodgers were on the radio but in the language of his new home! He quickly recognized the names of some of the other players: Cey, Garvey, and so forth. What he did not realize immediately was that he was listening to another legend of Dodgers baseball, Vince Scully. Soon, the Romero boys were tuning in on a daily basis to hear (and learning English through) the team's latest exploits. The English lessons combined with baseball parlance helped him sufficiently master this second language so effectively that by the end of the academic year in 1982, Francisco was confident enough to present a report on Cinco de Mayo to his classmates. It was during this time that he first began to conceive the notion that he might one day do the same job as Jarrín or Scully, "but that dream seemed very far away."[2] He would go on to graduate from Tucson's Pueblo High School with the class of 1987.[3]

Francisco then attended Pima Junior College and eventually on to the local university, graduating with his bachelor's degree in 1994. While in school, sport was always a part of his life, and he kept an eye on his beloved Wildcats. He dabbled in various areas, including taking classes in finance, media, and political science. He eventually took a job with the Pima County Board of Supervisors, interning with Dan Eckstrom. In his biography, Romero notes that this appointment provided him with extensive experiences in varied aspects of public service. Among his duties were attending to constituent request to various city departments, as well as working with the Sonoran Health Department and the same agency in Pima County to help stop a cholera outbreak in that Mexican state.

After graduation, this led to a post (in 1995) with the Arizona-Mexico Border Health Foundation for which he "implemented educational and training programs" on topics as varied as epidemiology, substance abuse prevention, environmental health, and other topics. The next year, he started working for the Pima County Department of Environmental Quality in the area of community outreach. His main task was to instruct residents and small businesses of South Tucson on proper disposal of household and other hazardous waste materials. All of these endeavors put the idea in Francisco's mind that he might ultimately want to run for public office. Still, by the late 1990s, the love of sports, as well as the seeds planted by Jarrín and Scully in the early 1980s, provided an opportunity to finally sprout through his hire with the Tucson Sidewinders (the Arizona Diamondbacks' AAA team) as head of Hispanic marketing. He would now put his knowledge of serving constituents to work in a totally different context.[4]

The Sidewinders replaced the old Toros (a franchise that existed between 1969 and 1997 and played at Hi Corbett Field in the downtown area) in 1998, playing their home games at Tucson Electric Park. Francisco was not only responsible for attracting Spanish-speaking fans to the stadium but also served, for the first time, behind the microphone of a baseball team. Simultaneously, the local Telemundo (Channel 40) hired him to serve as both sports director and a general assignment reporter. In this job, he not only worked on narratives dealing with athletics but also (continuing his interests from when he worked for Pima County) with political-social issues such as immigration, drug trafficking, and environmental health. He would remain at this post (while broadcasting MLB games as well) until 2008.[5]

With the establishment of the Arizona Diamondbacks franchise and their placement of spring training facilities in Tucson (along with the Chicago White Sox) came yet another opportunity for Romero to utilize his skills: this time as an instructor of English for young Spanish-speaking players. His responsibilities to these athletes also included something that Francisco faced as a young boy: coming to understand the cultural subtleties of life in the United States. The lessons involved not just being able to communicate in English but also how to fit into daily life, as well as how to deal with homesickness. According to Francisco, this effort by Arizona was one of the earliest, and most extensive, by any MLB team during the 1990s.[6]

The next step in Romero's career tied him even more directly to the Phoenix MLB franchise, as he worked as television play-by-play announcer (for around one dozen games) and producer for the team's Spanish-language broadcasts for the 1999 and 2000 campaigns. Meanwhile, as he continued to work at Telemundo, he assumed another chore: covering the University of Arizona's (UA's) athletic teams. He started working by doing UA hoops in 1999 and followed that with football the next year. Between 2005 and 2010, he would also cover the exploits of his alma mater's women's basketball, soccer, and softball teams. As a general assignment journalist, he also did work for NBC, Univision, Mundo Fox, Televisa, and CBS. Additionally, Romero worked on a civic committee for councilman José Ibarra. A highlight in the sports field also occurred when Francisco earned an Emmy Award nomination for a story he did on Yuliana Pérez, a triple jump specialist of Cuban American descent who starred at Pima County Community College and UA and was also a member of the 2004 U.S. Olympic track and field team in Athens. He became the first reporter to win this award in the history of Telemundo Arizona. Romero was nominated for another Emmy the following year.[7]

As if all of this were not sufficient, he continued to serve as a play-by-play announcer and postgame show producer for the Sidewinders for four seasons and eventually began to get opportunities to ply his trade at the MLB level. Starting in 2003 (until 2008), he would fly to Milwaukee to do the Brewers' weekend games for Telemundo Wisconsin. He considers this to have been his biggest early-career break.[8] Given all of his "free time," he also collaborated with the legendary Cuban ballplayer/broadcaster Tony Oliva in a similar capacity for the Minnesota Twins starting in 2003 (through 2007). He also did the same, briefly, for the Cincinnati Reds (for one month) in 2005. He also was the halftime Spanish-language reporter for the Arizona Cardinals for the 2005 season. These multiple opportunities, plus the quality of his work behind the microphone, helped to bring Romero well-deserved notoriety and facilitated opening the door to the Houston Astros post in 2008.[9]

The Houston club (originally bearing the moniker of Colt .45s) which started in 1962 was a pioneer in Spanish-language broadcasting, right alongside the Dodgers (both in Brooklyn as well as in Los Angeles) in this important trend. Francisco joined the Astros booth in 2008 and followed in the giant footsteps of personages such as René Cárdenas, Orlando Sánchez-Diago, Rolando Becerra, and Raúl Sáenz.[10] At first, he was not sure whether he should accept the post and still continued to work at Telemundo as well as in many "side gigs" with both MLB and other sports teams. It was his wife who ultimately pushed Romero to take the job. Recently, Francisco recalled that her encouragement helped him see that working for one team would be a wise move; after all, being in one place certainly was better than having to fly to various parts of the country as he did from 2003 through 2008. "I have broadcast for other teams in other sports, but my goal was to broadcast with one team, and luckily enough, it was the Astros."[11]

Francisco Romero (courtesy Francisco Romero).

As of the conclusion of the 2021 season in which he broadcast his second set of World Series games for the Astros, Romero had covered the team's two most recent trips to the Fall Classic, with a title (though tainted) coming in the hurricane-ravaged season of 2017 against the Los Angeles Dodgers and the team's recent defeat at the hands of the Atlanta Braves. In addition, he has also broadcast multiple no-hitters as well as one perfect game with the team. Another bit of history happened in 2015 as Francisco and Alex Treviño simulcast for both Houston and the Kansas City Royals as part of the Missouri club's Hispanic Heritage

Festival. By this point, Francisco has broadcast well over 2,000 MLB games for the Astros. This now brought him up to a total of six MLB teams who had employed him. They are the Diamondbacks, Brewers, Twins, Reds, Royals, and Astros. It seems that Romero has gone well beyond his wildest childhood dreams when he listened to Jaime Jarrín and Vince Scully. He continues to broadcast games for the Arizona Wildcats in multiple sports, with 2021 marking his 22nd campaign with his alma mater.[12]

While continuing to shine behind the microphone, Francisco Romero continues the practice that began while he was an undergraduate: he still seeks to make the world a better place for his fellow man. In 2006, he earned a Lifetime Achievement Award from the Instituto Tecnológico Regional de Nogales for his journalism. In 2007, he was nominated for another Emmy, this time for a story on immigration. In 2013, he received a humanitarian award for his service to the Spanish-speaking community as a journalist. The following year, he traveled to Nicaragua at the behest of the nation's journalistic association for a workshop on MLB broadcasting. He has also worked to improve life in southern Arizona and Sonora State by bringing UA students to border towns to participate in projects such as health screenings, painting over graffiti, feeding the homeless, constructing health clinics in Sonora, and helping to maintain facilities for an animal reserve. In Tucson, he also visits local schools and encourages students to complete their education and to follow their academic and career goals. One of his favorite endeavors along these lines is to visit his high school alma mater, Pueblo High, for Si Se Puede day in order "to show students that Pueblo is a very special place where strong foundations are built and that its students can succeed anywhere." In Houston, he does similar work, visiting schools with Astro players, as well as helping rebuild and maintain ball fields in underserved communities.[13]

In sum, Francisco Romero not only is an excellent broadcaster, as demonstrated by his efforts on behalf of Telemundo, UA, and multiple professional sports franchises, but he is clearly a man who is utilizing his talents and notoriety to "pay it forward" and make Tucson, Sonora, and the Houston area better and more equitable places. He is a Spanish-language version of the "hardest working man" in the business of sports broadcasting. The dream that started with listening to Jarrín and Scully has borne great and abundant fruit for the Romero family and those who listen to his broadcasts. It has also been a great way to bring more Latinos/as into the MLB family. Now, around two-thirds of these franchises have Spanish-language broadcasts, and as the demographics of our nation continue to change, there will certainly, eventually be more. As Francisco noted recently, "It's very hard for teams to believe they need a Spanish broadcaster or that they need to broadcast in Spanish. You have to convince the teams or organizations. You have to work twice as much as the English broadcaster so you can create credibility. Even though you do the same job, you have to do twice as much." Certainly, this is one *voz* who has done more than his share to bring professional and collegiate sports to the Spanish-speaking community in Texas, Arizona, and elsewhere. Although it has been hard work, Francisco summarizes his years behind the microphone by saying that "the journey has been very, very nice. It's been exciting to go through this to get to where I am now, which is the voice of the Astros. It's been a treat on this journey."[14]

Notes

1. La Vida Baseball, "La Vida Voices: Francisco Romero," May 23, 2019. See https://www.lavidabaseball.com/la-vida-voices-francisco-romero/. Accessed on October 26, 2021.

2. "Astros Broadcaster Francisco Romero Showcases Versatility as One of the Best Spanish Broadcasters in MLB," YouTube, August 9, 2021. See https://www.youtube.com/watch?v=cVEoXbQ-QE0. Accessed on October 26, 2021.

3. "Francisco Romero, Class of 1987." See https://phswarriorfoundation.wordpress.com/hall-of-fame/hall-of-fame-class-of-2017/francisco-romero-class-of-1987/.

4. Francisco Romero, interview with author, June 9, 2021. Also, "Francisco Romero Biography" by Francisco Romero. Copy of this document in author's possession.

5. *Ibid*. See also Francisco Romero's LinkedIn page: https://www.linkedin.com/in/francisco-romero-69580258. Accessed on October 28, 2021.

6. See "Francisco Romero Digs Deep with Russ and Jesus Ortiz," podcast, https://www.listennotes.com/podcasts/digging-deep/francisco-romero-digs-deep-H_QONymPoZJ/. Accessed on October 26, 2021.

7. Francisco Romero, interview with author, June 9, 2021. Also, "Francisco Romero Biography" by Francisco Romero.

8. *Ibid*.

9. *Ibid*.

10. Bob Hulsey, "The Men behind the Mic," undated. See http://www.astrosdaily.com/files/MenMic/. Accessed on October 25, 2021.

11. Kathleen Ortiz, "From Mexico to Houston, Francisco Romero Has Thrived," August 3, 2021. See https://ouresquina.com/2021/astros-broadcaster-francisco-romero-showcases-versatility/. Accessed on October 26, 2021.

12. Francisco Romero, interview with author, June 9, 2021. Also, "Francisco Romero Biography" by Francisco Romero. See also Francisco Romero's LinkedIn page.

13. "Francisco Romero Biography" by Francisco Romero.

14. Ortiz, "From Mexico to Houston."

Junior Pepén

Bill Nowlin

Nilson "Junior" Pepén has been broadcasting sports in the Greater Boston area since 1997, working on Red Sox broadcasts since 2006, and has been the primary *voz* of the Red Sox since June 2019.

He is a native of the Dominican Republic, born in Santo Domingo on February 9, 1971. He's always loved sports and played both baseball (first base) and basketball (as a guard) when younger, but his first sport was basketball and for a while he played professionally for Club San Carlos—"the best team over there."

"Everyone calls me Junior," he says. His father, Nilson Pepén, had the same name and worked as an accountant. "He was a politician, too," adds Junior. "He used to be vice secretary for health in my country. My grandfather, Amenodoro Pepén, was a congressman for 30 years" in the Congreso de la República Dominicana.

"My mother, Marina Morales Pepén, took care of the family. She lives in the Dominican Republic with my brothers. Sometimes she comes to visit, but right now she's 84 years old. Together, we are four brothers—Marino, Rafael, and José. One of my brothers was my father's son through a first marriage."

Junior studied law in the Dominican Republic, with a degree from the Technological University of Santiago (UTESA). His specialty in law was in civil law, but he also worked criminal cases. He spent four years working as a lawyer, both in the private sector and in the government.

When his father died in May 1996, however, Junior moved to Boston. His wife, Verónica—also Dominican born—was in Boston, and their first child was born the same year—in September 1996. He and Verónica have known each other since both were children; they lived on the very same street in the capital, Santo Domingo. She had come to Boston earlier because her extended family lived there. Junior followed, after the death of his father and for the birth of their son Enrique. In April 1997, he made the decision to move to Boston.

He had to start over, starting from nothing. All his paperwork was in order for law, but he was unable to continue his career because the nature of law as practiced in the Dominican Republic is quite different from English-based American law. "When I came here, I had to start over. I don't regret that. My first job here was in a laundry."

Within a year or so, he had begun broadcasting. "In 1997, a friend of mine—Víctor Canaan—had a TV program in Lynn, Massachusetts, and he invited me [to join him]. Just for a year. The show was *Latinos TV*, which was broadcast on local TV Channel 3 in Lynn on Tuesdays at 8:00 p.m. We covered the Celtics and sometimes here [Fenway Park]. That program covered everything—sports, politics, and everything.... I was looking for something else. I liked sports. It's my passion."

He soon came to cohost a TV show on a small channel in Boston, *Deportes de TV*. "It was every Sunday from 10:30 to 11:30 p.m. on Cuencavisión Channel 729. People liked it." His cohosts were Gustavo Terrero, Juan Óscar Báez, and Freddie Medina.

In 2003, Junior got more deeply involved with radio. "Juan Óscar Báez, he called me. 'Hey, we have a show on the radio. Why don't you work with us?' *Conversando de Deportes*. I love radio. But I did radio and TV. I had to do everything because that's part of the business. I started the same year. Radio and TV. He was the producer. He was everything *Conversando de Deportes*." It was Boston's only Spanish sports talk radio show, which aired on WJDA 99.9 FM and 1300 AM. Since 2003, Junior has been joined by his brother Marino. "In 2006, I became the producer and cohost. Currently, my brother Marino and I make them, he from the Dominican Republic and I from here. Monday through Friday—every week 5:00–6:00 p.m. I do it from here every night, too. I do my radio program remotely from here. *Conversando de Deportes*." He will do the program from Fenway Park before a typical weekday game—home or away—but will sometimes prerecord them. "When there is no baseball season, I do the program from the WJDA studios in Medford or from home, where I also have the facilities to do it."

Báez had done some work broadcasting Red Sox games. He was the number three man on the team, working for Bill Kulik and the Spanish Béisbol Network with J.P. Villamán and Uri Berenguer. Villamán had been part of *Conversando de Deportes*, too, but he was killed in an automobile accident after a Red Sox game in May 2005. Kulik needed to adjust the team. Juan Óscar Báez was named the "number one." He called Junior to ask if he would be willing to help, then talked to Bill Kulik: "I have a guy. Junior. He can do it." Junior Pepén became the number three man. He explained his role: "The number three guy is doing the pregame and sometimes the postgame and cover the fifth and sixth innings. Just in case Uri is missing or Juan Óscar is missing, I am here. Backup. 2006 to 2010."

He began to oversee a few other responsibilities but remained in the backup role until 2010, when he had another offer to do television for Univision. He left the work for Red Sox and started working with Univision as a sportscaster, doing a weekly program every Saturday—which he continued until the pandemic hit. That show ended in 2020.

In 2019, the Red Sox called him. Uri Berenguer had been suspended from his position—Junior was never told exactly what had happened—and on June 4, Pepén was assigned primary responsibility for the Red Sox Spanish-language broadcasts and finished out the year. He was invited back to broadcast in 2020 and has become a regular, through 2023, having completed five full seasons.

He's a Red Sox employee, working under Senior Vice President of Broadcasting and Marketing Colin Burch. Red Sox Spanish Radio Network shows in 2022 are carried on radio by WAMG 890 AM (Boston), WCCM 1490 AM (Haverhill), WLLH 1400 AM (Lawrence), WORC 1310 AM (Worcester), and WLAT 910 AM (Hartford). For those watching Red Sox television on the New England Sports Network (NESN), the voice of Junior Pepén is the voice one hears if one uses the SAP (second audio program) button to hear Spanish-language broadcasting.

Pepén went on the occasional road trip—such as to New York—before the Red Sox ran the network but now broadcasts every game—home and away—from the fifth-floor booth at Fenway Park, adjacent to the press box. For a ballpark with a seated capacity of 38,805, working a night game when the team is on the road can be an unusual experience, with as few as three people in the park—a security guard at Gate D, Junior Pepén, and his engineer. At times, there might be someone from the grounds crew working on the field.

Fenway Park has become an active venue for concerts and occasional other events. The sound from, say, a Zac Brown Band concert would penetrate the glassed-in broadcast booth, and the light from the booth might be distracting to some in the crowd, so Pepén broadcasts away games from what is essentially a utility room.

"I always come in three hours before because we have to prepare. I work alone here. I have an engineer, but I call the game by myself. I don't have a partner. That's why I have to take in all the information I can get." He had the same engineer for all the games in 2020 and 2021 but now has a small pool of three—though Alex Cohen is working most of the games in 2022. Colin Burch has helped as well.

He can glance out at an empty Fenway Park, one with all the lights turned out except the ones in his booth and the corridor from the elevator. He follows the game by watching the NESN broadcast, which allows him to better provide the SAP commentary—from the lineups through the game action. There is a backup, should he become ill.

With road games being broadcast remotely from Fenway Park, there have been limited opportunities to meet with other Spanish-language broadcasters, though he can catch up once a year at baseball's All-Star Game. "This is a small group of people. Everybody knows of each other. Before, I traveled for Univision, and we could meet together. I know almost every broadcaster in Spanish—the Dodgers' broadcaster Jaime Jarrín—he's a Hall of Famer—I used to meet him and Felo Ramírez, who's a Hall of Famer with the Marlins. I'll see them at the All-Star Game. That's the only time."

But he gets feedback from fans, listeners to the broadcasts. "People hear me—I'm surprised. People all the time text me or tweet me from Spain, from France, from DR, from Puerto Rico, from Mexico, from Argentina, from Chile, El Salvador, Panama, Venezuela, Cuba. They're crazy. They love the Red Sox so much."

Should the Red Sox make it to the World Series again, would he travel to broadcast from the road? "This is a good question. Maybe yes, maybe no. For me, it's better to stay here because I have to do my other show. It's better for me to stay here all the time because I can do multiple things. The only problem is that I can't interview the players in person."

Junior genuinely enjoys the work. "I love it. I like to call the game. I love Fenway Park. This has been part of me for the last 20 years. Before I called games here, I covered these games—for radio, for TV, interviewing the players. I've done so many interviews with a player like David Ortiz. He's told me 100 times, 'You're the guy who has done the most interviews with me.' We would talk every day." It's work, gathering information and perspective for better broadcasts, but there are personal conversations, too. "Sometimes you can relax and talk about life."

Junior and Verónica live in the Boston area. "We have two children—my son, Enrique Pepén, and my daughter, Lisa Marie Pepén. She is 20 right now. She goes to UMass Boston and is studying psychology. Enrique had some of the politician's blood. Right now, he's working in Boston City Hall. He likes campaigns. [Enrique is director of neighborhood services for the City of Boston.] He is married, and I am a grandfather. A beautiful girl named Penelope and a grandson named Enrique Jr." Although both children were born in the area and thus speak fluent English, the family speaks Spanish at home, which gives all the advantage of being truly bilingual.

His broadcast work is just part of Junior's life in the region. He adds, "One of my great passions is working for my Latino community, especially the Dominican community, where I have twice had the pleasure of being the president of the Dominican Foundation for Art and Culture, an institution that is responsible for projecting Dominican

Junior Pepén plying his trade at Fenway Park while the Red Sox are out of town (photograph by Bill Nowlin).

culture in Massachusetts. We also celebrate national holidays and teach English-language course and on American citizenship."

He has also been a member of the Dominican Festival in Boston and was president of the Dominican American Coalition of Massachusetts. For his work in the Dominican and Latino community and his work in the media, Nilson Pepén has received recognition from the governor of Massachusetts, the Massachusetts senate, the mayors of Boston, Lynn, and Salem, and the city councils of both Boston and Lynn, Massachusetts.

Acknowledgments

Thanks to Nilson "Junior" Pepén for an interview on May 7, 2022, and follow-up emails.

Jessica Mendoza

ROBERTO AVANT-MIER *and* PATRICK J. MCCONNELL

At its most basic, the right to speak about sports, to influence public perception, and to ideologically and practically lay claim to sport is not a male birthright. As an exercise in power, to control sport media—to speak, write, and represent sport in media dependent on images, information, and words—is to control the agenda of sport for both men and women.[1]

In a nod to Women's History Month events in March 2019, the U.S. women's national soccer team donned new jerseys for a match and instead of featuring each player's own surnames, the new jerseys featured the name of a prominent figure—a great or legendary woman, a trailblazing figure of sorts, or someone who was somehow inspirational to the new players.[2] Whereas some player jerseys featured the name of Sally Ride (the first U.S. woman in space), activists such as Audre Lorde, or other sports stars (Abby Wambach, Briana Scurry, and Elena Delle Donne), other tributes included sports anchor and now newscaster Robin Roberts and baseball broadcaster/analyst Jessica Mendoza.

Such an homage suggests that Jessica Mendoza is already a living legend, a great figure, even now as she's barely in her 40s at the time of this writing. Of course, to call someone "great" (or amazing or legendary) is a fairly common exaggeration in sports discourse which loves cliché and hyperbole, but honestly, what else can one say when describing someone who is exactly that—great, amazing, and legendary? What else can one say when a person seems to be great and to excel in multiple endeavors? What else should one say when it seems that everything a person touches turns to gold? This is genuinely how one could describe the work and career of baseball and softball broadcaster Jessica Mendoza.

A quick rundown will note that Jessica Mendoza is a highly accomplished softball player, was the winner of various awards and honors for her play on the field, and also an Olympic softball player, and then a reporter and analyst for radio as well as television (first for football and then for softball and baseball), and finally, the first female broadcaster to make it to national prominence through ESPN's Major League Baseball (MLB) broadcasts. But this chapter asserts that Mendoza is an important broadcaster and significant figure in ways that go further. This chapter will first describe the early life and career of Jessica Mendoza and then analyze her life work and career highlights. Finally, this chapter concludes with a necessarily brief summary of her career milestones and the significance of Mendoza for Latino/a sports broadcasting and for a conversation about women in sports media.

Early Life and Athletic Career

With Mexican roots, Jessica Ofelia Mendoza was born and raised (by Gil and Karen Mendoza) in Camarillo, California, into a Latino family that influences her to this day. For example, she says that she is all about family, that she is very close to her three siblings, and stated that her favorite foods include her father's "chorizo goulash" and her mother's tamales.[3] Her father, Gil Mendoza, by the way, is a first-generation Mexican American who grew up in the Watts area of Los Angeles and struggled with his bilingual, bicultural identity.[4] He is also a former college football player who was also her softball coach in her youth and must have provided countless hours of teaching, mentoring, and training in different sports because her talent in sports and hard work led her to heights in athletics—well before she ever excelled in sports broadcasting.

For example, by the time she graduated from Adolfo Camarillo High School in 1998, she was honored by the National Fastpitch Coaches Association (NFCA) as a first team All-American softball player. She made such a splash locally that the *Los Angeles Times* honored her as Player of the Year in 1998. In high school, she also played basketball and even was named most valuable player (MVP) in both her junior and senior seasons. Still, it's incredible to imagine that she would achieve far more when she moved up to Stanford University.

As a first-year softball player at Stanford, Mendoza stood out among her peers, shattering school records for home runs, average, doubles, hits, runs, RBIs, and even leading the team in stolen bases. Such on-field accomplishments during the season resulted in a national Player of the Week award, and she was eventually recognized with the Pac-10 Newcomer of the Year award. Ultimately, she was selected female Athlete of the Year for the conference and further honored by selection to the all-conference team (Pac-10) and then as an overall All-American selection (first team).

By 2000, during Mendoza's sophomore year at Stanford, she was a three-time Player of the Week winner and again selected to the All-Pac-10 Conference team. She was also honored that year as the Pac-10 Conference's Player of the Year (the first Stanford athlete to ever achieve such a feat) and once again broke or set new single-season records for home runs, doubles, hits, runs, and stolen bases. Arguably, the cherry on top of her second-year effort was a 19-game hit streak during the season.

During her junior season at Stanford (in 2001), the laurels once again included some Player of the Week honors during the season, and she was named a regional tournament MVP. Of course, she also garnered first-team All-Conference honors for a third straight year, and All-American honors for a third consecutive year. Once again, Mendoza led the Stanford team in runs scored, hits, home runs, total bases, slugging percentage, and on-base percentage; she was also near the top in doubles, extra-base hits, and stolen bases; and she led the team with multi-hit games and multi-RBI games and also another long hitting streak for good measure. During this season, she also became the university's all-time hits leader and all-time leader for stolen bases, home runs, and runs scored. And what about a "cherry on top" for the junior season? Well, she led her team to its first-ever appearance in the Women's College World Series.

For her senior-year effort at Stanford, Jessica Mendoza started all of her team's games and again led the team in home runs, triples, hits, total bases, runs scored, slugging percentage, and again, stolen bases. She also ranked near the top in batting average, doubles, on-base percentage, RBI, and a few other categories such as multi-RBI games and multi-hit games, and there was even another long hitting streak during this season, too. Naturally, Mendoza was again awarded first-team All-Pac-10 Conference honors (for a fourth consecutive year) and again All-American honors (for the fourth straight year). In summary, Mendoza left Stanford University as a career leader in several statistical categories (many for which she remains the overall leader to this very day).[5] And could there even be a "cherry" for her senior season? Remarkably (but perhaps not surprisingly), she was even recognized as a first-team academic All-American in 2002.[6]

From Athlete to Broadcaster

As described above, Jessica Mendoza's athletic career included a stellar college career that included various awards, four-time All-American (first team) honors, and an appearance in the Women's College World Series. Logically, right after her college run, she became a member of the USA women's softball national team (2001–2010), eventually becoming a two-time Olympic medal winner after winning a gold medal for the United States in 2004 and a silver medal in 2008. During this time, Mendoza was also a three-time softball World Cup champion (2006, 2007, and 2010), a three-time World champion (2002, 2006, and 2010), a two-time Pan-American Games gold medalist (2003 and 2007), in addition to garnering various other individual awards and accolades. For example, Mendoza was named the USA Softball Female Athlete of the Year in 2006 and was voted the Women's Sports Foundation Sportswoman of the Year in 2008,[7] all of which prompted one *USA Today* journalist to famously describe Jessica Mendoza as "arguably the most complete softball player in the world."[8]

Nonetheless, none of these important recognitions speak to her career in sports broadcasting or to her significance for Latino/a broadcasters. Yet, we believe that her athletic career and the achievements that followed were all a perfect base for a seemingly meteoric rise to a career in broadcasting that would see Mendoza stand out further, excel once again, and achieve even greater heights. Thus, we now turn to Jessica Mendoza's broadcasting career. For example, the basic facts show us that Mendoza began her career with Yahoo! Sports and Fox Sports.

Since around 2007, however, Mendoza has been somewhat of a fixture on ESPN, even if only part time at the beginning. Mendoza began her run on ESPN by providing color commentary for the Women's College World Series, while also doing some sideline reporting for football games on ESPNU in those early years. She covered the Women's College World Series for several years; she also was making on-air appearances to discuss softball (and/or baseball) on different shows throughout the network's programming empire such as their national flagship for MLB baseball (*Baseball Tonight*), the national daily show *SportsCenter*, and other popular shows on the network like *Get Up* and *First Take*. Of course, all of these appearances were allowing Mendoza to hone her skills as a baseball analyst and also to increase her profile as both a legitimate softball and baseball analyst with a growing national (and international) profile. And in all cases, it seems Mendoza was demonstrating an ease and familiarity with discussing sports and a genuine comfort with being in front of the camera—further foreshadowing her upcoming rise to star status and the forthcoming growth to the point of an increasingly important sports analyst and broadcaster.

Significantly, by 2014, Mendoza eventually made her way onto the network's long-running, baseball program *Baseball Tonight* (but also appeared on other programs), and then she also appeared in the 2015 Men's College World Series. Importantly, this notable appearance allowed Mendoza to become the first female color analyst to call the Men's College World Series. And then it seems, the world changed.

On August 24, 2015, ESPN was forced to suspend the regular color analyst Curt Schilling due to some controversial on-air statements and needed an on-air replacement for its *Monday Night Baseball* broadcast. Thus, the call came in for relief, and Jessica Mendoza was called up to become the very first female analyst to appear on a nationally televised MLB game (replacing Schilling). Interestingly, she also filled in for Schilling a few days later for ESPN's *Sunday Night Baseball*. Then some weeks later, in October of that same season, Mendoza became the first female to broadcast a nationally televised MLB postseason game (during an American League wild-card game).[9] Of course, this moment was such a huge "first" for baseball broadcasting history that the scorecard that Mendoza kept for that game was immediately sent to Cooperstown, to reside in the National Baseball Hall of Fame's Library Archive.[10]

Once again, it is important to note that in all of the aforementioned firsts, the legend of Jessica Mendoza has grown and is still growing, not merely because she's the first female broadcaster to reach such heights, but because once again she is a stand-out and is excelling at her craft. She seems to be transforming all the energy and magic from her on-field athletic career into a historic and noteworthy broadcasting career. And so, the legend of Jessica Mendoza just continues to grow. For example, in 2016, Mendoza officially joined the *Baseball Tonight* broadcast team as a regular contributor on Sunday nights.

Meanwhile, the accolades continue to mount. Mendoza was inducted into the National Softball Hall of Fame in 2019[11] and named to ESPN's greatest all-time college softball team in 2020.[12] In 2020, CNN also praised her when the network noted how she became the first woman to call an MLB World Series game for a national radio broadcast (on ESPN Radio).[13] By 2020, she was serving as a solo analyst (the first female ever) for some ESPN telecasts of MLB games (for a "package" of weeknight games and holidays). Currently (at the time of this writing), Mendoza is still a lead analyst for the Women's College World Series[14] and, of course, remains officially as part of the *Sunday Night Baseball* team. These days, a fan of baseball is just as likely to see and hear Jessica Mendoza during the broadcast of an MLB game during the week as they are to see and hear her analysis during the Women's College World Series … or even during a Little League World Series broadcast. Sometimes it feels like Mendoza is everywhere when it comes to baseball and softball telecasts.

A Conclusion of Sorts

This essay has served as a brief introduction to the early life, athletic career, and varied accomplishments of the famous athlete turned broadcaster Jessica Mendoza. Beyond her early life and career accomplishments, the next section discussed her transition from star college and Olympic athlete to sideline reporter, journalist, broadcaster, and now commentator and color analyst for different baseball- or softball-related telecasts on ESPN and/or ABC Sports. To conclude this chapter, the authors wish to suggest a final discussion point in order to further assess the life, career, and ongoing work of Jessica Mendoza. In this chapter's final section, we submit some final considerations regarding Mendoza's contributions for girls and women in sports and for women in the realm of sport media.

For example, this chapter began with an epigraph that points to discussions about who has the right to speak in sports, during sports, or about sports. Of course, some scholars have noted that historically, the speaking in sports mostly has been done by men. In the study mentioned here, researchers Staurowsky and DiManno recognize how the institution of sport generally has been slow "to fully recognize women" in sport and "extremely slow in allowing women to speak and be heard on the topic of sport."[15] As these authors also report, generally speaking, "female representation within the [sport media] industry remains relatively small."[16]

Meanwhile, citing the published research of other scholars as well as conducting and recording their own interviews, these scholars ultimately conclude that (a) the male-dominated sports media environment is still intimidating to women,[17] (b) old-fashioned or conservative attitudes toward women in the workplace often linger (even at the dawn of a new millennium),[18] (c) women in sports media are almost always in the minority and often feel that they are merely "tolerated" in the workplace,[19] (d) the industry frequently reveals "a marked division of labor" in which roles and specific tasks are assigned on the basis of sex,[20] and (e) women are still being sexually objectified or experiencing sexual harassment in locker rooms or in the general workplace,[21] among some other important findings and insights.

However, it is also true that "growth continues to occur among the ranks of women who write about sports, and provide sports commentary and sports talk radio [etc.]"[22] and also that "as the [U.S.] public is confronted with a more established female sports presence, the potential for girls to consider a career in sports media has increased."[23] As Staurowsky and DiManno further elaborate in their analysis, "the sport media workplace is an environment in flux, moving between exclusion, desegregation, and integration."[24] Thus, the optimistic view here, on our part, is that it is worth recognizing that the environment is changing with regard to the place and the potential for women in sports media. Even though it's not quite there yet in terms of complete equality for women, the research mentioned in this section indicates that things are changing—even if slowly.

Of course, returning to the analysis of the meteoric rise of broadcaster Jessica Mendoza, we submit that Mendoza's significance looms larger now given this context. As we discussed the stellar career accomplishments and the upward trajectory of her media broadcasting career, Mendoza seems to be further emerging as an iconic figure for women in sports media. As if all her athletic accolades and her quick rise in a career in baseball and softball commentary weren't enough, Mendoza is now on the verge of reaching superstar heights and perhaps an entirely new realm—as a legendary figure for women in sports broadcasting and as an icon for women in sports media.

Importantly, as Staurowsky and DiManno put it in their concluding remarks,

> The burden of changing the sport media workplace should not be left on the shoulders of individuals [women] who have the willpower, fortitude, and strength of identity and character to take on the system in isolation. As more and more women become part of the sport workforce, exploring ways for educational systems working in partnership with the sport industry should become a priority.[25]

Quite obviously, Jessica Mendoza appears to be an example of success through willpower, fortitude, and strength, as well as through her abilities and sheer talent. Yet we also hope that this chapter illuminating Mendoza's story eventually contributes to the goal of empowering and supporting women in sports media. Likewise, as educators, researchers, and sports fans ourselves, the authors believe that the compelling story of Jessica Mendoza is a contribution to not only the enriching story of Latinos in broadcasting but also to the story of legendary women in sports media.

No wonder, then, that Mendoza's name was evoked for a soccer jersey in 2019, honoring important women or iconic figures in women's sports. Even at such a young age, she is already the amazing, the great, and the legendary Jessica Mendoza.

Notes

1. E.J. Staurowsky and J. DiManno, "Young Women Talking Sports and Careers: A Glimpse at the Next Generation of Women in Sport Media," *Women in Sport and Physical Activity* (WSPAJ) Journal 11, no. 1 (2002): 127–161.

2. Dawn Ennis, "Lesbian Icons Honored with Jerseys Worn by USWNT," Outsports, March 4, 2019. See https://www.outsports.com/2019/3/4/18248520/lesbian-icons-honored-with-jerseys-worn-uswnt.

3. "Jessica Mendoza," TeamUSA.org (n.d.). See https://www.teamusa.org/usa-softball/athletes/jessica-mendoza.

4. Aimee Crawford, "Jessica Mendoza: Hispanic Girls Moving beyond Traditional Roles, onto Field," ESPN.com, October 11, 2011. See https://www.espn.com/blog/highschool/girl/post/_/id/334/jessica-mendoza-hispanic-girls-moving-beyond-traditional-roles-onto-field.

5. "Jessica Mendoza Profile," Stanford University Athletics (n.d.). See https://web.archive.org/web/20030609115232/http://gostanford.ocsn.com/sports/w-softbl/mtt/mendoza_jessica00.html.

6. "Jessica Mendoza (Analyst)," ESPN Press Room (n.d.). See https://espnpressroom.com/us/bios/jessica-mendoza/.

7. "Athletes: Jessica Mendoza," Women's Sports Foundation (n.d.). See https://web.archive.org/web/20101223095431/http://womenssportsfoundation.org/Content/Athletes/M/Mendoza-Jessica.aspx.

8. Lauren Verrusio, "The Complete Package: Olympic Softball Super-Star Jessica Mendoza," Women's Sports Foundation (n.d.). See https://web.archive.org/web/20100822095154/http://www.womenssportsfoundation.org/Content/Articles/Athletes/About-Athletes/J/The-Complete-Package-Olympic-Softball-SuperStar-Jessica-Mendoza.aspx.

9. ESPN.com News Services, "Jessica Mendoza, Aaron Boone Join 'Sunday Night Baseball' Broadcast," ESPN.com, January 13, 2016. See https://www.espn.com/mlb/story/_/id/14560502/jessica-mendoza-joins-sunday-night-baseball-full.

10. Matt Rothenberg, "Mendoza Blazing Trails for Women Broadcasters on ESPN," BaseballHall.org, https://baseballhall.org/discover/jessica-mendoza-makes-history-as-first-female-espn-mlb-broadcaster#:~:text=Jessica%20Mendoza%2C%20the%20first%20female%20Major%20League%20Baseball,%28Jean%20Fruth%20%2F%20National%20Baseball%20Hall%20of%20Fame%29.

11. "Bios: Jessica Mendoza," ESPN Press Room (n.d.). See https://espnpressroom.com/us/bios/jessica-mendoza/.

12. Graham Hays, "Lauren Chamberlain, Jessica Mendoza Voted to ESPN's Greatest All-Time College Softball Team," ESPN.com, June 9, 2020. See https://www.espn.com/college-sports/story/_/id/29281960/lauren-chamberlain-jessica-mendoza-voted-espn-greatest-all-college-softball-team.

13. Allen Kim, "ESPN's Jessica Mendoza Is the First Woman to Be a World Series Game Analyst on a National Broadcast," CNN, October 21, 2020. See https://edition.cnn.com/2020/10/21/us/jessica-mendoza-world-series-spt-trnd/index.html.

14. Ria Das, "Jessica Mendoza Becomes First Woman Analyst in World Series History," SheThePeople.com, October 22, 2020. See https://www.shethepeople.tv/news/jessica-mendoza-becomes-first-woman-analyst-in-world-series-history/.

15. Staurowsky and DiManno, "Young Women Talking Sports and Careers," 129.

16. *Ibid.*, 130.
17. *Ibid.*, 141.
18. *Ibid.*, 142–143.
19. *Ibid.*, 143–146.
20. *Ibid.*, 146–147.
21. *Ibid.*, 148–149.
22. *Ibid.*, 130.
23. *Ibid.*, 132.
24. *Ibid.*, 143.
25. *Ibid.*, 154.

Conclusion

Jorge Iber

The various essays presented in this anthology have provided an overview of the careers and contributions of individuals who have brought the national pastime to the hearts, minds, and ears of millions of baseball-loving *fanáticos* both within and outside our nation. Their task has been, and will continue to be, to link Spanish speakers to one of the sports that is at the core of their *Latinidad*. Given the demographic changes continuing to take place in the United States, it is not inconceivable that someday, perhaps in the near future, all 30 franchises will broadcast at least some of their games in Spanish.

If this editor might be allowed an opportunity to reminisce for a brief moment, it was my father, who played baseball for many years in Cuba and tried to teach me playing skills on the diamond, who engendered my love for the game. Unfortunately, my athletic aptitude was minimal. However, it has been a blessing that through academic research it has been possible for me to remain connected to the sport and to explore the significance of players and, now, Spanish-language broadcasters.

My father always spoke warmly of listening to Felo Ramírez during his youth in our homeland and was thrilled when the nascent Marlins selected him to be their *voz* starting in 1993. When he moved to Texas and lived the rest of his life with my family, he often recalled hearing Felo in his final baseball seasons in Miami, particularly when the late Cuban-born Marlins hurler José Fernández took the mound. It was painful to inform Dad that this young man, at the heart of the team's Spanish-speaking fan base, had died in a boating accident off Miami Beach in September 2016. As it was, I did not have to share the sad news of José's passing with my father, as Dad's death preceded his by a few months.[1]

A recent issue of *Baseball Digest* rightly honored the now 94-year-old Vin Scully with its second annual Lifetime Achievement Award.[2] Clearly, Scully's 67-year career speaks for itself, like the lives of other broadcast giants like Jack Buck, Harry Caray, and Milo Hamilton. Still, many baseball aficionados do not realize that when Ramírez succumbed in August 2017, that he had broadcast sports in Latin America for 72 years including games of the Cuban Winter League, the Caribbean Series, and leagues in Venezuela, Puerto Rico, Mexico, and the Dominican Republic. Ramírez earned the Hall of Fame and Museum's prestigious Ford C. Frick Award in 2001, the third Latino so honored, in addition to Canel and Jarrín.[3] This is not to compare Felo to any past or present voice; rather, it is to note that those who have broadcast the sport in Spanish also merit recognition for bringing the game to a different set of fans.

Fortunately, the research agenda is changing, and this anthology is a further step in that direction. As noted in the introduction, a recent book by Curt Smith expressly provides readers with an opportunity to hear comments and anecdotes by some of the broadcasters included in this anthology. In 2021, his official Hall of Fame and Museum book *Memories from the Microphone: A Century of Baseball Broadcasting*[4] expanded this inclusivity. The chapter on Spanish-speaking and other minority voices is titled, "1950s—Today: Opening Doors." Smith is hardly the only academician to recognize and write about this trend. Although not spending time specifically detailing the careers of Spanish-speaking announcers, Tony Silvia, in his concluding chapter in *Baseball over the Air: The National Pastime on the Radio and in the Imagination*, also takes note of this development. After spending time discsussing the game's ties to new outlets such as XM Radio, Silvia provides an excellent way to summarize this endeavor by arguing that

> one important aspect of baseball's future on the radio is its connection to fans of different ethnicities and national origins. In many Latin American countries, for instance, the dominant medium for exposure to baseball is radio, not television. As a result, radio's future means reaching out to those fans.... From its first year of operation, XM recognized what it termed "strong support from its Hispanic fan base," and broadcast games in Spanish.... Local teams do much the same over traditional broadcast stations. Larry McCabe, senior vice-president of sales and broadcasting for the Tampa Bay Devil Rays, points out that the team now transmits over eighty games per season totally in Spanish on one of several ethnic radio stations.[5]

Considering that Silvia made this assertion back in 2007 (heck, the Rays were still using the term "Devil" as part of their moniker!), it makes sense for scholars of media and history to spend even more time examining the growing significance of MLB's relationship to the Spanish-speaking aficionados via such broadcasts on radio and television.

As more Latinos play baseball at the highest levels and more of their countrymen come to the United States, it behooves franchises to examine ways to reach out to this booming fan base. It is certainly necessary for MLB to continue its work along these lines. Understanding the role and historical and current importance of *locutores* will only help to further strengthen the already deep-seated attachment between Spanish speakers and the various *equipos* (teams) of *las grandes ligas*.

Notes

1. Joe Frisaro, "Beloved Star Fernandez Dies in Tragic Accident," September 25, 2016. See https://www.mlb.com/news/jose-fernandez-killed-in-boating-accident-c203268704. Accessed on June 7, 2022.

2. Anthony McCarron, "Vin Scully: A Master at Work," *Baseball Digest 81*, no. 3, (May/June 2022): 36–42, https://www.mlb.com/news/jose-fernandez-killed-in-boating-accident-c203268704.

3. Richard Sandomir, "Felo Ramirez, Enduring Voice of Baseball in Latin America, Dies at 94," *New York Times*, August 24, 2017. See https://www.nytimes.com/2017/08/24/sports/baseball/felo-ramirez-dead-voice-of-baseball-in-latin-america.html. Accessed on June 7, 2022.

4. In addition to the work noted in the introduction, see also Curt Smith, *Memories from the Microphone: A Century of Baseball Broadcasting* (Coral Gables, FL: Mango Publishing, 2021).

5. Tony Silvia, *Baseball over the Air: The National Pastime on the Radio and in the Imagination* (Jefferson, NC: McFarland, 2007), 167.

About the Contributors

Roberto **Avant-Mier** has been in the Department of Communications at the University of Texas–El Paso since 2010. Prior to that post, he taught at Boston College. He is a graduate of the University of Utah. His research analyzes the discursive construction of Latino/Hispanic identities and cultural issues in popular music and film.

César **Brioso** is a digital producer and former baseball editor for *USA Today* Sports. In more than 30 years as a journalist, he has also written for the *Miami Herald* and the *South Florida Sun-Sentinel*. He is the author of *Havana Hardball: Spring Training, Jackie Robinson and the Cuban League* and *Last Seasons in Havana: The Castro Revolution and the End of Professional Baseball in Cuba*, which was the winner of the 2020 SABR Baseball Research Award.

Lou **Hernández** is the author of multiple baseball histories and biographies, including *Bobby Maduro and the Cuban Sugar Kings*, *The 1933 New York Giants: Bill Terry's Unexpected World Champions*, and *Manager of the Giants: The Tactics, Temper and True Record of John McGraw*. In addition to his work on baseball, he is the author of two young adult novels. He was born in Cuba and resides in South Florida.

Jorge **Iber** was born in Havana, Cuba, and raised in the Little Havana neighborhood of Miami, Florida. He taught in the public schools of Miami-Dade County for five years before pursuing a PhD at the University of Utah. He serves as associate dean in the student division of the College of Arts and Sciences and is professor of history at Texas Tech University in Lubbock. He is the author/coauthor and editor/coeditor of 17 books and has also published more than 30 scholarly articles.

Patrick J. **McConnell** is an associate professor of sports communication at High Point University in North Carolina. His PhD is from the University of Georgia. In a broadcasting career that spanned more than two decades, he served as a radio/TV play-by-play announcer for over 2,000 games of professional, collegiate, and high school sports. In addition, he was director of communications for a number of professional baseball organizations for over a 13-year period.

Scott **Melesky** has been a sports journalist for 20 years. He graduated with a BA in history in 1995 from the University of Syracuse. He earned an MA in education from Pacific Oaks College in 2021. He has written for numerous newspapers and worked in the Sports Information Department for several schools, including

Marquette University and Ohio University. He is also a member of the SABR Institute for Baseball Studies.

Bill **Nowlin** was one of the first fans to the mound when Jim Lonborg induced the final out and the Red Sox won the 1967 pennant. He was elected as SABR's vice president from 2004 to 2016 and served on the board as a director since that time. He is also the author of dozens of books on the Red Sox or Red Sox players, and has written more than 1,000 articles for SABR, including more than 700 bios for BioProject, and edited or coedited more than 50 SABR books.

Frank **Moreno** was raised in the shadow of the Los Angeles Memorial Coliseum. He attended Claremont Men's (now McKenna) College where he majored in political science and economics. In 1976, he was named district director for the Carter for President Campaign, and was national legislative director for Latino issues in Washington, D.C. He returned to Los Angeles as an editor and later associate producer for the *CBS Evening News with Walter Cronkite: Western Edition*. He is semiretired and is a strong advocate and consultant for small Latino businesses.

Juan Jose **Rodriguez** is a content developer and data analyst for Burgundy Group Advertising after working for three years as a consultant for Ernst & Young. He graduated from the University of Notre Dame in 2019 with a degree in business analytics, along with a second major in film, television and theatre and a minor in journalism. While on campus, Rodriguez worked for Fighting Irish Media as a play-by-play announcer and color commentator for more than 200 live events on ESPN and NBC digital platforms. He also served on the editorial staff of *Scholastic* Magazine, where he published 10 award-winning articles and led the staff as editor-in-chief during his senior year.

Luis **Rodríguez-Mayoral** has been a Major League Baseball scout, general manager for two Puerto Rican baseball clubs, and also served as a senior executive for two major league teams in his 45 years in pushing to expand Spanish-language baseball. He served as chief baseball correspondent for *El Vocero* of Puerto Rico for nearly 20 years and is the author of five baseball books. He coordinated MLB's Latin American Baseball Player's Day for 25 years. A veteran of over 2,000 MLB radio broadcasts, he currently does guest commentary for radio in Puerto Rico.

Francisco **Romero** was born in Nogales, Sonora, Mexico, and his family moved to the United States when he was age 12. He attended Pima Junior College and later, the University of Arizona. After graduation, he worked for various nonprofits/governmental organizations in Arizona. He also worked for Telemundo in the Tucson area. He toiled for a minor league baseball franchise and ultimately, the Arizona Diamondback and Cardinals. He joined the Houston Astros' broadcast booth in 2008.

Anthony R. **Salazar** is the chair of SABR's Latino Baseball Committee and editor of its publication, *La Prensa del Bèisbol Latino*. He has written on the Latino experience in the national pastime and has consulted with teams, museums, and programs looking to tap into the U.S. Latino market. He has also worked for the College of the Environment at the University of Washington in Seattle.

About the Contributors

Richard A. **Santillán** is professor emeritus at California State University at Pomona. He retired in 2018 and is an adjunct in the Political Science Department at East Los Angeles College. He was one of the founding members of the Latino Baseball History Project in 2005 and, since 2011, has served as the lead author of that series' book project on the history of Mexican American baseball and softball. As of the moment, this series has produced a total of 16 books on this topic in various parts of the country.

Index

Aaron, Henry 62
Adamack, Randy 98
Albarrán, David 23
Alicea, Juan 108
All-Star Games 184
Allen, Mel 23
Alonzo, Miguel 39
Alou, Felipe 86
Alvarez, Manolo 62
American Camp Association 134n11
Amorós, Sandy 37, 52n21
Anaheim Angels 98, 99
Angel, Joe 6
Aparicio, Luis 128, 134n15
Arechiga, Avrana 26
Arizona Cardinals 177–78
Arizona Diamondbacks 177
A's Amigos 99
assimilation 2
Avant-Mier, Roberto 13
Ávila, Eric 14–15

Báez, Juan 113
Báez, Juan Óscar 113, 116, 117, 182
Baltimore Orioles 94
Barber, Red 23
Baseball Hall of Fame 29–30, 42, 48–49, 53n38, 62–63, 77, 129–30, 150–51
Batista, Fulgencio 22
Bautista, Arturo 35
Baxter, Kevin 28, 168
Beaton, William 26, 38, 39
Becerra, Rolando 29, 87–88
Becker, Dan 96
Beckett, Josh 63–64, 170
Bellán, Esteban 3
Berenguer, Félix Augusto 102, 106
Berenguer, Irana 122n12
Berenguer, Juan 105, 106
Berenguer, Julian 119
Berenguer, Logan 119
Berenguer, Mark Howard 106, 122n12

Berenguer, Uri: becomes full-time regular announcer 114; early career 102; education 113; ends professional association with Red Sox 120–21, 183; fan club 119–20; first day of preschool 121n2; future plans 121; immigration status 122n12; on Juan Pedro Villamán 6–7; medical issues 2, 103–5, 111, 121; path to announcing for Red Sox 102–13; published works 122n35; and remote broadcasts 114–16; romantic life 118–19; and 2004 World Series and after 116–21
Berry, Jorge 166
Berryhill, Damon 105
Blake, John 130
Bogart, Humphrey 1, 60
Boston Globe 110, 111
Boston Red Sox 102–13, 114–21, 123n38, 181, 182–84
Boyle, Robert H. 1, 9–10
Briley, Ron 14
Buck, Jack 42
Burch, Colin 183
Burgos, Adrian 94
Bush, George 130, 131–32

Cagigal Calvo, Luis Manuel "Luisma" 119–20
Cambria, Joe 3, 147–48, 149
Canel, Colleen 24
Canel, Eloy "Buck" 1, 3–4, 10, 14, 21–24, 38, 59, 60, 129–30
Cannaán, Víctor 182
Canseco, José 131
Carberry, Ken 107, 108, 109
Cárdenas, Adán 25
Cárdenas, Jilma 27–28
Cárdenas, René 4–5, 14, 25–30, 38–41, 46, 82, 83–86, 87
Caribbean Series: (1948–49) 59; (1979) 61–62
Castiglione, Joe 104, 105–7, 111, 112

Castillo, Ángel 78
Castro, Fidel 1, 3, 60, 61, 66n7, 93, 147, 149
Cecil, Dick 128
Cedeño, César 86
Central Deportiva 166, 167–68
Cepeda, Orlando 86, 98, 126, 128
Chappell, Ben 54n51
Cheney, Dick 132
Chicago Bulls 138
Chicago Cubs 138
Chicago White Sox 129, 130, 133n4, 135, 138, 142
Cienfuegos 144
Cincinnati Reds 170, 177
Claire, Fred 54n42
Claro, Omar 57
Clay, Cassius 134n11
Clemente, Roberto 10, 37–38, 62, 87, 127, 128, 158
Cohen, Alex 183
Coimbre, Francisco "Pancho" 127, 134n10
Coleman, Ken 105
Colson, Gary 153–54
Conde, Carlos "Cuco" 58
Conversando de Deportes 182
Costas, Bob 2
Covid-19 pandemic 161, 170–71
Croquer, Francisco José 67n13
Cuban League 147
Cuban Revolution 93–94, 147

Dávila, Luis Antonio 137
Davis, Al 166
Davis, Willie 53n37
Delgado-Lizárraga, Gilberto 73
Denver Broncos 167
Deportes de TV 182
designated hitter rule 150
Detroit Tigers 131, 133
Día del Pelotero Latinoamericano 127–29
Díaz-Valdez, María Amparo 72, 73–74
DiManno, J. 191, 192
Doggett, Jerry 46
Drysdale, Don 53n37, 55n54
Duquette, Dan 111, 112

Eire, Carlos 93–94
El Mundo Boston 109
Elston, Gene 83
Elway, John 167
Enberg, Dick 77
Escobar, Chester 28
ESPN 189, 190
Evans, Stan 26

Fall Classics 60, 138–39
Favre, Brett 167

Feld, Joel 117
Feller, Sherm 107
Fernández, Alfonso 145, 146, 147
Fernández, José 65, 195
Fernández Tápanes, Roberto 147–48
Fernandomania 5, 42–45, 54n42, 54n45, 175
Ferreiro, Albert "Beto" 78
Finley, Charles 92–93, 95, 96
Florida Marlins 62, 64–65
Ford C. Frick Award 23, 24, 29–30, 53n38, 62–63, 77, 129–30
Frazier, Lindsay 104
Frick, Ford C., Award 23, 24, 29–30, 53n38, 62–63, 77, 129–30
Fuentes, Tito 168
Furillo, Bud 155

Gammons, Peter 4
García, José "Fats" 41, 46, 52n32
García, Rodolfo "Rudy" 38
García Márquez, Adrián 112–13
Garciaparra, Nomar 170
Garibay, Don Guillermo "Memo" 74
Giamatti, Bart 128
Gibson, Kirk 160
Gillette Cavalcade of Sports (GCS) 60, 67n11
Golden State Warriors 96–97
Gomez, Preston 86
González, Juan "Igor" 131, 132
González, Julio 92
González, Miguel (Mike) Angel 3
González, Olga 93
González-Echevarría, Roberto 83
Goodwin, Doris Kearns 3
Gran Stadium del Cerro de la Habana 58, 66n7
Green, George 155
Griffey, Robin 104
Gross, Jerry 71
Guardiola, Ángel 128
Guilfoile, Bill 24
Guillén, Ozzie, Jr. 141
Guillén, Ozzie, Sr. 141
Gutiérrez, Felix F. 12

Haak, Howie 127
Haas, Walter A., Jr. 95, 96
Hablando con los Dodgers 166, 167–68
Hall of Fame 29–30, 42, 48–49, 53n38, 62–63, 77, 129–30, 150–51
Halverson, Andrew 146–47
Harrington, John 113
Hawkins, Tom 165–66
HCJB 34
Healey, Jim 107, 108, 109, 110

Henninger, Thom 148
Hernandez, Sandra 5
Hershiser, Orel 53n37, 160, 161
Hildreth, Jaime 88–89
Hispanic Heritage Baseball Museum 97–98
Hoffman, Trevo 170
Hofheinz, Fred 6, 86
Hofheinz, H. Roy 6, 27, 81, 82, 83, 85, 87
Houston Colt .45s/Astros 14, 27, 29, 81–89, 165, 175, 178
Howser, Phil 149
Hoyos, Rodolfo, Jr. 41
Hoyos, Rodolfo, Sr. 41
Hull, Kevin 12

Iber, Jorge 13
Izenberg, Jerry 3

Jackson, Jesse 131
Jaime and Blanca Jarrín Foundation Golf Classic 158
Jarrín, Alfredo 33
Jarrín, Blanca Mora 34, 35–36
Jarrín, Jaime: appreciation for 49, 51n4; background 33; career trajectory 5–6, 34–37, 153; and current Spanish-speaking Dodgers broadcasters 48–49; and Fernandomania 5, 42–45, 54n42, 54n45; honors received 53n38, 53n41; influence on other announcers 160, 165, 175; interest in aviation 35, 51n11; Jaime and Blanca Jarrín Foundation Golf Classic 158; joins Dodgers 38–41; Jorge Jarrín works with 158–59, 161; legacy 32, 50; near-death experience 53n40; Ortega on 78–79; and Ramírez's induction into Hall of Fame 62–63; and René Cárdenas 28, 29; retirement 25, 49–50; signature calls 32, 51n2; and struggle against stigmatization of Spanish-speaking broadcasters 46–48; treatment of, by Dodgers 55n55; and Vin Scully 41–42; Yñiguez and 165, 168, 169
Jarrín, Jimmy 35
Jarrín, Jorge 34, 35, 48, 51n5, 55n55, 55n59, 78, 153–61, 169
Jarrín, Leopoldo 33
Jarrín, Mauricio 35
Jarrín, Stefan 48, 153
Jeter, Derek 65
Jimmy Fund 105, 121n8
Johnson, Lyndon 83

KABC 155, 156
Kasper, Len 139–40, 141–42
Kennedy, Kevin 158
Kershaw, Clayton 170
KIQI 96
KLVL 82
KOFY 92
KOGO 71
Koppett, Leonard 2, 3
Koufax, Sandy 35, 53n37
KSTS 96
KTNQ 45, 169
Kuhn, Bowie K. 23–24, 128
Kulik, Bill 110, 112, 113, 116, 117, 123n57, 183
KWKW 36, 37, 38–41, 46, 165

Larsen, Don 60, 62
LaRussa, Tony 96
Latin American Baseball Player's Day 127–29
Latino Baseball History Project 52n24
Latino surnames, pronunciation 75
Latinos TV 182
Liga de Beisbol Profesional Cubana (1946–47) 58
Llorente, Sonia 129
Lonborg, Rosie 2
Long, Howie 167
López, Edgar 145
Lopez, Manny 89
López-Moreno, Gustavo 74
López Portillo y Pacheco, José 43
Los Angeles Dodgers: Cárdenas and 25, 26, 28–29; current Spanish-speaking broadcasters 48–49; Jaime Jarrín and 35, 38–41; Jorge Jarrín and 156–57, 158, 160; move to Los Angeles 37–38, 81; Spanish-speaking radio channel and Latino fans 44–45; struggle of Spanish-speaking broadcasters for 46–48; treatment of Spanish-speaking broadcasters 55n55; Yñiguez and 164, 165–66, 168–70
Los Angeles Raiders 166–68
Los Angeles riots (1992) 155–56
Lucchino, Larry 121n8
"Luisma" (Luis Manuel Cagigal Calvo) 119–20

Maduro, Bobby 128
Magallanes Navigators 61–62
Márquez Estrada, Herón 145
Martinez, Dennis 168
Martinez, Ed 95
Martínez, Héctor 107, 108, 109, 111, 112
Martínez, Pedro 111, 122n35
Martínez-Pérez, Juan Manuel 72, 73
Matos, Gil 117
Mayoral, Radames 22

206 Index

Mayoral Goyena, Marvi 124
Mayoral Liera, Irasema 79
McCarthy, Jade 117
McConnell, Patrick J. 13
McGwire, Mark 97
McLane, Drayton 88
McMullen, John 87
Mejías, Roman 14
Mendoza, Gil 187
Mendoza, Jessica 15, 186–92
Mexican American Baseball History Project 52n24
Milwaukee Brewers 177
Minnesota Twins 128, 144–50
Miñoso, Orestes "Minnie" 133n4, 144, 150–51
Molina, Hector 135–43
Molina, René 59
Monday Night Baseball 190
Montana, John 167
Montano Fraga, Luisa Rafaela 59, 63, 64–65
Moraga, Jorge E. 12–13, 89
Morales Pepén, Marina 181
Mota, Jose 156
Mota, Manny 48, 54n42, 158

National League Champion Series (1986) 88
Nava, Milt 39
Navarro, Julio 126
NESN Daily 117
Nowlin, Bill 121n8

Oakland Athletics 92–93, 95–96, 98, 99
Oliva, Gordette DuBois 148, 149–50
Oliva, Tony 6, 144–51, 177
Olympic Games (Los Angeles, 1984) 154–55
O'Malley, Peter 128, 166
O'Malley, Walter 37, 46, 47
Operación Pedro Pan (Operation Peter Pan) 93–94
Orsillo, Don 113
Ortega, Eduardo 2, 6, 7, 71–79
Ortega-Becerra, Salvador 72
Ortiz, David 184
Ortíz, Jose de Jesus 78–79
Osorio, Efraín 95
Otto, Franklin 13

Pacheco, Tony 165
Pacific Coast League (PCL) 26, 38
Padrón, Pedro "Panza" 86
Palmeiro, Rafael 131
Parks, Rosa 131
Pascual, Camilo 144

Passe, Loel 83–84
Pepén, Enrique 184
Pepén, Lisa Marie 184
Pepén, Nilson "Junior" 120, 181–85
Pepén, Nilson, Sr. 181
Pepén, Verónica 181, 184
Pepperdine University 153–54
Pérez, Elias Díaz y 137–38
Pérez, Marco 35
Pérez, Tony 66, 111
Pi, Joaquín 93
Pi-González, Amaury 1, 4, 6, 92–100
Pittsburgh Pirates 127–28, 130
Podres, Johnny 64
Ponle Acento program 10
Portuondo Cala, Guillermo 23
La Prensa 25, 26, 38

Quintana, Luis "Yiky" 66

racism 149
Rafael "Felo" Ramírez Field 65
Ramírez, Rafael (Felo) 1, 4, 57–66, 67n24, 67n27, 93, 94, 99–100, 195–96
Ramos, Pedro 144
Ramos-Berenguer, Daisy Judith 102, 103–4, 106, 116
Reagan, Ronald 43, 109, 133n4
Red Sox Media Guide (2011) 117
Regalado, Samuel O. 81
Reguera, Manolo de la 58
remote broadcasts 114–16
Rentería, Edgar 5
Ribadeneira, Diego 122n35
"Ring of Honor" 48–49
Rivera, Mariano 160–61
Roberto Clemente Memorial Award 128–29, 134n15
Robinson, Jackie 42
Rodríguez, Pudge 131
Rodríguez de Tió, Lola 124
Rodríguez-Mayoral, Luis 6, 61, 124–33, 134n14
Rodríguez Vega, José 124, 125
Romero, Francisco 29, 30, 78, 175–80
Romero, J.C. 123n57
Rosario, Néstor 78
Rose, Pete 170
Ruiter, Brad 145
Ruiz, Francisco Ernesto 29, 89
Ruíz, Juan Félix 135–36
Russo, Billy 140–41, 142
Ruth, Babe 170
Ryan, Bob 110

Salamanca, Bobby 66
Salazar, Ruben 53n39

San Diego Padres 71, 72–73, 76
Sánchez, Olga 83, 86, 87
Sánchez, Orlando 82
Sánchez-Diago, Orlando 6, 14, 27, 29, 81–89
Sandinistas 28
Santiago, Benito 134n15
Santo, Ron 4
Schement, Jorge Reina 12
Schilling, Curt 190
Scully, Vin 5, 41–42, 45, 46, 55n55, 160, 169, 175, 195–97
Seattle Mariners 98
Selig, Bud 97, 128
Serrano, Bobby 107, 108, 109, 112
Serrano, José 132
Serrano, Rafael 137
Shea, Stuart 28, 81–82
Silvia, Tony 196
Sims, Frank 71
Smith, Curt 11, 196
Solamente Pelota 117
Soria, Oscar 78
Sosa, Sammy 97
Spanish Béisbol Network (SBN) 112, 117
Spanish Béisbol Productions 117
Spanish-language radio: change in audience 98–99; scholarship 11–15, 196; and stigmatization of Spanish-speaking broadcasters 46–48; ties between MLB and 10–11
Staurowsky, E.J. 191, 192
Steinberg, Charles 113
Stevens, Tito 122n35
Summer Olympics (Los Angeles, 1984) 154–55
Sunday Night Baseball 190
Surrey House 86
Swank, Bill 76, 79

Texas Rangers 130–31
Thompson, Chuck 3
Tiant, Luis 113
Tijuana Potros 73
Tonita's Restaurant 41
Torreón Algodóneros 74
Torres, Victor Manuel 92–93
Treviño, Alex 6, 29, 178–79
Trupiano, Jerry 106
Tucson Sidewinders 176–77

Ueberroth, Peter 128
University of Arizona 177

Valdez, Tirso A. 22
Valenzuela, Fernando 5, 42–45, 47–48, 50, 54n42, 54n45, 169
Vasallo, Alberto III 109, 116
Vassegh, David 158
Venezuelan Winter League 61
Vietnam War 136–37
Villamán, Juan Pedro 6–7, 109, 112, 114, 116, 119, 183
Vincent, Fay 128
Virdon, Bill 165
El Vocero 130

Walker, James R. 11
Wall Street Journal 98–99
Weddington, Elaine 110
Williams, Ted 121n8
Willow Elementary 76
Winfield, Dave 73
WLYN 113, 114
WOJO 138
women in sports and sports media 191–92
 see also Mendoza, Jessica
World Series: (1951) 60; (1997 to 2005) 168–69; (2004) 116–21
WRCA 109, 111
WRKO 110
WROL 109, 117
WVIB 110

Yawkey, Tom 129
Yñiguez, Jose "Pepe" 6, 48, 49, 52n23, 52n28, 164–72

Zapiaín, Mario Thomas "Don Mario" 71, 72, 74–75
Zoom meetings 170–71

www.ingramcontent.com/pod-product-compliance
Lightning Source LLC
Chambersburg PA
CBHW032044300426
44117CB00009B/1180